The Kennedy Circle

Edited by LESTER TANZER

With an Introduction by
DAVID BRINKLEY

LUCE

WASHINGTON, D.C.

EDITOR'S PREFACE

"PRESIDENT KENNEDY ANNOUNCES . . . ," A NEWSPAPER STORY MAY begin, telling of another action or decision by the thirty-fifth President of the United States. True enough, the decision in the end was made by the President. But rare is the presidential action that does not bear the influence, if not the authorship of others. Behind the President, any President, is a group of men whose ideas and thoughts are collected, compared, and accepted, rejected or modified by the Chief Executive.

Who are the men President Kennedy relies on? This book attempts to answer that question. It is the story of the people who, because of their personal relationship with Kennedy or their position in the government, will most influence the Administration, the nation, and the world in the coming years. All told, nineteen men are studied here in detail, including the ten members of the Cabinet and nine officials in and around the White House. Many other characters appear in these pages, too, in lesser roles.

Where did these nineteen come from? What paths did they follow to the New Frontier? Why were they chosen? What kind of people are they? What are their goals and ideas? How do they fit into President Kennedy's scheme of things? Thirteen of Washington's leading reporters sought the answer. The volume of facts they unearthed would have taken a single author a year or more to amass and digest.

Each of the nineteen personalities was interviewed one or more times. Trips were taken to ancestral homes and old stamping grounds. Family, working associates, friends—and enemies—were sought out. The public statements and writings of each man were examined, as were the recorded comments made about each. Then, after their stories were written, David Brinkley drew a composite image of the men around Kennedy to put them into perspective.

The trained professionals who wrote this book had the widest leeway in expressing their views. They had no axes to grind. By journalistic instinct and training, they looked upon the men they described as neither heroes nor villains, but fallible men trying to do their jobs. They have told the shortcomings as well as the virtues of the characters involved. As a result, the book is neither an apologia for, nor a diatribe against, the Kennedy team. It is an effort to put flesh and blood around the figures who will be responsible for the success or failure of the Kennedy administration.

As the Kennedy administration digs into its job, there will be other names in the headlines. Lesser appointees will be plunged into positions of prominence and importance—late-bloomers whose influence has yet to be felt. The chances are that most of these names crop up somewhere in the following pages.

One final note. This book is more than just a summary of the lives and thoughts of nineteen men. It tells much about President Kennedy and the way he is running the government. Though no one chapter is devoted exclusively to him, Kennedy's personality runs like a thread throughout the book. In the chapters by Alan Otten on Ted Sorensen and by Hugh Sidey on Bobby Kennedy, the reader will follow the road John Kennedy followed to the White House. Elie Abel's chapter on Robert McNamara provides the most thoroughly documented case study yet recorded of the way Kennedy conducted his talent hunt for men to fill his administration. Mary McGrory's story on Kennedy's right-hand men furnishes a perceptive glimpse into the informal, helter-skelter way the White House itself is run. In nearly every chapter the reader will discover another facet of President Kennedy, the man and his way of doing things.

In short, John Fitzgerald Kennedy is the center of *The Kennedy Circle*.

LESTER TANZER

Washington, D.C., 1961

CONTENTS

THE CONTRIBUTORS

ELIE ABEL
Washington bureau chief, *The Detroit News*

ALAN E. ADAMS
Washington correspondent, McGraw-Hill Publications

BEN H. BAGDIKIAN
Chief Washington correspondent, *The Providence Journal*

DAVID BRINKLEY
NBC News reporter

CARROLL KILPATRICK
National staff reporter, *The Washington Post and Times-Herald*

MARY McGRORY
National staff writer, *The Washington Star*

DON OBERDORFER
Washington reporter, Knight Newspapers

MICHAEL J. O'NEILL
Washington reporter, *The New York Daily News*

ALAN L. OTTEN
White House reporter, *The Wall Street Journal*

WALTER PINCUS
Washington correspondent, *News Focus*

THOMAS B. ROSS
Washington correspondent, *Chicago Sun-Times*

CHARLES B. SEIB
National editor, *The Washington Star*

HUGH SIDEY
Washington correspondent, *Time-Life*

DAVID WISE
White House correspondent, *The New York Herald-Tribune*

LESTER TANZER, Editor
Associate editor, *Changing Times,* the Kiplinger Magazine

INTRODUCTION

The New Men

By DAVID BRINKLEY

A NEW MEMBER OF THE PRESIDENT'S CABINET ARRIVING IN WASHington first sends his wife out to look for a house big enough for the entertaining soon to be demanded of him, and then he goes down to his office and bravely and hopefully enters into American history. He also enters a government department that is well aware it was there before he came and will be there when he is gone— where oil portraits of great secretaries from the past look querulously out from gilt frames seeing him, sitting there behind a ponderous desk and chromium water pitcher, wondering how to get control of an agency filled with people who know more about it than he does.

While he reflects on this, his wife telephones to say the really suitable houses are in Spring Valley and Wesley Heights, but they have racial covenants. While nothing really has been said, it is somehow understood that nobody in this administration may sign a covenant. He asks her to look down in Georgetown. A lot of the other fellows are moving in there, where the houses are quaint, if cramped, and while those with three small bedrooms begin around $60,000, they at least don't have covenants.

Now to try to see just what this agency he has been appointed to run is all about. One of President Kennedy's appointees tried to learn this by calling in his bureau heads and asking each one,

"What do you do and why do you do it?" The answers may boggle him. The Secretary of Commerce, for example, finds he has been put in charge of trade fairs, public roads, charting navigable waters, issuing patents, collecting business statistics, exports and imports, inland waterways, taking the census, supporting the merchant marine, and predicting the weather.

So there it is. While he is indeed Secretary, his is not the privilege of deciding what the institution he heads is going to do. It was decided for him long before he came—by Congress, in densely printed morocco volumes of statutes, by the encrustation of tradition, orders of Presidents long dead, sheer habit, and leaden bureaucratic dead weight. ("One of the first things he notices is an emphasis on procedure and routine. This is necessary and desirable, provided it does not make method an end in itself. When it does, overorganized bewilderment results."—ROBERT A. LOVETT)

He then finds that within these boundaries of law, tradition, and iron routine, his agency does have policies and objectives, or will have when the new administration has had time to choose them, but it will take months to see precisely what they are and how to direct them. ("I am not aware of any school for Cabinet officers, or Presidents either."—PRESIDENT KENNEDY) When, finally, the policies are known, he will try, with some frustrations, to get them to conform to those his political party proclaimed as it came to office. ("Nobody has been able to run the State Department in 150 years."—DEAN ACHESON)

Along about the sixth month, when he is settled and cramped in Georgetown, he is spending perhaps a fourth of his time testifying before Congress or preparing to, another fourth at meetings with people in his own agency and from others, and the rest of his time handling paper, reading and writing reports, including those brought home in a brief case. He finds that the only time he has for undisturbed thinking is while he is shaving, and he will begin to wonder if he has taken over an agency or if in fact it is not the other way around.

The first responsibility facing a President-elect is to find ten men for these Cabinet agencies who can do the work and survive the frustrations. ("I've been trying to do too much. My wife and I agree

I've got to slow down."—SECRETARY OF LABOR GOLDBERG, after
three months.) The ten must also be able to stay out of trouble,
contribute something to the success of the administration, collec-
tively represent a suitable geographic, religious, and ideological
spectrum, and, furthermore, demonstrate a devotion to the principles
stated or implied in the platform and the campaign speeches. In
this nearly impossible personnel task, President Kennedy, even in
the opinion of his enemies, succeeded brilliantly. With the exception
of two or three men he got every one he went after. And the ten
finally chosen make up what a good many people here believe
is the most talented Cabinet they can remember.

The level of ability found along the White House corridors and
the high-ceilinged warrens of the Executive Office Building next
door is also impressive.

Theodore Sorensen is there. He is no Sherman Adams in terms
of power, but he is the foremost of the presidential assistants. At
any given moment, he may be found looking over the papers on
a contested air-line route, on some ex-convict who wants a presidential pardon, or something on the wheat surplus. Or he may be
writing President Kennedy's next speech in a prose clear and lucid,
if slightly wordy.

Lawrence O'Brien may not be in his office, since his job is Congressional liaison. That is to say, he is assigned to roam the Capitol,
talk to people, see what is happening or about to, and occasionally
try to persuade somebody to do something—much like a routeman
for a wholesaler of household cleaners. He is more politician than
anything else, talks with pure pleasure, great expertise, and total
recall about the last campaign and seems almost unable to wait for
the next one to begin.

Walter Heller, of the Council of Economic Advisers, a talkative,
high-strung, ectomorph, may be heard saying exultantly that he
sent the President a twelve-page memorandum on some complex
economic problem and found at a Cabinet meeting one hour later,
"he had *read* it and was *quoting* from it."

What kind of people did John Kennedy choose to fill his Cabinet
and his White House secretariat? Contrary to some pre-election
forecasts, they are not New Dealers. Franklin Roosevelt came here

in 1933 at the head of a noisy column of hot-eyed reformers, intent on making over the basic institutions of this country, determined to end the depression and to change our class structure while they were about it. They brought with them the passions and the zeal that always go with immoderate loves and hatreds. They were tinkerers, experimenters, social workers, and agrarian reformers. There were geniuses and an occasional crackpot. They fell on Washington with zestful shouts of pure joy and began looking around for things and places that needed reform.

There is nothing nearly so gaudy as that in Washington now. In New Deal days, a good idea was a good idea, period. If it failed to work, it was because not enough money had been spent, or because no new alphabetical agency had been set up with an adequate budget to administer it. But in Washington now, a good idea is one that works. And the best idea is the one that works fastest with the least fuss while irritating the fewest people.

Pragmatism probably is the word. It is heard so often around Washington now it must be. At a party on one of the first hundred nights, the wife of a goverment official was heard to circulate the living room asking each guest in turn, "Are you pragmatic?"

Had Secretary of Treasury Douglas Dillon been at the party, which he was not, he might well have given the answer he has given since: "I believe in doing things the orthodox way when the orthodox way works. When you run into places where the orthodox won't work, then you try something else." Or, he might simply have said, "Yes."

Pragmatism (the word was literally invented at Harvard) has an honorable history. It has engaged the attention of such philosophers as William James, who proclaimed it to be "the attitude of looking away from first things, principles, supposed necessities, and of looking toward last things, fruits, consequences, facts." When James later felt he could say it in fewer words, he wrote, "Meaning, other than practical, there is for us none."

For nearly a century, then, the word and the philosophy have rolled off tongue and pen, but not until now, I believe, have they been applied to the governing of the United States.

Secretary of State Rusk, in his 1960 Elihu Root lectures, made

a formidable and almost unassailable case against summit conferences. He declared them to be unproductive, a waste of time and
Presidential energy, and even dangerous. But, pragmatic to the last,
he still refused to rule them out. Instead, his conclusion was that
worthless as summit conferences were, there might nevertheless be
times when they could be useful to us and might therefore be used
sparingly with suitable precautions against letting them become a
habit.

It recalled the ancient vaudevillian's firm statement: "I hate that
S. O. B. and I won't have him in the act, unless I need him."

Whatever the results of the Pragmatic System, or government by
The Palmer Method, large numbers of people in the early months
of the Kennedy administration professed astonishment that it was
not more radical than it was. A small-town Republican businessman of conservative taste, on hearing a visiting lecturer in the high-
school auditorium discoursing about the doings of the new administration, blurted out, "You know, that fellow hasn't done anything
Eisenhower wouldn't have done."

This judgment may not be pleasing to the New Frontiersmen,
but it is nevertheless one honest reaction to the careful unemotional
mood that now fills Washington as smoke fills a room.

It flows from the President himself and is further thickened by
the men he chose to staff his government. Something of Kennedy's
own taste and attitude can be seen in all of them. They are liberal,
but not very. Those of advanced liberal views have wound up in
secondary jobs. ("I'm glad they sent Soapy Williams to Africa.
If we'd been elected, that's exactly where we'd have sent him."—
SENATOR GOLDWATER)

This pragmatic trend could have been seen earlier, when Kennedy
after his nomination chose Lyndon Johnson for Vice-President, to
the intense distress of Walter Reuther. But American conservatives
did not want to see it, and there were confident predictions that
if Kennedy won, Reuther would get a solid gold passkey to the
White House. ("These people go to Walter Reuther for votes, to
Joe Kennedy for money, and to London for their clothes."—SENA
TOR GOLDWATER) As it turned out, during the early months of the
Administration at least, Reuther was not seen near the White House.

On the contrary, he was telling Congress more in sorrow than anger that the President's minimum-wage bill was just not good enough.

The liberal viewpoint is there, but it is concealed behind a concern for the possible. In his first months, when the President needed Southern congressmen's votes to open the New Frontier, Congress had not a word or a line from him about new civil-rights legislation. He came, like no President before him, direct from Congress, bringing with him a close knowledge of its ways and its means, its members, its rules written and unwritten, and a conviction that the thing to ask of Congress is what it is willing to give, or perhaps a shade more. Anything beyond that can be had, if at all, only at a cost too great to pay.

There is another factor: Franklin Roosevelt came at a time of urgency so great he could in his first week have seized and nationalized this country's banking system had he cared to. John Kennedy has no such power. If the urgency is that great, the American people have not yet come to realize it. Nor has Congress.

President Kennedy has therefore filled his administration with people who share his own style, who eagerly welcome new ideas, but who insist first on candling them like eggs held to a light.

Some other Kennedy characteristics can be seen in those he chose for his Cabinet and his White House secretariat. ("There can be few governments on earth equal to it in energy, youth . . . its new sense of serious dedication, its preoccupations with Asia and Africa, its correspondence courses in quick reading, Swahili and the diffuse nebulae. . . ."—*Manchester Guardian*) The concentration of campus intellectuals in soft jackets and easy shoes is perhaps unequaled in American history. Roosevelt never ran so heavily to men like this. He preferred experts in consumer economics, labor organizing, and hybrid corn. But now, those who twice were enchanted with Adlai Stevenson's eggheadedness find that in the administration he now has joined he is just one of the crowd.

One of the weekly news magazines briskly went about counting the Phi Beta Kappas among the officials Kennedy appointed, finding sixteen. It also found four Rhodes scholars and one Nobel Prize winner, and printed the names in a box at the bottom of a page with its conclusion: "In the new administration, the accent is on scholarship as well as on youth."

The Cabinet members and White House officials are a group (they *don't* call it a team) usually shown in print in the form of an organizational chart, made of many boxes connected by many lines, looking a little like the plumbing diagram for a twelve-room house. But Kennedy, on being asked, preferred to describe them as a wheel and spokes, all of them from time to time coming directly to him.

"One of the problems of any President," he said, "is that his sources of information are limited. I sit in the White House and what I read in the papers and magazines and memoranda, and things that I see, that is the sum total of what I hear and learn. So the more people I can see, the wider I can be exposed to different ideas, the more effective I can be as President. So, therefore, it is a mistake to have just one person working on one subject because then you don't get any clash of ideas and therefore have no opportunity for choice."

The Harun al-Rashid method of roaming the streets incognito and questioning the citizenry is not available to the President. As he says, the only information he can get is whatever is brought to him. (His brother, Attorney General Robert F. Kennedy, did try walking in shirt sleeves around the streets of New York and questioning juvenile gang members.) The President therefore has cast aside the Sherman Adams method of having information reach him through the fine-screen filter of a civilian Chief of Staff.

President Kennedy says, "I think President Eisenhower felt he could use his time most effectively by having the staff co-ordinate things at the secondary level and then for him to work through the chairman of the staff. I try to keep in contact with all these men individually because I think it enables me to keep in much greater intimacy with the various responsibilities we have."

The organization of the White House staff has over the years reflected the President's own personality. Calvin Coolidge, who liked the government quiet, had an adviser named Frank Stearns, who occasionally was summoned to the President's office, there to sit, the two of them, in a haze of cigar smoke for an hour or more in utter silence. Hoover, believing the government should be small, kept his staff down to three secretaries, military and naval aides, and forty clerks. Roosevelt vastly enlarged it, but never organized it. He kept it in a cheerful sort of confusion, with Harry Hopkins upstairs working on a card table set up in Lincoln's bedroom. In 1945, Truman found the White House offices so overcrowded and disorganized that one of his advisers, George Allen, was unable to get a desk or telephone and so chose to walk down Pennsylvania Avenue to a drugstore and transact his business from a telephone booth.

There is a federal law Congress never passed. The Law is that whenever two or more government officials meet more than once a month to say or do anything, their meetings quickly become Institutionalized. The process begins with the employment of a co-ordinator to insure that whatever decisions are made are carried out. The co-ordinator gradually acquires a deputy, a staff of assistants, a secretary for each, a wall or two of file cabinets, desks, chairs, glass-front bookshelves, and there, without anyone really knowing it, an entirely new institution has been formed with an identity, a payroll, and a letterhead all its own.

As The Law has worked over the years at the White House, Hoover's staff of forty-five people has grown into The Executive Office of the President, an institution of more than a thousand people and an annual budget of more than $5,000,000. Its functions, as listed in columns of type in the United States Government Organization Manual, run heavily to mobilizing, advising, and co-ordinating.

The resulting bureaucracy has come to be, in the view of several political scientists, an Institutionalized Presidency—a vast accumulation of people and agencies concerned in one way or another with the use of the powers the Constitution gives the President. Benjamin Franklin feared a President without responsible advisers and counselors would be "subject to caprice and intrigues of favorites and mistresses, etc." But so great was the prestige of George Washington that the writers of the Constitution left it entirely to him to choose his advisers, if any. So the President's secretariat, and indeed the Cabinet itself, has grown to the towering dimensions of today entirely through individual and widely spaced acts of Congress, Presidential decisions beginning with Washington, and through the inexorable workings of The Law.

Kennedy, on moving into this Institutionalized Presidency, has begun changing it to suit his own preferences, so far as change is possible to him. He has abolished a few co-ordinating bodies, declared formalized Cabinet meetings to be a waste of time, and done away with the chief of staff, substituting "a wheel and a series of spokes" with himself as the hub, each of his principal advisers in the Cabinet and White House coming direct to him, straight as a spoke, without first picking his way through a maze of boxes and lines, and bringing him the information he covets and finds hard to get. ("Many shall run to and fro, and knowledge shall be increased."—DANIEL, 12:4.)

These spokes now converging at the hub of presidential power are, by general consent, men of outstanding ability and intelligence whose pragmatic planning and careful candling may or may not please the American people. The application, however cautious, of the scholar's intelligence to institutions that often grew up without it will inevitably cause distress, outcry, and perhaps blunders, as in the first attempts to undermine Castro in Cuba. ("Great intellectual gifts mean an activity pre-eminently nervous in its character, and consequently a very high degree of susceptibility to pain in every form."—SCHOPENHAUER)

Whatever history's judgment of this new breed of leaders, the job is there. It has to be done. And they are the chosen.

PART
I

The
White
House

1.

"WHAT DO YOU THINK, TED?"

Theodore Sorensen

By ALAN L. OTTEN

JOHN FITZGERALD KENNEDY, AS PRESIDENT, DOES HIS OWN thinking and makes his own decisions. In the Cabinet and on the White House staff he has a number of trusted and valued advisers from whom he draws the raw stuff he refines into national policy. No one of them, however, can remotely be considered *the* power behind the President—a puppet master, all-important, indispensable.

Yet in any organization, even one as vital and effervescent as the White House today, there is always one man on whom the boss relies particularly, whose word counts just a bit more, whose advice is most consistently sought, who seems to be most thoroughly attuned to the ideas and attitudes of the man on top. In the maelstrom at 1600 Pennsylvania Avenue that man is thirty-three-year-old Theodore Chaikin Sorensen, a brilliant, bespectacled, and somewhat brittle egghead from Nebraska.

This reserved, almost ascetic-looking young lawyer is virtually unknown outside Washington. Yet since 1953 he has come closer than anyone else to being Kennedy's political alter ego, first in the pursuit of the Presidency and now in the exercise of presidential power.

Sorensen is the Special Counsel to the President, a legal-sounding title that covers a vast range of policy-making and advisory chores.

After the President himself, he is the White House official most directly concerned with formulating administration policy, particularly in the domestic field. He provides a constant sounding board for presidential ideas and a constant cushion of advice for presidential actions. "What do you think, Ted?" is one of the President's most frequent questions at staff meetings.

Subject to the President's final judgment, Sorensen shapes White House recommendations to Congress, basing them on the suggestions of Cabinet and agency heads, adding his solid knowledge of Kennedy's goals and methods and lacing them with his own ideas. He writes most of Kennedy's special messages to Congress, speeches, and other public statements; the masterful Kennedy State of the Union message was largely a Sorensen product.

During the early days of the new Administration messages outlining new legislative proposals for education, health, agriculture, tax revision, the budget, defense, foreign aid, and many other subjects were sent to Congress at the rate of two or three a week. Agency proposals for all these were funneled into Sorensen's office, digested there, chewed over once more with the President, and a final, polished product forwarded to Capitol Hill. The work required an ability to shift on a moment's notice from a meeting on price supports for feed grains to a lengthy phone discussion on the United States balance-of-payments situation, to arguments on federal aid for medical students. Sorensen stage-managed it all without blinking. "Ted has the clearest, most authentic claim to the title of 'genius' of any man I've ever met," one Cabinet officer admiringly declares.

Sorensen attends Cabinet meetings and the President's weekly conferences with Democratic Senate and House leaders. Cabinet members, budget and economic advisers, and other administration officials each week take to Sorensen dozens of problems that need White House attention but can be solved short of going to the President himself. Interagency disputes are frequently refereed in his office; he takes these family quarrels to the President only when he can't bring the agencies together himself, and then his suggestions carry immense weight with Kennedy. Sorensen, among others, helps brief the President before his weekly press conferences, going over the probable questions and possible answers.

His job includes recommending to the President whether bills passed by Congress should be approved or vetoed. He keeps in touch with idea men throughout the government and in universities and foundations, restlessly searching for new approaches that might serve the Administration. His office performs a vast complex of routine legal tasks—checking over executive orders to government agencies, suggesting presidential action on international air-route awards, proposing the President's course on pardon applications by criminals, and reviewing some court-martial judgments.

Yet close as he is to the President, Sorensen does not approach the position of influence and importance held by Sherman Adams in the Eisenhower administration. Adams was in fact, as his title proclaimed him to be, not *an* assistant to the President but *the* Assistant to the President; many thought the title might more appropriately have been the Assistant President. Kennedy, who came to the White House a far more energetic and politically-tuned President than Eisenhower, did away with the Adams post, and no one now has the title or the power held by the granite-faced one-time governor of New Hampshire.

"Adams had a hunting license to go just about anywhere in the White House, or for that matter in the entire Eisenhower administration," according to a Kennedy aide who had studied the previous regime. "No man on Kennedy's staff will be over all the others, as Adams was, or have quite so broad a grant of power. But there's no question that Ted has the broadest job of them all. That's the way it's been since 1953, and that's the way it will be through 1968."

From the first day of the Massachusetts Senator's service in 1953, Sorensen's mark has been on Kennedy's career. In fact, if Kennedy were not a dynamic, powerful personality in his own right, there would be an almost irresistible temptation to paint Sorensen as a master manipulator. As it is, the relationship must be viewed instead as a highly effective partnership, with the President the senior member but with the junior member exercising an unusually strong and active role.

A complete intellectual, Sorensen has a wide-ranging but orderly mind supported by an incredibly retentive memory, and a deep, almost intuitive understanding of political power and the ways of manipulating it. He is Kennedy's chief ambassador to the nation's intellectual liberals. Yet he knows the habits of the most hard-shelled southern senator or tough-talking northern ward boss.

From the day he joined the Kennedy staff Sorensen has charted a course most likely to win attention and acclaim for his man. He arranged thoughtful speeches on the Senate floor and planted magazine articles. He researched the material for Kennedy's *Profiles in Courage,* which won a Pulitzer Prize and made its author a politician with more than average celebrity appeal.

He skillfully managed the Kennedy vice-presidential boomlet at the 1956 Democratic nominating convention and, the day that failed, helped launch the Kennedy-for-President drive that was to reach fruition in Los Angeles in July 1960. Cross-country speaking tours were arranged for the candidate, more magazine articles produced, attention-getting Senate floor speeches readied. Political leaders were cultivated in every state. Bit by bit the organization needed to deliver the presidential nomination was built, with Sorensen a principal architect and builder.

And once the nomination was assured, he turned to selling the country the winning image of Kennedy—the likable, intelligent, cautiously liberal, vigorous young candidate. During the campaign Sorensen wrote most of the major statements Kennedy issued and edited the rest. He briefed the candidate daily on the problems ahead and masterminded the arduous drilling that preceded each of the crucial TV debates with Richard Nixon.

The tightly-knit Kennedy-Sorensen alliance is possible only because of an unusual harmony of view and purpose. On practically any subject Sorensen now will react as the President himself would, partly because their political and ideological views are virtually identical, and partly because Sorensen has schooled himself to react the way his chief does. "It's hard to figure," one high-ranking official mused, "when Ted is expressing something he really feels himself or something the President feels. Maybe the answer is that there's no difference."

In the process of mastering the Kennedy philosophy, Sorensen has also mastered his speaking and writing mannerisms. He can produce on incredibly short notice speeches that express the Kennedy ideas and bear the stamp of Kennedy's style and yet require only minor editing by the President himself before they are delivered.

During the Indiana presidential primary in the spring of 1960 Kennedy's voice gave out and Sorensen was called on to substitute. Reading from papers in his hand, he gave a typical Kennedy campaign speech, including Kennedy-style jokes and some of Kennedy's favorite quotations. Actually, reporters learned later, the papers were blank. The speech came directly from a mind so saturated with Kennedy's thoughts and approach that it could speak perfect Kennedy.

Physically, the President and his number-one assistant are quite different. Youthful, wearing horn-rimmed glasses, a boyish grin only occasionally lighting his studiedly serious face, Ted Sorensen looks more like a bright young college instructor than a White House power. A slightly stooped stance makes him seem shorter than the six-feet-one-and-a-half inches he actually reaches, and slighter than his 185 pounds.

But like Kennedy, he is physically and mentally tireless. Both men like ideas, books, intellectual argument. Both are quickly bored by pointless small talk. Both speak directly, sometimes almost brusquely. Both have a sly, brainy sense of humor. Both, too, would admit to the same political label, a highly-pragmatic liberalism, although they arrived at it from different poles. In the President's case, an innate political shrewdness was fused, as he matured and widened his horizon, with a New Dealing liberalism; the shrewdness and realism, however, never permit the doctrine to stand in the way of immediate gains. Sorensen developed as a devoted liberal largely by inheritance from his agrarian reformer parents. But his liberalism was gradually tempered by the realities of doing business in the Senate and the national political arena.

Like Kennedy himself, Sorensen is an internationalist in foreign affairs and a cautious advocate of government intervention in the domestic arena. Receptive to new ideas, he is not wild-eyed, embracing newness merely because it is new. He is a political realist willing to compromise and even retreat when the situation dictates this. "Ted is an intelligent, rational liberal, not the kind you have to lock the Treasury door against," says an old friend. "He was brought up in a liberal, new-idea atmosphere, and new ideas have lost their forbidden-fruit tang for him."

Sorensen has recently carried his political and philosophical kinship with Kennedy over into other areas. One now hears in his flat Midwest speech the overtones of Boston—an occasional "hahf" for half or "fo-wer" for four. He gestures now as Kennedy does, explaining a proposal with upturned palm, making a point with finger cutting the air. Sitting at ease, he'll drape his leg over the arm of the chair and begin massaging his ankles, à la Kennedy. Long an abstainer except for a rare glass of wine, he has begun drinking an occasional daiquiri or Heineken's beer, the President's own favorite drinks. (He still, however, does not smoke, not even the cigars Kennedy has cultivated in the last few years.)

Certainly the two men have benefited from their association. Sorensen has helped Kennedy achieve the highest office in the nation, and he has himself moved there at Kennedy's right hand. Their relationship, based on mutual understanding and respect, seems secure and solid. It is true that Sorensen has never been part of the Kennedy social world, but there is no sign he ever particularly sought or wanted to be. Although Kennedy, during the immediate preconvention period in 1960, pushed Sorensen a little into the background, the campaign put him back in his old close role, and there he remains.

Certainly Sorensen's devotion to his chief is single-minded and all-enveloping. This attitude is not uncommon among the men around Kennedy, but perhaps Sorensen carries it farther than most; family, friends, relaxation have at various times all been slighted or ignored to further Kennedy's career. He tends to judge the rightness or wrongness of a development not so much by absolute moral standards as by the extent to which it advances or retards Kennedy's cause. Frequently facts are bent to push his Kennedy-minded plan.

During the preconvention period Sorensen would leak public opinion polls favorable to Kennedy and suppress those that weren't advantageous, maintaining throughout that all polls were being made available as fast as they came in. "Let's never forget," he once told a reporter, "that as good friends as you and I are, our objectives are different."

Other people have been unconcernedly sacrificed. When the Wisconsin presidential primary was at its most bitter, Sorensen and other Kennedy aides encouraged Governor Gaylord Nelson to believe he was Kennedy's choice for keynoter at the Democratic nominating convention; Nelson was suspected of leaning toward rival candidate Hubert Humphrey of Minnesota, and had to be kept neutral. But once the primary was won, Senator Frank Church of Idaho was told that he was Kennedy's keynoter choice; the decision on how Idaho's delegates would go was still ahead.

"For the past eight years," a friend said soon after the inauguration, "Ted had only one thought—to elect John F. Kennedy President of the United States. Now his only thought is to make sure Kennedy goes down in history as one of the greatest Presidents."

Although he still works long hours, Sorensen seems able to relax a bit more now that he's in the White House. After the physical rigors of years of cross-country traveling in Kennedy's cause, he enjoys sleeping in the same bed each night, eating three meals a day (even if one or two are at his desk), and occasionally finding time for a movie or party.

Moreover, like the President himself, Sorensen basks in the relative peace and seclusion of his new quarters. His high-ceilinged office is spacious and quiet, with a huge desk, conference table, and sofa among the furnishings. The White House gate is an effective barrier to droppers by; secretaries filter out phone calls. It's all very different from the crowded Room 362 in the Senate Office Building, where he had to share a small cubicle with two other staff members, where callers grabbed him to ask questions or pour out their thoughts each time he wandered out of his cubbyhole, where the phone was always bringing some problem that Candidate Kennedy just couldn't ignore.

"There are so many people you just don't have to talk to any more," Sorensen exults.

To understand this White House pillar one must look long and hard at his parents. Ted, his three brothers and one sister, grew up in an atmosphere of intellectual liberalism and public service that left its stamp on all of them. His Danish-descended father, Christian Abraham Sorensen, was born in a sod house on the western Nebraska prairie, the eldest of ten children. He became a liberal lawyer, a key lieutenant of the famed progressive Republican Senator George Norris and the father of rural electrification in Nebraska. A civil libertarian and free thinker, he quit his lifelong Republicanism in the mid-thirties to become a strong Franklin D. Roosevelt supporter; F.D.R., he felt, was only putting into practice all the projects he himself had long believed in and worked for.

Ted's mother, born of Russian Jews, was also a liberal and dedicated feminist. (All her children carry as their middle name her maiden name of Chaikin.) She was active in the woman's suffrage movement, the League of Women Voters, and similar liberal causes. Looking back now, her children think that Annis Sorensen always resented being just a mother and housewife and would have liked a career, too.

Liberalism, in fact, was one of the bonds between Ted's father and mother. C.A., as most Nebraskans knew him, was among other things counsel for the state women's suffrage movement, which brought Nebraska women the right to vote well ahead of the federal constitutional amendment. Miss Chaikin was a leading member of the movement. She was also secretary to the University of Nebraska Alumni Association during World War I, and a few of her stray remarks brought charges of pacifist and radical sympathies. The attorney who helped her defend herself against these charges was young C. A. Sorensen. The two were married in July 1921.

C.A. was a liberal from the start. He was expelled from Grand Island College in 1912 for making too liberal a speech in an oratorical contest. He had suggested that each generation should re-examine the "truth" as it had been handed down by previous generations—in politics, economics, religion, and other areas. Only this way, he argued, could man progress. Several ministers denounced him from the pulpit, a few newspapers wrote fulminating editorials, and the authorities of the school, which was church affiliated, suggested it would be better if he continued his education elsewhere. C.A. switched to the University of Nebraska. He also quit the Fundamentalist faith in which he had been reared and became a Unitarian. Ted and the rest of the family are still Unitarians today.

In Nebraska in those days a liberal in politics automatically joined the Norris wing of the Republican party, and C.A. took his talents and enthusiasm there. Regarded by many as the Senator's heir, in 1928 he was, over the objections of the Republican right wing, nominated and elected state attorney general. With clever use of press relations he promptly made a reputation as a fire-eating crime buster, was re-elected once, but lost out in the Roosevelt landslide of 1932. He was Senator Norris' campaign manager in 1936, when the Senator won as an independent, and was co-campaign manager when the elderly Senator finally lost out to conservative Kenneth Wherry in 1942.

His children still don't know how C.A. voted in the 1932 and 1936 elections, but they suspect he voted for F.D.R. at least in 1936, if not the earlier year. Roosevelt's New Dealing zeal captivated C.A. completely, making a strong internationalist out of a man who had been a zealous isolationist and a member of Henry Ford's Peace Ship expedition in World War I. In 1940, when Senator Norris was co-chairman of a nationwide group of independents for Roosevelt, C.A. was regional vice-chairman. His political activity taught the children that party label wasn't as important as liberal principles. Asked whether they were brought up as Republicans, Democrats, or what, one Sorensen sibling says, "Or what."

Ted grew up in this liberal, politically-charged atmosphere. He and his older brothers occasionally accompanied their father on his political trips or visits to public power groups, and were sitting on the platform and taking occasional bows at tender ages. Liberal magazines were everywhere in their house. *Time,* the *Reader's Digest,* the *Literary Digest,* and other traditional journals were there, but so were the *New Republic, Nation, Harper's, The At-lantic,* and *The Progressive.*

Devotion to public service was deeply indoctrinated. The eldest brother, Robert, now in charge of market research for a New York magazine, was formerly research director of Radio Free Europe and of the Johns Hopkins Operations Research Office. The next oldest brother, Thomas, is now a deputy director of the United States Information Agency and was previously in charge of its Middle East operations; he speaks Arabic. Ted was the third child, followed by a sister, Ruth, now the wife of Derek Singer, an International Cooperation Administration official who has worked on foreign-aid projects in South America and Africa. The youngest brother, Philip, practices law in Lincoln. He was for some time clerk to a federal district judge.

At one point several years ago, if the elder Sorensens had wanted to visit all their children, they would have had to circle the globe. Robert was in Munich, Tom in the Middle East, Ted in Washington, Ruth in South America, and Philip was serving with the Coast Guard in the Far East.

Except for the unusually intellectual, liberal atmosphere, Ted had a normal small-town upbringing. There were always five or ten friends playing baseball or football with the Sorensen brood in the yard behind the Sorensens' house on Park Street in Lincoln, where the elder Mrs. Sorensen still lives. Ted's enthusiasm for touch football, a game he still enjoys despite a trick back, long predates his service on the Kennedy staff. He was a counselor at the Y.M.C.A. and other summer camps, and there is still a touch of the earnest, clean-living, and right-thinking Y counselor about him.

All the Sorensen children were uncommonly bright. Tom Sorensen recalls being told by teachers he would have to do extremely well to match the pace set by brother Robert, and Ted, in turn, was told he would have to be fabulous to live up to the achievements of both Bob and Tom. And so it went. The youngest brother, Philip, says he spent his whole life running to catch up with his older siblings.

At the University of Nebraska Ted was Phi Beta Kappa, editor of the *Law Review* and top man in his law class. His calm reason was obvious even then; when the students held a convention to draft a new campus constitution, Ted was unanimously chosen moderator of the drafting session.

In the fall of 1949, while in law school, Ted married Camilla Palmer, a college classmate and daughter of a University of Nebraska professor. The Palmers were also church companions of the Sorensens; actually, they were Quakers, but there was no Friends' meeting place in Lincoln, and so they turned up frequently at the Unitarian Church the Sorensens attended. Ted and Camilla in short order had three boys—Eric, now eight, Stephen, seven, and Philip, six. Too young for World War II, Ted also escaped Korean War service; he had just had a tumor removed from behind his ear when the Korean War broke out, and draft authorities wanted to be sure it wasn't serious.

There was never any doubt of his liberalism. He was active in a group seeking to outlaw racial discrimination in Lincoln, was a member of Americans for Democratic Action, and contributed articles on academic freedom to *The Progressive* and on civil rights to the *New Republic*. "The Supreme Court during its present session has the opportunity to strike its mightiest blow against racial segregation," an article in the December 15, 1952, *New Republic* declared. Entitled "School Doors Swing Open," it reviewed the extent to which southern and border-state schools and universities had already integrated with comparatively little trouble. "It is a roll call which refutes word for word the specious arguments of the Byrneses and their lawyers, who say they want to protect innocent Negro children," Sorensen asserted. "Legally-enforced orders ending educational segregation have not resulted in widespread violence. The public schools have not been destroyed by withdrawal of parental support."

The article concludes that "these many schools and colleges demonstrate that there is no need to wait another one hundred years to desegregate successfully and peacefully throughout the South. As a representative of the New Jersey Department of Education said, 'The best way to integrate is to do it.'"

Ted Sorensen's ability, his upbringing, his views, and probably some great inner push to success all made him look beyond Nebraska. His father wanted Ted to join him in law practice in Lincoln, but Ted had other ideas. "Lincoln was a good place to grow up in," a friend relates, "but if you have itchy feet, dream big dreams, and are a liberal, you leave. Ted left." That was the summer of 1951.

The place he left for was the nation's capital, and he had no trouble, in the closing days of the Truman administration, landing a job as a lowly lawyer in the Federal Security Agency, the predecessor of the present Department of Health, Education, and Welfare. But he was restless there, too, handling routine paper work, and he soon managed to find a temporary opening on the staff of a special Senate subcommittee investigating the Railway Retirement System. His job was to study the relation between railroad retirement and regular social-security benefits, and to do some general research on the economic problems of the aged. The subcommittee chairman was Senator Paul Douglas of Illinois.

That fall of 1952 Dwight D. Eisenhower was elected President, and Sorensen's old F.S.A. job seemed out of reach. Fortunately, however, a young Democrat in Massachusetts, bucking the nationwide Republican tide, had defeated the incumbent Republican senator, Henry Cabot Lodge, and was ready to take his seat as the junior senator from Massachusetts. John Kennedy needed some expert staff help. In particular, he needed a research assistant and speech writer. Senator Douglas, whose judgment he respected highly, recommended Ted Sorensen, then a tender twenty-four. Kennedy hired him almost sight unseen.

Sorensen still marvels at the casual beginning of what turned out to be so vital a relationship. Kennedy needed a research aide, and Sorensen was available. Sorensen wanted to start swimming in the turbulent Washington main stream, and the position on Kennedy's staff was open. Neither knew too much about the other, and certainly neither knew how basic and close their kinship would become. The decision to join talents was made largely on the basis of an intuitive, off-the-cuff appraisal which would have been remarkable for any area of government or industry let alone one which almost immediately began pointing toward the White House.

As a Massachusetts congressman, Kennedy had not shown himself a particularly crusading liberal, although some seeds of liberalism were readily visible. Nor had he presented the picture of a devout internationalist; in fact, he had opposed some of the Truman administration's foreign-aid and foreign-trade proposals. His advance to a more solid liberalism and internationalism came gradually, though steadily, in the Senate. Even then he never approached the degree of sloganeering liberalism represented by such senators as Douglas or Clark of Pennsylvania.

No one knows for sure just how much of Kennedy's growing liberalism resulted naturally from his own intellectual and philosophical development. Many think his election to the Senate sparked national ambitions which he believed he could achieve only with a more liberal springboard. Others are convinced that when Sorensen began to beam the pure light of his own profound liberalism on the Senator, the latter took his first sure steps toward the New Frontier. In any event, Kennedy's shift to a more consistent liberalism and internationalism did come after Sorensen joined his staff. Perhaps the Senator would have moved in the same direction in any case, but Sorensen's presence no doubt accelerated and reinforced the movement. Certainly the young research assistant would not have had so much impact if he had joined the staff of a senator basically more conservative than Kennedy; nor would Kennedy have evolved precisely the same philosophy of government if his key staff aide had been someone more conservative than Sorensen.

To gain attention for this freshman senator from Massachusetts, Kennedy and Sorensen mapped a careful public-relations program, starting with a series of speeches on the problems of New England. Sorensen, with his relentless, steel-trap memory for anything seen or read, quickly collected the views of economists and other regional experts. He deluged the Library of Congress reference service with requests for books and information; Library staff members still recall him as the man who took out more books than anyone else on Capitol Hill.

Starting in May 1953, just a few months after Ted Sorensen joined his staff, Senator Kennedy began a series of New England speeches on the Senate floor. Gradually he broadend his appeal, claiming that New England's needs were those of other depressed areas throughout the nation, and that the problem therefore was national and not merely regional. Kennedy and his aide followed up these speeches by publicizing the program, and the Senator, in articles in the *New York Times Magazine, The Atlantic,* and the *New Republic.*

Much of the Kennedy-Sorensen program was a typical liberal one: extension of such New Deal measures as federal minimum wage and social security, increased federal development of natural resources, and other steps which were both popular and also calculated to reduce the South's competitive advantages over New England by raising southern manufacturing costs. But there were some nonstandard proposals; for example, a scheme for regional development corporations.

But the speeches and magazine articles received comparatively little national recognition. "Leaders of national opinion dismissed it as just another push in the endless scuffle for local or regional advantage," declares James Macgregor Burns in his authoritative political biography of Kennedy.

Adding to Kennedy's problems at this time was the recurring pain in his back, injured first at football in college and then severely aggravated when a Japanese destroyer rammed his PT boat during World War II. In the fall of 1954 he decided on surgery and spent the next seven months first in a hospital in New York and then recuperating in Florida. During this time Sorensen took over all the Senator's legislative work, keeping an eye on the doings of his committees, answering correspondence, having the Senator's name put on bills he was interested in, and arranging to get Kennedy's views made known on the major issues that were coming before the Senate.

But his chief effort during this period, both in terms of time and later political impact, was research for the project that finally made Kennedy a national figure: the series of vignettes of courageous senators who put principle before personal gain, *Profiles in Courage.* Sorensen again combed the Library of Congress and other sources, checked with historians, talked to senators and other authorities, and fed a flood of raw material to the Senator in Florida.

The introduction to the book liberally and frankly acknowledges Sorensen's help. "The greatest debt," Kennedy declares, "is owed to my research associate, Theodore C. Sorensen, for his invaluable assistance in the assembly and preparation of the material upon which this book is based." Both Kennedy and Sorensen violently deny any suggestion that anyone but Kennedy himself actually wrote the book.

Sorensen and several other aides and friends urged Kennedy to use his newly-found national reputation to seek the Democratic vice-presidential nomination; according to Burns, Sorensen argued that even if Senator Kennedy lost, the national publicity would stand him in good stead later. Kennedy finally decided against trying for the nomination openly himself, but told Sorensen and other aides to go ahead on their own. It wasn't until the convention itself had begun in the summer of 1956 that Kennedy personally committed himself to the race.

The Kennedy-for-Vice-President drive was largely masterminded by Sorensen, with help from Kennedy's administrative assistant Ted Reardon, brother Robert, Connecticut Governor Abraham Ribicoff, Kennedy's brother-in-law Sargent Shriver, and a few others. They worked on the assumption that Adlai Stevenson would be the presidential nominee and would pick his own running mate. So they directed their efforts to persuading Stevenson and his top advisers that Kennedy was their man.

One of the major weapons in this campaign was a fascinating, statistic-studded document that Ted Sorensen researched and wrote on "The Catholic Question." Recognizing that his boss's religion was considered by many a major stumbling block for national nomination, Sorensen decided to meet the issue head on. He produced a lengthy study, bolstered with tables and footnotes, designed to prove that far from being a handicap, a Catholic running mate would be a major asset to a Protestant presidential nominee.

The study claimed that Catholic voters were decisive in the states with the largest number of electoral votes, and that these Catholic voters, once overwhelmingly Democratic and the source of Roosevelt and Truman victories, had deserted Stevenson in substantial numbers in 1952. A Catholic vice-presidential nominee, the study argued, would bring many of these back to the Democratic fold, adding far more strength to the national ticket than would a running mate with primary appeal to the South or to the farm belt. Planted in several news magazines shortly before the convention, the study helped focus still more attention on the young man from New England.

Sorensen supplied other fuel for the Kennedy fire, too. He, Reardon, and others talked tirelessly to friendly politicians to line up support for their man. They operated a small hotel headquarters where delegates could get buttons and literature. When Kennedy agreed to make the main nominating speech for Stevenson, Arthur Schlesinger Jr., a Stevenson speech writer, turned out a proposed nominating talk that was top notch Stevenson but impossible Kennedy; Sorensen overnight whipped out a first-rate Kennedy-style nominating address.

But Stevenson, once nominated for President, did not, of course, tap the young Massachusetts Senator for his running mate. Instead, he threw the convention open for vice-presidential balloting, and Senator Estes Kefauver of Tennessee nosed out Kennedy in a seesaw, spine-tingling contest. The failure to win the vice presidential nomination for his boss jarred Sorensen only momentarily. He rebounded rapidly, and almost immediately launched Kennedy's 1960 presidential campaign. Leaving his erstwhile legislative chores to other staff members, Sorensen began an intensive study of the sources of political power across the country and an equally intensive cultivation of these sources.

To attract public attention, Senate speeches and more magazine articles were ground out. Detailed memos were prepared setting forth, in the most favorable possible light, of course, Kennedy's views and record on McCarthyism, labor legislation, farm problems, civil rights, and other thorny topics. Magazines wanting to put Kennedy on their cover or otherwise publicize him found Ted a ready source of anecdotes and other useful material.

To attract the attention of politicians, an arduous, incessant cross-country speaking schedule was laid out for Kennedy, and his aide also supplied the raw material for these appearances. Sorensen himself was on the phone tirelessly, talking to old friends and new allies across the country. He began attending regional and state Democratic meetings, attempting to convert local leaders and potential delegates. His efficiency and political savvy won the respect of many old pros, even though they never felt at ease with this sober, intense young fellow.

More and more he became the Kennedy emissary to liberal groups—organizations which found his obvious intellectualism and past liberal affiliations reassuring in the light of their doubts of Kennedy's own liberal credentials. Late in 1958 Sorensen began recruiting a brain trust of university professors for the candidate. This accomplished many objectives: it brought Kennedy and Sorensen valuable ideas and ammunition on many campaign issues; it gave an aura of intellectualism to the Kennedy movement; and it brought into camp many men who otherwise might have thrown in with Stevenson, Humphrey, or some other presidential candidate.

Probably Sorensen's darkest months came in early 1960 during the period of presidential primaries and preconvention maneuvering. He was still writing, traveling, contacting. But somehow he wasn't quite so close to Kennedy as he had been.

Kennedy obviously felt that the shaping of a public image was fine for the long haul but that organization was the key to winning primaries and conventions. He regarded Ted as overserious, a little too stiff for backslapping and small talk with the delegates, too intent on marshaling arguments and figures, and not ready enough to relax with the local leaders in the nearest bar. Old pros moved in—Brother Bobby, just finished with his own book, *The Enemy Within;* Bobby's college and Senate Rackets Committee sidekick, Kenneth O'Donnell; long-time Massachusetts political expert Larry O'Brien, and Connecticut Democratic state chairman John Bailey. Sorensen felt more than a little left out of the show, and although he tried to cover it, he worried about his future relations with Kennedy.

But the presidential campaign revived the old close relationship. While the pros ran the political end, Ted Sorensen took charge of

the once-again vital job of building the public image. He traveled
everywhere with the candidate. Each morning he briefed him on
the latest news developments, charted the issues likely to be brought
up at each stop, discussed speech ideas. Usually he would talk to
Kennedy in advance only about the general subject matter, then
write a first draft. After showing it to the candidate, who usually
changed no more than a few words, Sorensen would write the final
draft. Unlike many speech writers, he rarely requires as much as
three drafts to satisfy the boss. Sorensen wrote almost three-fourths
of all the major speeches and statements during the campaign,
although Kennedy always ad libbed considerably in actually delivering them. Aides turned out the rest, with Sorensen riding herd
and editing their product.

While Kennedy would be delivering one speech, Ted Sorensen
was usually working on the next two or three speeches. When the
candidate finally went to bed, Sorensen would stay up working on
the following morning's needs. Frequently he got only a few hours'
sleep; twenty-hour days were routine. In fact, one night near the
end of the campaign, when he managed somehow to get a full
ten hours of sleep, he found himself so groggy in the morning from
the unaccustomed luxury that he packed and shipped off to the
plane all his clothes—including those he was to wear that day. He
had to call frantically for a bellman to get the luggage back from
the truck.

With Myer Feldman, a long-time Kennedy aide and now White
House Deputy Special Counsel, Sorensen also briefed the Democratic candidate for the crucial television debates with Nixon. The
two would sit with Kennedy for several hours, going over likely
questions and possible answers, suggesting statements he could
make, arming him with facts to repel expected Nixon charges,
priming him with attacks he could make on the Republicans. Certainly Kennedy himself deserves the major credit for his brilliant
TV performances, but a good share of the plaudits must go to the
superb briefing jobs.

One of the very first appointments Kennedy made, following his
election, was to name Ted Sorensen his Special Counsel. And his
first two assignments were typical of the vital and varied role the

young Nebraskan was to play. One was to start thinking immediately about the content of the Inaugural and State of the Union addresses. The other was to recruit and supervise some two dozen special "task forces," which were to study and prepare policy recommendations on a wide variety of foreign and domestic problems ahead of the new administration.

The job Sorensen now holds is one that, despite the title, has had relatively little to do with strictly legal chores. Sorensen, who has never really practiced law himself, recognizes this. Congratulated on his appointment, he replied with typical wry humor, "I thought it was time I got back to practicing law."

The post was created by Franklin D. Roosevelt during World War II, when Judge Samuel I. Rosenman, his long-time confidant and speech writer, moved into the White House setup on a permanent basis. The title was a reflection of Judge Rosenman's past background, rather than a description of his actual White House work. "The title," declares an unpublished study by the Brookings Institution on *The White House and the Executive Office of the President,* "was in deference to Rosenman's profession; the actual job was to ride herd on the stream of messages and public documents flowing from the White House. A full-time senior staff member was thought essential. To control the public expression of policy is to have a major voice in the formulation of policy, as Rosenman well knew." Judge Rosenman drafted the President's messages to Congress and orders applying to the war agencies, passed on legislation, wrote speeches, and generally did troubleshooting jobs for his boss.

President Truman tried to do without such an aide for a time, but soon, the Brookings study continues, "found it impossible to get along without a senior staff member in the sensitive role of watchdog over the preparation of speeches, messages to Congress, and other public papers. He named Clark Clifford to this spot. Since Clifford was a lawyer, the 'abolished' title of Special Counsel was resurrected, although, just as in Rosenman's case, it was adopted as much to fit the man as to describe the job."

Clifford and his successor, Charles S. Murphy, built up a staff of five to eight associates. "All," says Brookings, "were expected to, and did, move with rapidity from a speech on civil rights to a congressional message on foreign policy to a veto of a labor bill to discussing the strategy of dealing with Capitol Hill. All were expected to view every problem and every assignment from the point of view of the President, wearing all his hats."

Under President Eisenhower the Special Counsel title was continued, but with more strictly legal tasks. The functions of message preparation, speech writing, policy making, and legislative liaison were dispersed among many other White House aides. The three men who held the job under Eisenhower, Bernard Shanley, Gerald Morgan, and David Kendall, were essentially lawyers, advising their client on bills, pardons, executive orders, and other legal business.

Sorensen's assignment goes back to the Roosevelt-Truman concept. His primary task is to write the major speeches, messages, and other public documents that help shape the public image of the President. There has always been a debate on the extent to which the man who writes the speeches makes policy. But whether narrow or extensive, there is little doubt that he does have some impact. "The first thing a new Cabinet member should do," one Washington observer once remarked, "is to get to know the President's speech writer."

Friendship with the speech writer probably has less value for a Cabinet member under Kennedy than under many another president. The Chief Executive has his own ideas and sets the guide lines. He is highly literate and thoroughly informed on a vast number of topics. Yet even for Kennedy the importance of the speech writer is immense. There are endless variations possible within the broad framework of policy.

The State of the Union message was a good example. As each Cabinet member was appointed, Kennedy and Sorensen urged him to bear in mind that the new President would have to give a State of the Union address soon after inauguration, and to submit suggestions for it. As these came in Sorensen organized them by topic, and then talked further to the Cabinet members. Combining all this with the task force reports the President-elect had been receiving and with his own knowledge of Kennedy's attitudes and desires, he drafted a proposed message. Kennedy made substantial changes. Another draft resulted, and the President made some additional changes. That was largely it.

Even aside from the powers of the speech writer, Sorensen has a major voice in helping to shape the policy he must put into words. The messages and speeches are not merely an opportunity for the President to state his views but also an opportunity for him and his staff to develop those views. In Sorensen's office discussions go on endlessly among Cabinet members, undersecretaries, agency heads, and lower echelon officials. Problem after problem is thrashed out, issues that must be resolved before new administration policy is ready to be announced.

Day-to-day developments in foreign policy and national security are largely left to presidential assistants McGeorge Bundy, Walt Rostow, and Jerome Wiesner. But Sorensen and his deputies sit in and have a voice in the preparation of long-range policy in these fields—a new look in foreign aid, revision of the reciprocal-trade program, overhaul of the defense budget, steps to halt gold outflow, or how to cope with Communist threats in Latin America.

In the domestic area Sorensen is immersed in both long-range and day-to-day policy making. Agencies in disagreement over new policies bring their controversies to him. He sits, listens, summarizes the discussion. "He analyzes and mediates," a fellow staff member reports. "Sometimes he'll let the discussion go on two or three hours, then tell them where they agreed, where they disagreed, and perhaps a possible solution. It's immensely impressive." Some disputes are worked out this way, and some he takes to the President, giving the pros and cons and his own thoughts. If he doesn't make any recommendations of his own, the President will usually turn to him anyway and ask, "What do you think, Ted?"

To help him in his myriad special counsel chores Sorensen has a three-man staff of long-time associates. Top man is forty-four-year-old Myer (Mike) Feldman, a tall, affable lawyer who started his government service after World War II as an attorney with the Securities and Exchange Commission. Feldman, one of Sorensen's closest personal friends, gradually moved up to the top S.E.C. staff job, executive assistant to the chairman, and then switched to Capitol Hill to help run the Senate Banking Committee's investigation of stock-market practices in 1955 and 1956. He moved over to the Kennedy staff as legislative assistant in 1958, and headed the Kennedy research operation during the 1960 campaign.

Richard Goodwin, a twenty-nine-year-old former law clerk to Justice Frankfurter, is another assistant. A brilliant lawyer and perceptive student of government, Dick Goodwin has mastered the Kennedy style almost as thoroughly as Ted Sorensen himself, and was the maestro's chief speech-writing assistant throughout the 1960 campaign. The third member of Sorensen's staff is thirty-seven-year-old Lee C. White, a University of Nebraska classmate of Sorensen. When Sorensen became Senator Kennedy's legislative assistant in 1953, he summoned classmate White from a job as a Tennessee Valley Authority lawyer to be his helper. After a few years White decided to strike out on his own, shifted to the staff of the Senate Small Business Committee, and later became the administrative assistant to Republican Senator John Sherman Cooper of Kentucky. After inauguration he returned to the Kennedy fold.

How does Ted Sorensen strike people personally? He is not a simple character. He talks in measured syllables uttered so softly that the listener frequently has to strain to hear him. Very often he will hesitate long before answering a question or remark, and then come out with rather cryptic comments. This is partly the result of a cautious desire to avoid committing the President, partly perhaps to give an impression of wisdom and maturity beyond his years. He has long avoided the limelight. But more recently he seems to be enjoying the power and prestige of his position.

To many he has seemed surly, highhanded, abrasive, abrupt. "Countless people feel he has engaged in psychological warfare against them for years," one acquaintance says. Senatorial aides are a clubby lot, frequently lunching together or pausing to chat in Capitol corridors to trade the latest gossip. Sorensen rarely took time for this, and some colleagues complained that he would pass them in the halls without so much as a nod. When Kennedy's speech writers first met to hear their future role in the presidential campaign, Ted Sorensen came in to address them. The group included some of the biggest names in the writing field, including *Look* magazine editor, William Attwood, now Ambassador to Guinea. But Sorensen talked to them as though they were freshmen in a college composition course.

"I'm sure," he said, according to one authoritative report, "you all have ideas of what the campaign issues should be and how they should be presented to the people. But remember, the campaign issues are what Senator Kennedy says they are, and they'll be presented the way he wants them to be. If you don't think you can do that, you have no business here." Then he turned and left.

Sorensen himself doesn't recall having been quite that brusque. But he'd argue that even if he had been, he was merely saving everyone's time.

Friends defend him as being direct but not haughty. They say he just never learned the art of small talk, tends to be shy and reserved anyhow, and so covers this up with a brusqueness that frequently seems arrogant. "He has to go to the heart of the matter," one colleague asserts. "You can call this arrogance, or you can call it efficiency."

Some acquaintances feel that his abruptness fed on feelings of insecurity. Now that he has arrived and his future seems safe, they suggest, he'll mellow. Early experience seems to bear this idea out. Anyhow, close friends insist, he has always been warm and relaxed with them, the best of companions. He doesn't have a large circle of friends, but sees a lot of those he has—a few office associates and one or two reporters. He likes to play softball or throw a football with colleagues and their offspring. Gifted with an unusual ear for a tune, he can play practically any piece on the piano after hearing it once.

Ted has an excellent sense of humor, as does his boss. Kennedy is a fast man with a quip or ad lib, and drops many of his own jokes into speeches. But Sorensen has supplied a good number of the most effective gags used by Kennedy during the presidential campaign and in appearances since he took office. Sorensen and

Dick Goodwin frequently have sat around trying out old joke-book lines on each other, but Ted has also written or adapted many jokes himself.

One of his best contributions were those he made to the running stream of witty remarks with which Kennedy opened his speech at the Al Smith Memorial dinner in New York in October 1960. There, with Nixon also present, Kennedy thawed out a predominantly Republican audience with a series of audacious but apt gags, many of them Sorensen's.

Their host, Cardinal Spellman, was, Kennedy noted, "the only man so widely respected in American politics that he could bring together, amicably, at the same table, for the first time during this campaign, two political leaders who are increasingly apprehensive about the November election, who have long eyed each other suspiciously, and who have disagreed so strongly, both publicly and privately"—and as the audience looked expectantly at him and Nixon he paused and then added—"Vice-President Nixon and Governor Rockefeller."

Nixon, he declared, was being criticized for his campaign tactics by even such friendly sources as the *Wall Street Journal,* "like the *Osservatore Romano* criticizing the Pope." He said the worst news the Republicans had that week was that Casey Stengel had been fired: "It must show that experience doesn't count." And so on for about five minutes.

Sorensen loves to write light verse and comic parodies, and grinds out poems on almost any occasion. This year he composed comic valentines for most of the White House staff. When an old friend, Elliot Richardson, quit as assistant secretary of the Department of Health, Education, and Welfare to become district attorney in Boston, Sorensen penned a rather lengthy effort that began:

> *Rejoice all ye widows and orphans,*
> *Ye victims of fraud and decay.*
> *Rest easy, ye helpless and homeless.*
> *Old Elliot's to be the D.A.*

Avaunt all ye Hoffas and hoodlums,
Gather ye hot goods while ye may.
For your syndicates and empires are crumbling,
Old Elliot's to be the D.A.

and ended:

So, friends, let's toast to his future.
A future as bright as can be.
We're glad he'll be D.A. up in Boston.
'Cause he then can't be D.A. in D.C.

Another effort was whipped out just before Inauguration Day,
when Arthur Goldberg, designated to be Labor Secretary in the
Kennedy Cabinet, invited the entire Cabinet and some other top
Kennedy aides to a Sunday brunch. This was the Cabinet's first
meeting together. Mrs. Goldberg read an ode an old friend had
written her husband on his selection by Kennedy, and thus inspired,
Sorensen took five minutes to dash off "Men of the New Frontier":

All hail the men of new frontiers—
The hardy Kennedy pioneers.
The Georgia cracker known as Rusk.
The courtly Hodges, never brusque.
Orville Freeman, farmers' friend.
To Stu Udall, sleeping bag lend.
Send racy books to Edward Day.
Send lazy crooks to Bobby K.
Take health needs to Abe Ribicoff.
Blame Dillon if your checkbook's off.
McNamara's Ford is in his past.
Art Goldberg, not least, though mentioned last.

Ted Sorensen will not have much time for poems and parodies
in the coming years, as he toils at President Kennedy's right hand

to sell Congress and the American public on the Kennedy program and the Kennedy personality. The problems he faces are essentially the problems Kennedy himself faces. This is undoubtedly exactly what Ted Sorensen and the President of the United States expect and want.

2.

SCHOLARS OF THE NUCLEAR AGE

McGeorge Bundy
Walt W. Rostow
Jerome B. Wiesner

By DAVID WISE

DIRECTLY ACROSS WEST EXECUTIVE AVENUE FROM THE WHITE
House, in one of the ugliest buildings in Washington, sit three
men whose brains and judgment may influence the fate of America.
The three are the President's cold-war, politico-military, and scientific advisers.

One, McGeorge Bundy, is the former dean of Harvard, a
polished, proper Bostonian with family roots that go as far back
as the time of the Indian Squanto. He is the grandson of one of
the founders of the Daughters of the American Revolution, although his mother canceled her membership when the D.A.R. demanded a $25.00 fee to verify her genealogy.

Another, Walt Whitman Rostow, is the son of a Russian immigrant. He helped found the O.S.S. in World War II and currently
spends much of his time trying to anticipate the next move of
the Russians.

The third, Jerome B. Wiesner, is the son of a dry-goods shopkeeper in Dearborn, Michigan, a relaxed pipe-and-sweater man
who has the perpetual expression of a sleepy poker player but
who knows every card in the deck. He is a quiet, gentle man who
likes to eat blintzes with his family for Sunday breakfast—and who
helped develop wartime radar and the atomic bomb.

If their backgrounds are different, there are nevertheless some remarkable similarities. All three men are products of the war. All served President Eisenhower in varying part-time capacities before they came to work full time for President Kennedy. All have been in and out of government and intelligence work over the past decade. All are expert beyond their own immediate academic discipline, and all are activists as well as thinkers. None is violently partisan.

"We are all almost substitutable for each other," says Rostow. "We are interchangeable parts."

These are, in short, the scholars of the nuclear age. Each has left his university for the political arena to focus his brain and skills on the central problem of his time: survival in a world that has learned how to split the atom. In a sense, they are high priests in a booby hatch; brilliant witch doctors tending to the ailments of a civilization that pretends it is civilized but is not. They must provide logical, rational answers to essentially irrational problems. They are, at best, practitioners of an indefinite art. But witch doctors are necessary in an uncivilized society; in Bundy, Rostow, and Wiesner, Kennedy has selected three whose feathers, rattles, masks, and amulets are of the highest craftsmanship.

A MONTH AFTER JOHN F. KENNEDY'S ELECTION IN NOVEMBER 1960, Adlai E. Stevenson called on the President-elect at his red-brick home in Georgetown. "I'd like you to be United States Ambassador to the United Nations," Kennedy told his visitor.

"Whom will I be working for?" Stevenson asked.

The President-elect ticked off the names of Dean Rusk, David K. E. Bruce, Senator J. William Fulbright, and McGeorge Bundy as possible choices for Secretary of State.

Stevenson was visibly annoyed. "How," he asked Kennedy, "do you expect me to work for a forty-one-year-old Republican?"

The forty-one-year-old Republican, of course, was McGeorge Bundy, who ended up, not as Secretary of State, but as Special Assistant to the President for National Security Affairs, a sort of day-to-day overseer of foreign and defense policy. Actually, in that post Bundy is closer to the throne than either Stevenson or Rusk, the man Kennedy finally chose as Secretary of State. Bundy, whose

Republicanism is a sometime thing, but whose age, at least, was accurately described by Stevenson, is the top cold-war adviser to the President. He holds an awesome, chilling responsibility in a push-button era, when nations are poised on the brink of oblivion and tomorrow is an uncertainty.

The man who holds this tense nuclear-age post is a sandy-haired, bespectacled Back Bay Yankee who is carrying on his New England family's tradition of mixing public service with the academic life. One of Nathan M. Pusey's first acts as president of Harvard was to name Bundy dean of Harvard's Faculty of Arts and Sciences, at the unbelievably young age of thirty-four. Bundy left that post to go to work for Kennedy.

Walking through the White House outer lobby in his ivy-league clothes, Bundy, six feet and lean as a track star, could easily be mistaken for a graduate student rather than one of the most powerful men in the inner circle of advisers with direct access to the President of the United States. Two adjectives, aggressive and brilliant, are those that crop up most often in descriptions of Bundy. (A leading jurist, Learned Hand, once termed Bundy "the brightest man in America.") Neither is ill applied. Nor, in fairness, does either tell the full story.

Already there have been rumblings to the effect that Rusk will have to do some fancy diplomatic two-stepping to avoid being shunted aside by the eager Bundy. Some have speculated that with Bundy around, Theodore C. Sorensen, Special Counsel to the President, may face the same problem as Rusk. Said a colleague: "Kennedy and Bundy are very much alike—the pace at which they work, their disdain for irrelevant detail. Before this administration is over Bundy will be closer to Kennedy than Sorensen."

A similar view is taken by an astute observer of the Boston scene: "Bundy is a take-over guy. They say Pusey was glad to see him go. He'll take over in Washington, too."

Bundy is well aware of the overlap between his job and Rusk's, and of the potential for friction stemming from this hard fact. On the other hand, he is not by temperament and training the sort of man who will hold back, or refrain from plunging into a situation because he might risk stepping on someone else's toes.

A measure of Kennedy's confidence in Bundy is the fact that he did indeed consider Bundy for Secretary of State. Stevenson's objections to working for a forty-one-year-old Republican helped to knock Bundy out of the picture. And once Kennedy had selected Douglas Dillon to be Treasury Secretary and Robert S. McNamara as Defense Secretary, the choice of a third Republican for the Cabinet would have been politically hazardous.

At one point in the Cabinet-making process Kennedy told Bundy he wanted him as Under Secretary of State. This time it was Bundy who asked who his boss might be. Kennedy mentioned Rusk and Bruce. Bundy confessed that while he was dean at Harvard, he and Rusk had squabbled, mostly over Bundy's desire for more Rockefeller Foundation money for Harvard.

Quipped Bundy: "I admit I have an interest in seeing Dean Rusk Secretary of State. It would get him out as head of the Rockefeller Foundation."

Kennedy replied in the same vein: "As an overseer of Harvard, I have an interest in seeing you out as dean of the faculty."

In the end Bundy turned down the offer of appointment as Under Secretary of State for Administration. "It's too much like being dean again," he told Kennedy.

The Bundy name may be Swiss, French, or Scottish, no one is sure. But the family's roots are as deeply New England as clam chowder. On his father's side, the first Bundy landed at Ipswich, north of Boston, more than two hundred years ago. Bundy's mother is a Putnam, one of New England's oldest families. He is a descendant of the illustrious Lowell line, which included James Russell Lowell, poet, critic, and diplomat, and poetess Amy Lowell.

Bundy's father, Harvey Hollister Bundy, was born in Grand Rapids and brought up in Michigan. He was graduated from Yale and in 1915 married Katharine L. Putnam, the sister of his roommate at Harvard Law School. At the time he was secretary to Justice Oliver Wendell Holmes. Four years later, on March 30, 1919, McGeorge Bundy was born in Boston.

At the age of eight Mac was trundled off to the Dexter School in Brookline, Massachusetts, where his playmates included his elder brother, Bill, who was a grade ahead, and a skinny youngster named John Fitzgerald Kennedy. William P. Bundy, who went to the Pentagon after Kennedy's election, was on the Dexter football squad with the future President and remembers Kennedy well. Mac's memory of Kennedy is hazier. "I knew there was a Kennedy in the school," Mac says, adding a trifle stiffly, "I don't consider it very significant."

In 1931, after four years at Dexter School, Mac Bundy went to Groton. His father, who had achieved prominence as an attorney in Boston, was in Washington as Assistant Secretary of State in the Hoover administration under Henry L. Stimson. The elder Bundy held this position until Franklin D. Roosevelt was inaugurated in March 1933. Later, Harvey Bundy returned to Washington to serve as special assistant to Stimson during World War II when Republican Stimson was Roosevelt's secretary of war.

At Groton young McGeorge played the title role in Shakespeare's *Henry V*. ("Even then he was aiming for the top," said one friend.) And as brother Bill recalls, "He became very good at tennis." He still is. At Yale Mac majored in mathematics and classics, dabbled in politics as an active member of the Liberal Party in the Yale Political Union. Bill was already at Yale; both compiled excellent academic records. "There was an intense rivalry between them," recalls one classmate.

"Mac was two jumps ahead of everyone else even at Yale," says another close friend. "Bissell [Richard M. Bissell, Jr., now a top C.I.A. hand] gave some abstruse course; you had to be a mathematical genius even to get a glimmer of it. Naturally Mac took that."

"He was the most active spokesman for the Liberal Party in the Political Union," says another associate of college days. "A Republican? Bunk. In college he was the most ardent supporter of the New Deal and F.D.R."

Bill Bundy disagrees that his brother was quite that violently New Deal, but sums up Mac's Yale years this way: "Mac was something of an iconoclast. He took Senator Taft on once in a debate, just after Taft was elected to the Senate, and bested him in the opinion of most who heard him. But Mac was only middling New Deal at Yale. . . . He wrote a column for the *Yale News* in his junior year recommending the abolition of football at Yale. It was not popular."

Mac was tapped for Skull and Bones, the exclusive secret society about which grown Yale men still speak in whispers. In 1940 he was graduated Phi Beta Kappa into a world in ferment. A year later, after a trip to South America with a friend, Bundy took his one-and-only plunge into elective politics. He ran for City Council in Boston as a Republican—and lost. "It would probably be a good contender for the worst campaign in history," Bundy says now.

After Pearl Harbor Bundy entered the Army as a private early in 1942. Extremely myopic, he was accepted only after wangling waivers on his eyesight. He was trained as an intelligence officer; brother Bill was at the same school. Mac was yanked out by Admiral Alan G. Kirk, commissioned an officer in the Signal Corps, and assigned as an aide to the Admiral. "I was sort of a general handyman," Bundy recalls. "I was stationed in Norfolk, Virginia, first, then Sicily, and then to London in the fall of 1943. I helped plan Operation Overlord, the invasion of Europe. By the time I caught up with my battalion, the war in Europe was over." Bundy was also in on the planning of the Allied invasion of Sicily (Operation Husky). He emerged with the rank of captain.

Even in wartime England there was time for some intellectual and social activities. Bill recalls, "On Tuesday nights Mac went to Harold Laski's soirees, and Lady Astor's on the weekends. It was a balanced ticket."

After the war Mac returned to Boston. His father had just completed four years in Washington as Stimson's assistant. Mac moved into a cottage on the Stimson estate, where for a year and a half he had daily talks with Stimson while the two men co-authored *On Active Service in Peace and War,* a biographical account of Stimson's government career.

In April of 1948 Bundy came to Washington for his first job in the capital. He worked until September on the Marshall Plan under Richard Bissell, who had taught that abstruse course at Yale. That fall President Harry S. Truman was running for re-election against New York Governor Thomas E. Dewey, and Bundy got his first taste of presidential politics. He went to work for Dewey as a member of a high-powered foreign-policy team. The other members were Douglas Dillon, John Foster Dulles, Allen W. Dulles, and Christian A. Herter. The election returns brought catastrophe.

Bill Bundy remembers his brother's activity in those days this way: "Mac wrote speeches on China but Dewey never used them. After the campaign Mac wanted to go back to the Marshall Plan office but Truman said no. Truman said he didn't mind people contributing to the G.O.P. but he drew the line at writing speeches against him."

In view of Truman's unreasonable attitude toward hiring Dewey speech writers, Mac left Washington and went to work in New York for the privately-run Council on Foreign Relations. During 1948–49 Bundy was a political analyst for the Council in a study of the Marshall Plan. The chairman of the panel was Dwight D. Eisenhower, then president of Columbia University.

In 1949 Bundy made an important decision: he returned to Harvard to teach the basic undergraduate course in American foreign policy. There, at thirty, bachelor Bundy made the same discovery as many a Harvard man before him: Radcliffe girls can be dangerous. Mary Buckminster Lothrop was associate director of admissions at Radcliffe. She and Bundy were married June 10, 1950.

The following year Bundy was named associate professor of government. That was the year conservative William F. Buckley, Jr., turned on his and Bundy's alma mater and attacked Yale for "collectivism" and "atheism." Bundy struck back, blasting Buckley in the *Atlantic Monthly* as a "violent, twisted, ignorant young man." The *Saturday Evening Post,* in those days when "McCarthyism" was becoming a household word, editorially accused Bundy of "McGeorge Bundyism."

In 1952 Mac Bundy edited the public papers of Dean Acheson, Truman's Secretary of State, into a book published under the title *Patterns of Responsibility.* In the book Bundy carefully noted his family relationship to Acheson. (Brother Bill had married Acheson's daughter.) Then he proceeded to enter a strong defense of the embattled Secretary of State against charges of softness toward communism and friendliness toward Alger Hiss.

Senator Joseph R. McCarthy was aroused by the Bundys. At the height of his power in 1953 he went after Bill Bundy, by this time a key employee of the Central Intelligence Agency. Alarmed at the fact that Bill Bundy was Acheson's son-in-law, McCarthy attacked him on security grounds and tried to block his passport. He failed. Mac Bundy stood up to McCarthy, too, when other men were keeping quiet. He told a Senate committee, "The national security is not served when the security program becomes an instrument of insecurity and mistrust among men of good sense and high character. It is high time for us to recover from a timidity which has led us to give a world-wide impression that we do not trust ourselves."

While stoutly defending Acheson's conduct of foreign policy in his book, Mac Bundy made it plain that he disagreed with him on Communist China. "I do not believe," he wrote, "that our policy toward China from 1945 to 1950 adequately assessed the probable character of a communist regime in that country."

"Very near the heart of all foreign affairs," he also wrote, "is the relationship between policy and military power." And Bundy made it plain that he felt the United States could deal with the Soviets only from positions of strength.

In 1952 Bundy also tackled his first big job in the field of national security. He served as secretary for a year to a special and super-secret M.I.T. panel named by Acheson to explore the alarming growth of Soviet missile capacity, the possibility of arms control, and other related military and political problems. This was the Oppenheimer panel, so-called after its chairman, J. Robert Oppenheimer, whose security clearance as a consultant to the Atomic Energy Commission was removed two years later in a bitterly controversial case.

"It was," says Bundy, "the first time I was involved with highly-classified security aspects of defense planning." This is a fairly frank statement for a man who, eight years later, was named the top national security adviser to the President. On the edges of the Kennedy team there is some grumbling to the effect that one year in defense planning and seven as a Harvard dean do not qualify Bundy as a security expert. One friend of the Bundy brothers feels that "Bill was far more qualified by training for the job Mac got. But I don't think there's any jealousy between them. Bill is less aggressive. He doesn't have Mac's salesmanship."

In his own defense, Bundy points out that "the conduct of American foreign affairs has been my specialty since the war." Perhaps more pertinent is the fact that Kennedy apparently prefers advisers who are able to tackle problems in more than one area; men of ability and judgment, who mesh well with his own style and personality, rather than specialists.

Bundy became a Harvard dean in the summer of 1953. At thirty-four he found himself responsible for overseeing a staff of 1,000, including 288 full professors, most of them much older than he. Bundy worked hard to help meet Harvard College's goal of $82,-500,000 in new funds for expansion. He conducted a popular freshman seminar in United States foreign policy, and revamped the rules to permit bright students to move ahead at their own pace. He established, in short, a reputation as an able and energetic administrator.

He also found time to join the Republican drive against Foster Furcolo, a Democrat, during his 1958 campaign for re-election. Said Bundy in a newspaper ad: "Furcolo is not a wicked man. He is something more dangerous than that. He is a bad governor." Furcolo won, anyway.

Bundy and Kennedy saw each other a few times a year after Kennedy became an overseer of the university. At commencement in 1960 Bundy sat next to Kennedy; the two men talked for a long time, and Bundy liked what he heard. Although he had backed Ike in 1952 and 1956, Bundy helped organize a scientific and professional committee for Kennedy. However, he never became part of the "Cambridge group" of some twenty-five intellectuals who actively fed ideas to Kennedy during the campaign.

After the campaign a fairly painful period of waiting began for Bundy. First Secretary of State went by the board. Then he turned down the offer of an under secretaryship. Kennedy also discussed the post of Assistant Secretary of Defense for International Security

Affairs, a job that eventually went to Paul H. Nitze. (Bill Bundy became Nitze's deputy.) There was also discussion of Bundy directing the United States disarmament team, a job that went to John J. McCloy.

In the meantime, John K. Galbraith, one of the key Cambridge brain trusters, was quietly pushing Harvard Historian Arthur M. Schlesinger, Jr., for the post that Bundy finally got. "Arthur wanted it," said one Kennedy aide, "but Kennedy wanted Bundy."

Bundy was preparing to leave for a Jamaica vacation the Friday after Christmas. On Wednesday before, the President-elect tried to reach him. Bundy was off making a speech, but he telephoned Kennedy back at Palm Beach the next day. He agreed to take the security post. Kennedy told Bundy to write a press release announcing the appointment, which was made public by the President-elect on New Year's Day.

The following week Bundy flew back to Boston for an important meeting with Kennedy and other members of the Cambridge group at Schlesinger's home. There Kennedy was to settle on jobs for Schlesinger, Wiesner, and other denizens of Cambridge. The day was bitter cold. As secret-service men crowded the front yard, and spectators shivered on the icy street watching the house, Bundy, the dean of Harvard, came wheeling up on a bicycle. It was his favorite mode of transportation at Harvard.

Kennedy gave Bundy the responsibility of streamlining the staff organization of the National Security Council, the nation's top strategy board. Within a month Kennedy abolished the Operations Coordinating Board, an arm of the Council, at Bundy's urging. Bundy became a one-man replacement for the O.C.B., charged with the task of making sure the Security Council's decisions are carried out.

Bundy thinks his job will be different from what it was under Eisenhower. "The temper of the man is different. Broadly speaking, the N.S.C. is an instrument of the President. The fellow in my job is expected to be the President's staff officer in the N.S.C. My problem is to try to find a way of using the Council and the Council staff that will conform to the style of this President."

Serving as major domo of the Security Council is only one of

Bundy's major functions. He is a prolific idea man in the field of security and foreign affairs. He channels information from the State and Defense departments and other security agencies to the President. Most important, he monitors all security decisions of the President to see they are fulfilled.

As evidence of Bundy's central position within the Administration, he was one of the few men at Kennedy's elbow when the President met hurriedly with British Prime Minister Harold Macmillan at Key West in March 1961, during the tense crisis in Laos that threatened to trigger World War III. Several weeks earlier Bundy was among the group that urged Kennedy to react quickly, firmly, and publicly to threats of Soviet intervention in the Congo. Kennedy took the advice.

Because of the nature of his job, Bundy is reluctant to discuss his views on dealing with the Soviet Union. But he believes a starting point is that neither side desires mutual destruction. Bundy is troubled by what he has termed the Soviet's "ruthless control of science and technology," its demonstrated ability to focus its resources on a given problem and thereby achieve enormous results. He has faith, however, that the United States can match and surpass the Soviets once it is aroused to its tasks. And, as his writings have suggested, he feels that the United States must build up its military might to improve its position for dealing with Russia.

The aggressiveness that White House associates have noted in Bundy comes as no surprise to his personal friends. Some of his companions of earlier days remember his manner as dogmatic, bordering even on arrogance. "Mac is so facile, but also so aggravatingly sure of himself," one associate says. "Once, at a suburban party, Mac was bored with the chitchat of mothers about their children. So he said, 'All children should be farmed out, disposed of between infancy and twenty-one.'

"It horrified some of the wives, but I don't think he meant any of it. Now he's one of the most adoring fathers you'll ever meet. [Bundy and his wife have four sons.] Most of us who admire him used to be aggravated by his dogmatic attitude. The trouble was he was often 100 per cent right. Now he's much more inclined to admit there is more than one point of view. Maturity and marriage have softened the edges somewhat."

"He's always got something to say," says another friend, adding, "even when its something he doesn't know much about. He has an excellent sense of humor but quite a temper. He is always very conscious of the fact that he has gone much farther more quickly than any of his classmates."

Bundy, who speaks French and Spanish, reads German, and has a "first-year knowledge of Russian," is clearly an academic man, concerned with matters of the mind. His world is the world of ideas, of intellectual give and take. But those who know him best say he has a tough, stubborn inner core. "I'll never forget," one friend said, "the time his college classmates tried to toss Mac into the river. It took ten men to do it. We were all astonished later," the friend added, "at what a hell of a fight he put up."

ON THE LONG FLIGHT FROM WASHINGTON TO BOSTON ABOARD John F. Kennedy's Convair, the *Caroline,* a mild-mannered, bespectacled professor was engaged in earnest conversation with the 1960 Democratic candidate for President of the United States. Walt Whitman Rostow, an economic historian by profession and a key member of Kennedy's Cambridge brain trusters' group, was telling the Massachusetts Senator about his idea for a campaign theme. Rostow's suggestion: "Let's get this country moving again."

To roaring millions Kennedy repeated those words in varying form in every high-school auditorium, outdoor rally, shopping center, and football stadium he spoke at in the next few months. Rostow watched with some satisfaction. His satisfaction was increased when Kennedy won on November 8 and later named Rostow Deputy Special Assistant to the President for National Security, under McGeorge Bundy.

Actually, Rostow first broached the "Let's get this country moving" theme to Kennedy at a cocktail party of the Cambridge group in Boston June 16. As Kennedy himself later recalled it, Rostow also mentioned another little idea at that party, while Kennedy sipped a ginger ale and listened. "Call your program the New Frontier," Rostow suggested.

Not long after the party, Kennedy, confident of victory at Los Angeles, asked his staff for drafts of an acceptance speech. Several were submitted; only two contained the phrase "New Frontier." One was written by Rostow; the other by Max Freedman, Washington correspondent of the *Manchester Guardian.* Kennedy liked the phrase. And so, at Los Angeles Coliseum, on the night of July 15, Kennedy told a cheering throng in his acceptance speech: "We stand today on the edge of a new frontier—the frontier of the 1960's. Are we up to the task? Are we equal to the challenge?"

The easygoing professor who provided Kennedy with the two most important motifs of the presidential campaign was born in New York City October 7, 1916, the son of a Russian immigrant, Victor Aaron Rostow. "My father," says Rostow, "came to this country when he was eighteen and worked his way through Pratt Institute. He became a metallurgical engineer. My mother was born here. My parents were young and enthusiastic. They named their three boys after three men they admired."

That is how Rostow came to be named Walt Whitman Rostow. His brother Eugene V. Rostow, dean of Yale Law School, was named after socialist Eugene V. Debs. A third brother, who runs a clothing store in Plymouth, Michigan, is Ralph Emerson Rostow.

Walt was graduated from Yale in 1936 at the age of nineteen. While at Yale he made a decision that was to influence the course of his life. "I decided as an undergraduate I would work on two problems. One was economic history and the other was Karl Marx. Marx raised some interesting questions but gave some bloody bad answers. I would do an answer someday to Marx's theory of history."

It was twenty-one years before Rostow provided his own answers in a series of lectures at Cambridge University, England, in 1958, that touched off a world-wide dispute and helped focus major attention on Rostow.

In the fall of 1936, aged twenty, Rostow went off to England for two years as a Rhodes scholar. One morning in 1937 a letter arrived from Dr. Max F. Millikan, now director of the Massachusetts Institute of Technology's Center for International Studies, and author of the first report on the Peace Corps for Kennedy.

Millikan had sent a clipping from the *New York Times*. It was a picture of a Barnard girl who had won a scholarship to a summer school at Geneva. She was Europe-bound, and her name was Elspeth Vaughan Davies. Millikan wrote: "Dear Walt: Enclosed you will find one sample seminar student. She may not be a dodo. Most of them are."

Rostow met Elspeth in Paris in 1937, while they were both en route to summer school in Geneva. Not till ten years and one war later did they marry, however. Mrs. Rostow is a distinguished American historian in her own right. She has taught at Barnard, Sarah Lawrence, and M.I.T., where she was the first woman professor.

Back in the United States, Rostow earned his Ph.D. at Yale, then became an instructor in economics at Columbia in 1940–41. In *Who's Who in America* Rostow's biographical sketch shows a blank for the next four years. But Rostow was rather busy. "I helped start the O.S.S.," he said. "Then I went overseas." By 1943 Rostow was an Army major in England, a staff officer assigned to work with the British Air Ministry. Rostow's job was to help select bombing targets in Europe.

After the war's end Rostow went to Washington for a year as assistant chief of the German-Austrian economic division of the State Department. Then he returned to Oxford, this time as Harmsworth professor of American history. At the end of the academic year Harvard beckoned. Rostow, at thirty, was offered a professorship, but declined. This was the era of the start of the Marshall Plan; much was happening and Rostow wanted to be part of European recovery. He was asked to help set up the Economic Commission for Europe, a U. N. offshoot under the direction of Swedish economist Gunnar Myrdal.

On June 10, 1947, at the home of Sir Oliver Franks, a close friend of Rostow, and provost of Queens College, Oxford, Walt married his Elspeth, the girl in the *New York Times* clipping. They returned to the scene of their first summer, Geneva, where Rostow served as Myrdal's assistant for the next two years. Then it was back to England, where Rostow taught American history for a year at Cambridge.

In 1950 Rostow returned to the United States to be professor of economic history at M.I.T. A year later Millikan left C.I.A. to direct M.I.T.'s Center for International Studies. He invited Rostow to become a staff member. For the next three years Rostow studied the Soviet Union and Communist China at the Center.

Some of Rostow's work during these years involved assignments for C.I.A. and psychological warfare, although Rostow is not free to talk about it. He served as chairman of a panel that worked up the "Open Skies" plan of aerial inspection that President Eisenhower proposed at the Big Four summit meeting in Geneva in 1955. Nelson A. Rockefeller, then psychological warfare assistant to the President, had established a panel of government and outside experts to study proposals the United States might make at the summit. The hush-hush group met at the United States Marine base at Quantico, Virginia; with Rostow as chairman, the panel evolved the idea of an "Open Skies" plan that would demonstrate the United States' peaceful intentions without weakening its nuclear power.

In 1957 Rostow and Millikan published a book together, entitled *A Proposal: Key to an Effective Foreign Policy,* that was responsible for Rostow's first meeting with Kennedy in March 1958. The book interested senators on the Foreign Relations Committee, of which Kennedy was a member, during their study of the foreign-aid problem; in fact, it provided the intellectual underpinning of the Development Loan Fund. The D.L.F. was set up in 1957 and began operating on a large scale in 1958, lending money to the newly-developing nations. Rostow in 1958 also drafted the program President Eisenhower laid before the UN General Assembly to bring peace to the Middle East. It included a regional economic assistance plan to raise the Arabs' living standards.

The book and the later Cambridge lectures were part of Rostow's work in focusing global attention on the importance of underdeveloped areas to world peace and United States survival. (During 1958 and 1959 Kennedy was a strong advocate of economic aid to India, with Rostow as his chief adviser.) In September 1958 until the following spring Rostow was off to Cambridge, England, for lecturing and traveling, on a sabbatical from M.I.T. It was in Cambridge, in the autumn of 1958, that Rostow delivered his now-famed lectures, later published in book form as *The Stages of Economic Growth.* This was Rostow's "non-communist manifesto," the falling into place of the answers he determined to seek more than two decades earlier as an undergraduate at Yale.

In his lectures Rostow set forth his view of history. His theory touched off a rarefied controversy still raging among economists and intellectuals. He argued that societies pass through five identifiable stages of economic development:

The traditional society, in which men have not yet come to know that the external world is subject to a few knowable laws and that it is possible to manipulate environment through this knowledge. Almost all the resources of such societies are devoted to agriculture. Medieval Europe and the most remote areas of the world today are examples of traditional societies.

The preconditions for take off, in which a traditional society is gradually transformed so it can "exploit the fruits of modern science." Western Europe went through this phase in the late seventeenth and early eighteenth centuries; most underdeveloped countries are now in it. "The idea spreads not merely that economic progress is possible but that it is a necessary condition for some other broader purpose," such as national dignity, private profit, or the general welfare. Banks and other institutions for mobilizing capital appear. Commerce widens. Here and there modern manufacturing enterprises appear. But all this activity proceeds at a limited pace within a society still sticking to the old social structures and values.

The take off, "when old blocks and resistances to steady growth are finally overcome." The forces making for economic progress come to dominate the society, and growth becomes its normal condition. There is a surge of technological development in industry and agriculture, and political power passes to the groups who regard modernization of the economy as the first order of business. The United States passed through this stage around the 1850's; China and India are going through it now. Total investment rises to 10 per cent or more of the national income. New industries expand rapidly, stimulating other new industries to service them. Profits are plowed back into new plants. Agriculture is commercialized, too, and the population moves from the farm to the city.

The drive to maturity, during which the economy grows steadily over a prolonged period and modern technology extends over the whole economy. From 10 per cent to 20 per cent of the national income is invested, permitting output to outstrip the increase in population. "New industries accelerate, older industries level off." Coal and iron give way to machine tools, chemicals, and electrical equipment. A society usually reaches maturity about sixty years after the take off begins. The United States attained maturity early this century; the Russians only a decade or so ago. Western Europe, Canada, and Japan have also progressed this far.

The age of high mass consumption, when the economic emphasis steadily shifts to durable consumers' goods and services. The mass-produced automobile is a symbol of this stage. The United States reached it in the 1920's, western Europe a decade ago, and Russia is now engaged in an "uneasy flirtation" with it. A greater proportion of the population works in offices or in skilled jobs, less in factories or unskilled labor. Further extension of modern technology loses some of its savor, and a society may choose to spend more of its resources for social welfare and security.

In the spring of 1959 Rostow, with his wife, traveled to Moscow for the first time, visiting also Yugoslavia and Warsaw. Rostow hadn't even unpacked his bags at his home in Belmont, Massachusetts, the first night back in the States, when the telephone rang. It was Senator Kennedy, calling to say hello, and also as one Kennedy aide later put it, "to make sure Rostow was still his property." Rostow assured Kennedy he was.

On January 2, 1960, at the Harvard Club in Boston, a group of the nation's top brains gathered to hear Kennedy. This was the nucleus of what later came to be known as the "Cambridge group." It operated out of a smoke-filled faculty room that provided the gray matter for the Kennedy juggernaut during the presidential campaign.

"It was a very interesting meeting," recalls Rostow. "The Senator said he had committed himself to running for office, that he would enter the presidential primaries, and that he expected to win in November. He wanted not our political support but our views on what the public policy of the United States should be. It was very impressive and straightforward."

Rostow himself says he kept in "close touch" with Kennedy from 1958 onward. During the campaign he describes himself as a "behind-the-scenes adviser. . . I stayed at Cambridge at my desk but I did a lot of chores. I did the basic stuff on military policy and threw some other ideas into the pot."

During the campaign Rostow kept the memos coming on defense, foreign aid, and other subjects. He and Kennedy seldom saw each other, but they talked on the telephone. One of the most important and longest phone conversations just before the campaign was on the birth-control issue. Kennedy sought, and got, Rostow's advice on how to handle the delicate controversy.

After the election Rostow was invited along with other American scholars to participate in the sixth Pugwash International Conference of Scientists and Scholars in Moscow. The conference, which afforded valuable contact between Soviet and American intellectuals, got its peculiar name from the town in Nova Scotia where industrialist Cyrus Eaton had his summer home and where the first conference took place. Eaton's political romance with Khrushchev had embarrassed American participants to later conferences, so by 1960 the United States delegation was brought together by the respectable American Academy of Arts and Sciences.

The Russians were anxious to get another look at Rostow, knowing that he was likely to be one of Kennedy's top strategists in the cold war. Before going to Moscow Rostow cleared his attendance with both Kennedy, then President-elect, and Allen W. Dulles, C.I.A. director. Rostow had sent a memo to Kennedy proposing his attendance at the Pugwash conference. When Allen Dulles went to Palm Beach to see Kennedy shortly after election, the two men discussed Rostow's memo. Dulles, who has the highest regard for Rostow, instantly approved the idea. Although the Administration later described the Rostow mission to Moscow as the act of a private citizen, the fact that both Kennedy and Dulles approved it in advance endowed the trip with a semi-official aura.

On the day after Rostow returned from Moscow, he came to Washington to see Kennedy. It was the same morning, December 9, 1960, that Mrs. Kennedy came home from Georgetown Hospital with her new son, John F., Jr., and the President was not too interested in talking about Moscow. He kept Rostow waiting while he went to the hospital to fetch Jackie.

When he finally returned to his Georgetown home, Kennedy said to Rostow, "I want you to be head of the policy planning staff of the State Department. I'll call you again in a few days."

Kennedy also talked about the problem of selecting someone to be Secretary of State. He asked Rostow's judgment, but Rostow said he had no strong preference. Rostow emerged from the meeting and told newsmen he had been offered a high post by the President-elect. Asked whether he would take it, Rostow replied, "We'll see."

Afterward Rostow went to the State Department to brief officials there on Pugwash. Then Rostow went back to Boston, "under the impression," a friend said, "he would be chosen policy planning chief." Later, Rostow had two meetings with Dean Rusk, whom Kennedy had named as Secretary of State. Rusk indicated he had another man in mind for policy planning. This turned out to be George McGhee, former United States Ambassador to Turkey. Rusk urged Kennedy to persuade Rostow to be McGhee's deputy.

Rostow, a bit annoyed at the palace intrigue by now, declined. In January Kennedy was to fly to Boston on a Monday morning to attend a meeting of the Harvard Overseers. At the last minute Kennedy abruptly changed his plans and flew up from New York to Boston on Sunday night. He wanted to confer with Rostow, which he did early Monday morning in Kennedy's 122 Bowdoin Street apartment, a voting residence the President maintains on the hill opposite the State House. In an hour-long chat Kennedy straightened out the problem, and Rostow, who had reached the point where he was not sure he would take any post on the New Frontier, agreed to become Bundy's deputy.

Rostow's experience at Pugwash convinced him that something new is in the Soviet air. "For the first time I was prepared to contemplate the possibility that there was an element of seriousness in their disarmament proposals. I had the feeling it was on their minds quite seriously, that they were concerned particularly over the spread of nuclear arms to Germany and Communist China." His feeling was reinforced by two private talks with Soviet Deputy Foreign Minister Vasily V. Kuznetsov.

Rostow was well aware, however, that while the Soviets were conferring with him in Moscow on disarmament they were shipping arms to underdeveloped areas of the world and to trouble spots such as Laos and the Congo. This was underscored by a meeting going on simultaneously in the Soviet capital. "At the same time the dignified scientists of fifteen nations were meeting to discuss disarmament," says Rostow, "the world's eighty-one communist parties were meeting nearby trying to figure out how to take us to the cleaners. I did not come back with the notion that peace was about to break out."

The 4,600-word *aide memoire* that Rostow prepared for Kennedy told the President of Rostow's feeling that the Soviets might be serious about disarmament. He cited five reasons: the Russian fear of the spread of atomic weapons to other nations, which scientists call the "nth power" problem; the danger of accidental war; the belief that neither side can win in an arms race; the fact that disarmament would free resources for domestic use and for underdeveloped areas; and, finally, the unspoken Soviet hope that disarmament would throw the United States economy out of whack.

Rostow warned Kennedy that whether the Russians are serious about disarming or not, the United States must strengthen its military power, in the meantime, to develop a "second-strike" capability so it could retaliate effectively even after suffering a devastating first blow. Rostow also suggested a United States get-tough attitude on communist arms deliveries to underdeveloped areas.

In all, it was a balanced, liberal viewpoint toward the Soviet Union; a healthy mistrust tempered by hope and the belief that progress can be made on specific issues as more common ground emerges between the two great powers.

Rostow sees his present job this way: "You have a President whose problem is to have the widest range of alternatives for action. The choice presented to him is not and should not be predetermined. He is struggling, as Churchill did, to find a wide range of vision, a bifocal view." Rostow considers it his task to tell the President, "Here are the questions you must answer before you make a decision. My job is to present alternatives, not solutions," he adds. "We ought to be able to make something out of this administration, to build forward planning into day-by-day work so that each crisis is not a fresh surprise."

Rostow argues that the underdeveloped areas can either turn to communism, or, with the active help of the West, develop as free societies. Unlike Marx, Rostow does not believe that economics alone determines the acts of man. "Communism," writes Rostow, "is a kind of disease" that can strike a country ready for modernization.

The real hope for peace, Rostow thinks, lies in the fact that the atomic club is getting bigger, and Russia cannot control all the new members. As this occurs, he feels, "the Russian national interest shifts closer to that of the United States and the West." The logical policy for Russia, he argues, is to join the United States in "an effective international system of arms control," before the nth power problem gets completely out of hand.

In an eloquent finale to one of his lectures at Cambridge in 1958 Rostow summed up his view of the challenge: "The problem posed by contemporary Russia lies not in the uniqueness of its story of modernization, but in whether the United States and the West can mobilize their ample resources to do the jobs that must be done; resources of spirit, intellect, will, and insight quite as much as steel and electronic gadgets; and jobs which extend not only to missile arsenals . . . but to . . . the far reaches of Asia, the Middle East, Africa, and Latin America. The problem lies not in the mysterious East, but in the inscrutable West."

AT THE KREMLIN A FEW DAYS AFTER JOHN F. KENNEDY WAS elected President, Dr. Jerome B. Wiesner called on Soviet Deputy Foreign Minister Vasily V. Kuznetsov at the Foreign Office. The meeting was quite unofficial in that Wiesner, at the time, was not a spokesman of the United States government. Rather, he was in Moscow as a member of the American delegation attending the sixth Pugwash International Conference of Scientists and Scholars.

Nevertheless, the Russians were quite well aware of the fact that Wiesner, and Rostow, who accompanied him on the visit to Kuznetsov, were in line for top White House posts and spoke, at least in an informal way, for the new administration. Kuznetsov solicitously inquired what the Soviet government could do to help out the Kennedy administration. "Do nothing," replied Wiesner.

Even Kuznetsov joined in the general laughter, but the story illustrates two important points about Wiesner: First, he is a scientist with a conscience. His very presence in Moscow at the Pugwash Conference, which is scorned by many conservative scholars, was evidence that Wiesner, who knows more about the power of atomic bombs than most men, deeply believes every possible effort must be made to prevent their use.

Second, his succinct reply to Kuznetsov underscores the fact that Wiesner is a practical, hardheaded man, quite aware of political realities. He is in no sense an absent-minded scientist toiling in some far-removed vineyard. Rather, he has for most of his adult life devoted the bulk of his energies and scientific skills to the preservation of the United States in a perilous world.

Now the Special Assistant to President Kennedy for Science and Technology, Wiesner will have considerable opportunity on the job to put his rare combination of idealism and pragmatism to the test. In his post as White House adviser, Wiesner is the scientist with the most influence in the federal government. He coordinates the scientific data that flow to the President from the executive agencies and adds his own advice on the proper course for the United States in such areas as missile development, satellite programs, exploration of outer space, nuclear testing, disarmament, atomic energy, development of American science and technology, and a host of other subjects any one of which, if mishandled, could spell defeat and disaster for America.

A passionate advocate of phased, inspected disarmament, Wiesner can be expected to push his views within the Administration whether or not it pleases the Pentagon or the missile makers. "A lot of people don't want disarmament," Wiesner says bluntly. "They don't want to turn off the cold war." Wiesner's impassioned efforts for disarmament stem from a firsthand knowledge of the instruments of death. At Los Alamos, New Mexico, in 1945, Wiesner helped to develop components of the atom bomb. Something else happened at Los Alamos. Wiesner's second son, Zachary, was born there. Somewhere in this intimacy with life and death lies the key to Wiesner.

"Disarmament for Jerry is not an abstract concept," says a close friend. "He has a tremendous moral concern." Accompanying the moral concern is Wiesner's practical conviction that disarmament offers the nation more real security than a continuation of the headlong armaments race. "If you look ahead ten years and see where this is taking you, you find this is really a mirage," says Wiesner; "the security you think you buy just won't be there.

"If you try to project an all-out arms race of the kind that we're engaged in, if the country were to do all the things that it should be doing to stay in such a race, here's what you would do. You would first of all start a massive shelter program to protect yourself. But about the time you finish that shelter program you'd find you aren't protecting yourself against one megaton or two or three or four megaton warheads. You would be protecting yourself against the 100 or 1,000 megaton bombs which we think could be developed if we continued. You then would be faced with the prospect of crawling into the fallout shelters and being cremated by these enormous new weapons. If you project this for ten or fifteen or twenty years you see what appears to be a short-run security is a long-term threat and danger."

The man who spoke these words has come a long way from his boyhood in Dearborn, Michigan, where his father, the late Joseph Wiesner, ran a small dry-goods store. Jerry was born May 30, 1915, in Detroit but grew up in nearby Dearborn. His mother, Ida Friedman Wiesner, still lives with her son and his family.

Wiesner is now well off, thanks to a scientific research company he has formed. But in Dearborn, as a youth, he peddled newspapers, caddied on the golf courses (sometimes for Henry Ford), and tended bar. In his spare time he kept telephone company repairmen busy hunting for the lines of a private phone network he devised to talk to his friends. To outsmart the repairmen Jerry sometimes flew a kite to haul his lines over the rooftops. Once the kite broke down. To Wiesner's dismay, the wire plunged across a power line and disrupted Dearborn's electricity.

The disaster did not discourage Wiesner's ambition to be an electrical engineer. He entered Fordson High School in 1929 at the start of the depression, studied at Michigan State Normal College at Ypsilanti, and then switched to the University of Michigan at Ann Arbor, where he earned his keep waiting on tables and washing dishes. Wiesner also puttered around the college radio station, and became its chief engineer. He graduated in 1937 with a Bachelor of Science degree in mathematics and electrical engineering. He earned his Master of Science degree there in 1940 and his Doctorate in 1950.

While he was a student at Michigan, a classmate invited Wiesner home for lunch. A pretty coed from Johnstown, Pennsylvania, named Laya Wainger, was invited to lunch, too. "There was Jerry and that was that," says Laya Wainger Wiesner. They were married in 1940, after Laya graduated from Michigan.

The same year Wiesner took his first Washington job as chief engineer of the Acoustical and Record Laboratory of the Library of Congress. There Wiesner met the Lomaxes, Alan and his father John, and became interested in folk music. "I tramped around the South with them, more as a sociologist than a musician," recalls Wiesner.

By the start of World War II the British had invented radar. In 1942, at M.I.T., Wiesner was tapped to develop a more sophisticated version. The M.I.T. Radiation Laboratory was one of two large installations that developed the components for the land, sea, and airborne radar that later proved invaluable in the war. Wiesner concentrated on microwave electronic components that were the heart of the new radar systems developed at the lab.

He also took occasional trips to Los Alamos to work on some of the complex electronic problems involved in the development of the atom bomb. In the fall of 1945, after the end of the war in the Pacific, Wiesner moved to Los Alamos full time. There he supervised the instrumentation of the atomic tests on Bikini Atoll in July 1946.

After the war Wiesner returned to M.I.T. as assistant professor of electrical engineering. He became a full professor in 1950. The following year he helped establish the university's Lincoln Laboratory, which developed the complex radar, computer, and communication systems that make up the nation's continental air-defense system. In addition, he helped to create the "scatter-communications" system that made possible the DEW line warning system against enemy bombers across the northern rim of the continent.

Wiesner also found time to form, with two friends, the Hycon Eastern Corporation, a research company that later merged with the ITEK Corporation, Lexington, Massachusetts, a multimillion-dollar leader in the new field of information technology. "Wiesner is a wealthy man, thanks to Hycon and ITEK," says one close friend in a position to know.

During the early 1950's Wiesner became one of Senator Mc-Carthy's targets, when the Wisconsin Senator was trying to find communists in the Voice of America. The Voice had decided to locate in Seattle a key transmitter beamed at Communist China. A disgruntled Voice engineer told McCarthy that the transmitter would have worked better in Los Angeles. The government asked M.I.T. to review the decision. Wiesner supported the Voice of America's expert's decision to locate in Seattle. He refused to testify against the Voice despite implied threats that he might lose his security clearance. "I just dug in and refused to back down," recalls Wiesner. "It was a period of terror the like of which I haven't lived through before or since." The transmitter is still in Seattle.

In 1956, after the Democratic national convention at Chicago which almost nominated Kennedy for Vice-President, an event took place that was to have an important bearing on Wiesner's future. Professor Abram Chayes of Harvard Law School, a Kennedy brain truster now legal adviser to the State Department, returned from the convention and suggested to Wiesner, "Go to work for Kennedy."

Wiesner took the advice of Chayes, a close friend, and began advising Senator Kennedy from Cambridge in 1957 on military policy, disarmament, and scientific matters. The same year Wiesner was picked by the Eisenhower administration as staff director of a study of the United States defense posture headed by J. Rowan Gaither, Jr., then board chairman of the Ford Foundation. The top-secret report called for a greatly stepped-up defense effort. A month after it was handed in Eisenhower named Wiesner to his Science Advisory Committee.

It was a significant period for Wiesner. During the Gaither study he became convinced for the first time that it was not possible to protect the American people in the event of a global nuclear holocaust. As long as the Soviet Union was prepared to match America's military effort, Wiesner decided, "there was no hope of avoiding a terrible loss of life in the event of a major nuclear war, regardless of the magnitude of our defense effort."

Said Wiesner: "Even at best, if we did all the things we could think of, if we built fallout shelters, worked very much harder than we are now doing on air defense and missile defense, even if we committed twice the resources we are now committing to defense, we could not prevent a major nuclear war from being history's greatest catastrophe. The task we must work on is to assume that such a war does not take place."

During the M.I.T. years Wiesner escaped the tensions of nuclear-strategy problems by taking off for Martha's Vineyard with his family in the summer for their home at Chilmark, on Menemsha Pond. "At the Vineyard," said a friend, "Jerry smokes a pipe and sails. He has the ability to forget his work and compartmentalize his life. When he relaxes, he relaxes." Skiing in the winter and amateur photography year round also helped Wiesner relax. The Wiesners lived simply in a rambling sixteen-room, sixty-year-old house in unfashionable Watertown, Massachusetts. Wiesner also managed to run and win as Democratic candidate for the town planning board. On Sundays he cooked the family breakfast, usually blintzes.

In 1958 Eisenhower sent Wiesner to Geneva as staff director of the United States delegation to a conference on surprise attacks. Wiesner was impressed by United States lack of preparedness at the conference table. It helped solidify a growing conviction in his mind: disarmament proposals have to be backed by solid scientific knowledge and detailed planning. A lot of time, money, man power, and effort are spent in military planning, Wiesner argues, and similar painstaking preparation must go into disarmament proposals if they are to have any chance of success.

During the campaign Wiesner, by this time an important member of Kennedy's "Cambridge group," handed in his resignation to Eisenhower as a member of the Science Advisory Committee in order to avoid any political conflict of interest. It wasn't accepted. So Wiesner continued to work for Ike while advising Kennedy.

Immediately after election, with the full approval of Kennedy and United States security officials, Wiesner left for the Pugwash Conference with Rostow. Although no longer Cyrus Eaton's project, Pugwash was still viewed with alarm in conservative academic quarters. Also, there was always the danger that in the event of a sticky propaganda blowup at Moscow, those who took part would be stigmatized politically. Wiesner went to Moscow nevertheless. "Jerry decides what needs to be done and does it," a colleague said of Wiesner's decision to attend the conference. "He doesn't ask 'suppose this gives me a black eye before some congressman?' "

Wiesner urged a new principle at Pugwash: that international inspection increase proportionally as disarmament proceeds. It was an ingenious proposal, designed to calm the Soviet fears of foreign inspection teams but at the same time insure United States security.

In a serious answer to Kuznetsov's question about what the Kremlin might do to better relations with the new administration, Wiesner and Rostow urged that the RB-47 pilots be returned without President-elect Kennedy having to bargain for them. Wiesner and Rostow set this forth as the first step necessary to smoother relations. The secret conversation laid the groundwork for the release of the two surviving pilots five days after Kennedy was inaugurated. Wiesner and Rostow also warned that pressure on Berlin would forestall any serious disarmament negotiations or relaxation of tensions. And they emphasized that Russia would have to agree to a generous number of test-ban inspections.

Returning from Moscow, Wiesner discovered that joining the

New Frontier involved, as for all prospective appointees, a waiting game. Wiesner had confidently expected to be named science adviser to the President a week after election. Actually he didn't hear from Kennedy about the appointment until he met with the President-elect at Schlesinger's house in Cambridge in January. Kennedy had asked Columbia Professor Richard E. Neustadt to look around for a science adviser. Several names were dropped into the hopper, but in the end Kennedy chose Wiesner, as had been expected.

Shortly before Kennedy took office he made public the report of a task force headed by Wiesner on the nation's space and missile effort. The panel's verdict: the missile program was "lagging," and it was "unlikely" that the United States would be first in placing a man into orbit around the earth. Wiesner called for a drastic streamlining of the nation's space efforts.

In Watertown Wiesner's mother was proud of her son's selection as science adviser to the President. But she made a revealing comment to a friend. "You know with all this fuss about Jerry in the papers," she said, "nobody says what a marvelous father he is."

Actually, Wiesner had precious little time for being a father at the start of the New Frontier. Temporarily, he had to leave his daughter Lisa, eleven, and son Joshua, eight, behind in Watertown with his wife while he plunged into the job in Washington. His other two sons are away at school, Zach at Andover and his eldest son Stephen, eighteen, at the California Institute of Technology.

From his headquarters in the Executive Office Building Wiesner operates at the standard pace for New Frontiersmen: he reports in at 8:30 A.M. and leaves twelve or fourteen hours later. A visitor finds Wiesner, who has the pushed-in nose of an inexpert boxer, sitting in shirt sleeves with his feet up, puffing on a pipe and giving orders in a quiet, almost inaudible voice. It is a deceptive appearance of lassitude. The next minute he is up, jacket on, and dashing off across the street to see the President, or to sit in on one of the endless round of meetings and conferences at the White House. "I never thought I'd ever be working as hard again as I did in the war," Wiesner told an aide recently.

As science adviser, Wiesner is also chairman of the eighteen-man Science Advisory Committee which meets two days a month. To manage his wide-ranging job, Wiesner has nine assistants who handle the scientific aspects of foreign affairs, space rocketry, disarmament, and military matters. And the day isn't necessarily over when he leaves the office. One night not long ago, when Wiesner was riding home in a White House car at the end of a wearying day, a voice crackled over the car's two-way radio: "Dr. Wiesner, the President wants to talk to you." Wiesner stopped the car, hopped out, dashed into a drugstore, and telephoned Kennedy at the White House.

"Jerry," says one good friend, "is not a theoretical scientist, but he is high in the ranks of the applied scientists. To my mind, he is one of the few authentic great men I know. Not only for his knowledge and performance in his field, but also for his emotional commitment. He has deep human understanding."

A top government scientist, a much older man who knows Wiesner intimately, says, "Jerry is relaxed. He hasn't any question about why he is doing things. Perhaps how, but not why. It's a big job Jerry has. The ability of a man to destroy himself has created a new situation. So many of the old ways are obsolete. We need new approaches to meet the change. I think Jerry can do it."

3.

THE RIGHT-HAND MEN

Pierre Salinger
Lawrence O'Brien
Kenneth P. O'Donnell

By MARY McGRORY

WHAT THE IRISH POET WILLIAM BUTLER YEATS WROTE OF Byzantium goes in spades for the New Frontier: "This is no country for old men."

The average age of the Kennedy administration is, in fact, so tender that there are millions of American citizens who can see that they are being governed entirely by their juniors. And even these young men have trouble keeping the pace set by the President.

Between the Eisenhower and Kennedy days in the White House there is the difference between a slow march and a jig. The Eisenhower times were marked by spit and polish and high ceremoniousness. With Kennedy in charge, life has taken on a highhearted, helter-skelter air not known since Teddy Roosevelt. The President himself is informal and accessible. Unlike his predecessor, who apparently found life in the Executive Mansion so oppressive he frequently fled it, Kennedy likes his job so much he can scarcely tear himself away from his desk.

All sorts of people are welcome at the White House these days. Poets and painters have supplanted brokers and bankers. Earthshaking news comes out—about salamanders and chefs and Caroline Kennedy's rag doll in the President's chair in the Cabinet room. Reporters roam through the back corridors, enjoying the freedom Eliza Doolittle dreamed of in Buckingham Palace.

Keeping up with the President is the staff's greatest challenge. They follow his lead in long hours and try to anticipate the wide leaps of his mind. Everyone has to be on tap and on his toes at all times. This especially holds true for the three men who serve him most closely on practical matters: his press secretary, Pierre Salinger; his congressional contact man, Lawrence F. O'Brien; and his appointments secretary, Kenneth P. O'Donnell.

When the President is dealing with crises far away or not yet matured, he calls in representatives from the intellectual wing of the White House—men such as McGeorge Bundy, his national security affairs assistant, or Jerome Wiesner, his science adviser, or Arthur M. Schlesinger, Jr., the Harvard historian, who is a special aide. But when there's trouble at home, right under his hand, it is Salinger or O'Brien or O'Donnell he wants.

These three are the President's technicians. They are as essential to his official daily life as the policeman, the fireman, and the television repairman are to the existence of the ordinary citizen. These are men who see him every day, who are expected to come up with the right answer at the snap of his fingers.

Two of them, O'Donnell and O'Brien, are, like himself, Massachusetts Irishmen with politics in their blood. Salinger is a cosmopolitan San Franciscan of French and German-Jewish origin who, like O'Donnell, was brought under the Kennedy banner by the President's brother Bobby, the Attorney General. O'Donnell and O'Brien are old political allies who have conspired and operated together since the President's first victory for the Senate in 1952. Late-comer Salinger cut his teeth on the presidential campaign in 1960.

All share the tempered, practical liberalism of their boss. In Salinger's case, this represents a moderation of earlier, more extreme views. O'Brien and O'Donnell have always been more interested in what works than in what should be.

What the three have in common besides the nature of their work is the perhaps disquieting realization that the President could do their jobs as well as or even better than they. Pierre Salinger is the first to say that he doesn't think the President, a man with scores of reporter friends and an eerie sense of public relations, really needs a press secretary. Larry O'Brien, who must transmit the President's will and wishes to congressmen, spends much of his time arranging to bring his charges face to face with the President, their old colleague. And Kenny O'Donnell can keep the public out but not the President in. The restless Kennedy is constantly wandering out of his office, scooping up visitors waiting for other people and carrying them back to his oval study for a cozy if slightly para-lyzing chat.

If the President's acquaintance with their tasks gives him a certain understanding of their problems, it also gives him a standard to judge them by. If they fall short, they hear about it in that saltiness of expression and directness of address that are peculiarly the President's own. "The one thing he can't stand is stupidity," says Pierre Salinger, who regards Kennedy's attitude as a "reasonable intolerance."

SALINGER IS THE MAN BEST KNOWN TO THE PUBLIC OF THIS practical trio. He reflects the President to the people.

Pierre Emile George Salinger, thirty-five, is a roly-poly, cigar-smoking piano player with dark blue eyes, pointed ears, and a sense of proportion unusual in one of his calling. Some people think he resembles Napoleon without the imperial dyspepsia; others think he looks like Grover Cleveland without the mustache.

What interests the Washington press corps much more, however, is his professional resemblance. It is generally agreed he bears practically none to his immediate predecessor, James C. Hagerty, who not only enunciated Eisenhower policy, but, by the President's own admission, helped to make it. Pierre does not help make White House policy; occasionally he doesn't even know what it is, and what's more he admits it.

Whereas Hagerty attempted to overwhelm reporters with the wealth of his information and the virtuosity of his technique, Pierre contents himself with disarming them by his wit and good humor. Hagerty, who spoon-fed the press for eight years, was renowned for his ability to make the trivial seem portentous—a trait brilliantly lampooned by columnist Art Buchwald in a column that made Hagerty furious. Pierre sometimes makes the trivial seem even more trivial than it actually is. "It's wonderful how quickly these briefings degenerate into the insignificant," he said one day after a strenuous go round with the press on *Honey Fitz,* the new name of the presidential yacht.

Sometimes, consciously or not, he parodies Hagerty's solemn, oracular style. When Caroline Kennedy's pet cat came to the White House, Pierre announced the following day that "Tom Kitten slept well."

Hagerty was an awesome figure who inspired a certain sycophancy among those seeking his hard-won favor. He ran a tight shop. White House callers from the fourth estate were sometimes checked through, and occasionally blocked, by him. Reporters don't even tell Pierre where they're going as they hurry by to have a word with a confidential presidential adviser. Pierre's secretaries talk back to him, and reporters bicker with him in a manner that would have occasioned severe reprisals in the Hagerty regime. In anger Pierre is given to bursts of loud truculence. They never last.

At Mrs. Kennedy's request (although she has her own press secretary), Pierre has taken over the disbursing of the women's news. So it is that tidbits about interior decorating and nursery affairs are woven around matters of state. One reporter who was vainly trying to focus on appointments to high office kept stumbling into the appointments of Caroline's room. Finally he complained, "Pierre, we don't know what you're talking about and we don't think you know what you're talking about half the time." Pierre chuckled with the rest.

Reporters are less amused by what they consider sloppiness on Pierre's part. They complain of inaccuracies in press releases, of misspellings and misstatements. They grumble about his failure to be punctual, a failing he shares with the President. One ploy that Pierre has borrowed from Hagerty they say he does not execute so well. It is the business of announcing news of government departments, if it is good, from the White House, to create the impression that all the action comes from the President. The difficulty is that Pierre sometimes fails to acquaint himself with all the facts with the result that reporters are left with an item rather than a story, something the highly professional and seasoned Hagerty would never have done.

Even so, Pierre is enormously popular. "You can't snarl at Pierre," said a regular who has often corrected the press secretary on matters of fact, "and it's quite impossible to hate him." What has ingratiated Pierre with reporters is his willingness, even alacrity, to admit a mistake. He never alibis and he never passes the buck —a most winning quality, virtually unheard of in official Washington.

When, for instance, he volunteered the information that all members of the White House domestic staff had been required to sign a pledge not to write their memoirs, the matter was front-page news all over the country. From a press secretary whose public utterances have usually related to "the expansion of communication" it was a *gaffe* of some proportions. It was, moreover, a gratuitous blunder.

"I knew I made a mistake the minute you began being so polite to me," said Pierre to Merriman Smith, the veteran United Press International White House correspondent. He then sought an emergency audience with President Kennedy. Pierre told the President he had done something awful, and the President vigorously agreed.

The next morning the press secretary, who happens to be a gifted cook, opened his briefing with the announcement that it was not true that he had been fired as press secretary in order to take over as White House chef. He also said he had taken a pledge not to discuss the pledge any further. He refers to the matter as the "silent-butler, dumb-waiter affair."

"I can just tell you one thing," he said when the matter inevitably came up again, "even if I have to sign a document that I can't write my memoirs afterward, all I have to do is publish the transcripts of these briefings."

Others share his feelings about the briefings' special, random charm. Robert J. Donovan, chief of the Washington Bureau of the *New York Herald Tribune,* one Sunday published a column of transcript. One exchange gave the flavor:

A reporter asked, "May I ask if Caroline calls her nurse Nanny and why isn't she calling her by an American name since that is a British term?"

Pierre never lost his aplomb. "Maybe that's her name," he suggested.

The press secretary regards his twice-daily briefings, which are scheduled for noon and 4:30 P.M., and hardly ever occur at those hours, as a kind of verbal Indian wrestling.

A reporter will ask if it is "usual" for Pierre not to announce the substance of the President's conference with McGeorge Bundy and Secretary of State Dean Rusk. "I do it sometimes," Pierre responds.

Or a reporter, noting that Mrs. Roosevelt has made a statement about the admission of Red China to the U.N., asks if she can ever speak for herself now that she is a member of the United States delegation to the U.N. "She said she was speaking for herself," says Pierre noncommittally, and the matter is dropped.

Such inconclusive grapplings have made the transcripts must reading for a little group of connoisseurs. Kenneth O'Donnell, not a frivolous man, reads them for relaxation the way another man would lose himself in a P. G. Wodehouse novel.

Thanks to his excellent sense of humor, Pierre gets along very well with the President. Although he does not share the Kennedy cult of toughness, the two have a pleasant, easygoing relationship. Despite his tough-guy background as a crusading crime reporter and an investigator for the Senate Rackets Committee, Pierre, having been adjured throughout his childhood by his French mother not to be *barbare,* is very civilized. He likes good music, good food, and good wines. He is a doting husband and father and he loves to speak French.

He is undone by small kindnesses. He respects the President's desire for some privacy and he guards it. The President appreciates Pierre's gaiety and quickness of mind. Pierre always tries to have something funny to tell or show him at their twice-daily meetings. He never can point out anything in the press the President hasn't read. The President devours newspapers.

The President thinks it was clever of Pierre to suggest the live television broadcasts of the President's press conference. The press has complained of the cold setting in the new State Department Auditorium, and James Reston, the Washington correspondent of the *New York Times,* has said that it is "like making love in the Grand Central terminal." But the public is enchanted with this weekly glimpse of the Chief Executive and has written in savage denunciations of the boorish reporters who pester him with questions.

The President is happy that Pierre has contented himself with passing the word along instead of trying to put words into his mouth. In Pierre's disordered office there is a portrait of Kennedy with a cordial inscription to "The Voice of the White House."

"The Voice of the White House" was born in San Francisco, on June 14, 1925, the first child of Jehanne and Herbert Salinger. His mother, from whom he inherited his *joie de vivre* and his nostalgia for the thick of things, was the daughter of a member of the Chamber of Deputies. The family moved to Indo-China where her father established a newspaper. On his death, she became its editor. She met her husband, a mining engineer of German-Jewish ancestry, in San Francisco when she was attending a Pan-Pacific Conference as a representative of Indo-China in 1923. They were married the same year.

In 1930, work being scarce, Salinger *père* took the family to Canada, where it was discovered that Pierre was a musical prodigy. Enrolled in the Toronto Conservatory of Music at the age of five, he made his debut a year later, playing a Haydn sonata at the Canadian National Exposition.

For the next six years Pierre practiced three or four hours a day, studying at home with his tutor. He was brought up as a Catholic, and always spoke French in the home. When he was twelve he and the family, then augmented by a French grandmother and three small brothers, decided it was no life for a boy, and Pierre gave up the idea of being a concert pianist. He did not give up the piano, however.

In 1936 the Salingers returned to San Francisco, where Pierre was sent to a "marvelous" progressive school called the Presidio Open Air School. He was less happy when he went on to high school, where he was younger and smarter than his classmates. He was completely out of things until a teacher named Jack Patterson started a journalism class. Young Pierre became his prize pupil, and decided then and there newspapering was for him.

In his seventeenth summer he triumphantly entered the office of the *San Francisco Chronicle* as a copy boy. His first managing editor, Lawrence Fanning, recently told a luncheon at which Pierre was guest speaker that on his first day in journalism Pierre crashed into the publisher, spilled coffee down an editor's neck, and lost a valuable piece of copy. Pierre admits it was something like that, but at least everyone knew he was around. Within three months the brash youngster was put on the staff.

The war took Pierre out of the city room and sent him to the Pacific, where as skipper of a subchaser at nineteen he became the youngest commanding officer in the Navy. Upon his return, caught up in years and experience with his classmates, he finished college at the University of San Francisco. He also went back to the *Chronicle* as a police reporter. He became a star. His first feat was to expose a bail-bond racket. Then he masqueraded as a bum named Émile Flic and got himself arrested all over California so he could investigate jail conditions at firsthand. His stories resulted in prison reform, reconstruction, and administrative changes. They also brought him the McQuade Memorial Award for reporting.

He also crusaded successfully to liberate a Negro who had been wrongfully accused of setting fire to a hotel. For three years he was city editor of the *Chronicle,* a job he forsook to return to reporting.

Concurrent with his exertions in this field, he was dabbling in politics. He began in 1947 by managing Congressman Frank Havenner's campaign for mayor of San Francisco, did some work on reapportionment for a labor group, and in 1952 was press secretary for Adlai Stevenson's California effort.

Mrs. Elizabeth R. Smith, who is now Treasurer of the United States, remembers him as an exuberant figure of contagious good will, who was not just a writer of press releases but a great morale builder "who never thought of defeat." When he was press secretary for Richard P. Graves, an unsuccessful candidate for governor against Goodwin J. Knight, Pierre discovered that Knight was consulting a swami and facetiously cast a horoscope for him. When his own candidate was sent to the hospital, Pierre issued a steady stream of statements on all sorts of subjects.

In 1955 he quit the *Chronicle* to become western editor of *Collier's*. A year later, sent to New York by the magazine, he hurried right down to the West Side Democratic Club, asked for a job "that nobody else wanted," and went around speaking on the street corners of Manhattan for the Stevenson cause.

That year, too, he began a series of articles on Teamster President James R. Hoffa. The series changed his life. By December 14 *Collier's* was about to die. Pierre, with the articles in type, got a call from the then chief counsel of the Senate Rackets Committee, Robert Kennedy, asking to see the Hoffa story. Pierre made it available, and a month later Bobby hired him as the committee's first investigator.

The partnership was a success. Pierre and Bobby liked each other on sight. Pierre testified more than any other staff member before the committee. "He was careful in his work," Bobby says approvingly, and adds, "Pierre is jolly, too."

The friendship goes on. Every day Pierre and Bobby talk on the telephone. The President's press secretary is still grateful to the President's brother. "He disciplined me in a subtle but kind of wonderful way," Pierre says. "I wasn't disciplined and generally not a detail man."

With Bobby's brother Jack, a member of the committee, Pierre's relations were remote. In April 1959 Senator Kennedy, to whom Pierre had occasionally suggested questions that might be asked of witnesses, called Pierre on the telephone. "I'd like you to be with us during the campaign," he said. Pierre was somewhat mystified by this cryptic request but assented because "by that time my personal commitment to Bobby was so total that if he had asked me to work for his brother Louie, who was an idiot, to be President, I would have done it."

By September of that year Pierre realized that he was to be the candidate's press secretary. The first three months in the new role were miserable. The Senator, he reports, "never knew I was there." Pierre was never consulted, seldom knew what the candidate was doing. All policy decisions were made in concert with either Ted Sorensen or Kenny O'Donnell. Everyone was oblivious to Pierre.

But in November, when the candidate was desperate for a fast statement for the press, Pierre came through and there was a breakthrough in their relationship. Thereafter Pierre, who had been suspected of self-centeredness, a crime in the Kennedy camp comparable to lukewarmness, was accepted. Pierre jogged along in the campaign with the press, solaced by cigar smoke and his aesthetic enjoyment of the Kennedy speeches, which he said "had a minimum of baloney."

He was delighted upon victory to become press secretary, a job he realizes isn't much to the public with a press wizard like Kennedy in charge. What he likes about it is the access to the President and the insurance of being in the middle of things. Because he has the President's ear he was able to play a leading part in sending an emergency mission to Bolivia, to alleviate a situation called to his attention by a friend of his mother's, who came here seeking help with the Vice President of Bolivia, Juan le Chin.

The President includes him in meetings Pierre thinks he should attend. He attends the legislative meetings on Tuesday and the occasional Cabinet meetings. Pierre, as always, has a finger in many pies. He has instituted weekly meetings of the press representatives of the Vice President, Defense, Treasury, United States Information Agency, and the Space Agency, some of the sessions devoted to formulation of possible Wednesday press-conference questions. He envisions international powwows someday of chief government press chieftains. He has sparked a movement for a White House music award. He makes numerous public speeches. He has institutionalized meetings with foreign correspondents in Washington, so they will feel at home, and is working on plans for an international press center in New York.

Pierre and his wife, Nancy Joy, enjoy going to Washington parties, and frequently entertain at their split-level house in Lake Barcroft, Virginia, where they live with the three children of Pierre's first marriage. (He was divorced in 1957.) The Salinger home contains many original paintings presented by artists to his mother who had befriended them while she was a newspaper art critic.

Pierre cooks on Sunday, plays the piano (favorite composers are Bach, Purcell, Handel, and Vivaldi) and a little tennis.

He likes his job, and according to Robert J. Donovan, biographer of the inner workings of the Eisenhower White House, "is handling it as well as anyone ever has."

LAWRENCE F. O'BRIEN'S EARLIEST MEMORIES ARE POLITICAL. HE grew up in a household where the overwhelming preoccupation was politics. A frequent visitor to the house was Boston's Mayor James Michael Curley, the durable leprechaun who inspired *The Last Hurrah*. Another was Senator David I. Walsh to whose coming young Larry looked forward somewhat less. Senator Walsh, ensconced in the parlor of the Roland, the small hotel run by the O'Briens in Springfield, Massachusetts, would summon Larry, just home from school, and command him, "Tell me what you know about American history."

One day, as the familiar charade was being enacted, Larry noticed out of the corner of his eye that a coal truck was drawing into position before the house. At that time the Senator grandly put in a call to the White House. Larry figured that just about the time the Senator was paying his respects to Herbert C. Hoover the coal would be delivered. It happened just that way. The Senator had hardly bidden the President good-day when the coal rattled down the chute, obliterating his silvery tones and making Larry as happy as ever he had been during a Walsh visit.

He has been making precise calculations ever since.

Larry O'Brien was born into politics as surely as the President he serves as Special Assistant for Congressional Relations and Personnel. His father and mother both brought from County Cork the Celt's abiding interest in public affairs. His father, also Lawrence F., never wanted to run for office, but he had a passion for organization, and he often took his son along when he did his door-to-door canvassing on his tours of the wards. "The votes are there," he told the boy, "if we can only get them out."

O'Brien senior was elected to the Democratic state committee and in 1932 backed Franklin D. Roosevelt for the Presidency, in the face of bitter opposition from the townsfolk who favored Alfred E. Smith, the idol of the Irish Catholics.

It took courage, even though O'Brien had the companionship of James Michael Curley in his unpopular stand. The pair were defeated as delegates and James Michael later turned up as a delegate from Puerto Rico. O'Brien had a harder time, because none of his neighbors would speak to him until his political judgment was vindicated by the Roosevelt victory.

Young Larry attended Cathedral Grammar School and Cathedral High School. He was a basketball player and a debater. He worked his way through Northeastern University Law School, served for a while as a bartender, later being elected president of the bartenders union in his only bid for office. In 1943 he went into the Army, and was assigned to the Classification Center at Camp Edwards.

During those years he formed a crucial friendship with Foster Furcolo, a bright, mercurial young lawyer who shared his mania for politics. In 1946, with Larry managing the campaign, Foster Furcolo ran for Congress and lost. In 1948 they tried again and made it, and Larry O'Brien came to Washington as Furcolo's administrative assistant. The two were close friends. Furcolo was best man at O'Brien's wedding to Elva Bressard in 1944 and stood as godfather to Lawrence O'Brien, III.

But in 1950 they fell out. Why, neither will say. It was a complete break and of such a serious nature that Larry O'Brien took an extraordinary step for a Bay State Irishman: he swore off politics. He went to work administering a fund for hotel workers and doing public relations.

His abstention from politics was of short duration. In January 1951 a slender congressman named John F. Kennedy came to him and asked him if he would like to help him run for state office. O'Brien had met Kennedy four years before—in 1947 at a labor meeting in Springfield, where they were introduced by Representative Edward P. Boland, who told O'Brien at the time that Jack Kennedy would someday be President.

Kennedy wanted O'Brien to be his western campaign manager. Although Massachusetts is a small state which can be traversed in a morning, the difference between East and West is Kiplingesque.

The East, with Boston at the hub, is traditionally Irish and Democratic; the West, "Yankee" and Republican. Kennedy knew he
must win the West, where he knew no one, and he needed O'Brien's
help. At the time he had to cool his heels while Paul Dever, then
the governor, made up his mind whether to seek re-election or run
for the Senate against Henry Cabot Lodge.

Eventually, Dever decided for the governorship, and O'Brien
decided to join the Kennedy campaign for the Senate as western
campaign manager. Foster Furcolo told Kennedy he could have
either O'Brien or himself in his efforts. Kennedy chose O'Brien.
By the spring of 1951 O'Brien was spending most of every week in
Kennedy headquarters in Boston and had been named state-wide
director of organization under Bobby Kennedy, his brother's campaign manager. "Larry was indispensable," says Bobby. "I didn't
know the politicians and I must say I seemed to alienate the few
I knew. Larry knew everybody and got along with them all."

O'Brien took the candidate and his brother all over Massachusetts. With them on many of these excursions was Bobby's classmate, Kenny O'Donnell, who also owes his initiation to O'Brien.
The problem then was to work through and yet around the men
whom O'Donnell calls "the cute pols," who were all committed to
Dever. In every city and town they hunted up bright young professional men who would not appear menacing to the politicians as
future candidates and who could be trusted to work both with them
and without them.

The bright young men, whose counterparts have been the back-
bone of every Kennedy effort ever since, were called "Kennedy
secretaries." They headed Kennedy committees and reported direct
to O'Brien, who provided them with a list of mimeographed instructions which, like every subsequent O'Brien manual, guided
them from their first coffee party to the last ride to the polls on
Election Day. Kennedy beat Henry Cabot Lodge by 70,000 votes
after one of the hardest-fought campaigns in Bay State history.

Three years later O'Brien and O'Donnell began to plot to take
over the Massachusetts State Committee, which was then firmly in
the grip of John W. McCormack, House majority leader and an
old-school Irish politician who was hardly ecstatic over the rise of

young Kennedy in the party. Senator Kennedy was not especially interested in the maneuver. His chief Washington adviser, Theodore C. Sorensen, opposed it, on the ground that the Senator should be consolidating himself in New England with area legislation. The Senator's father, Joseph P. Kennedy, did not think it wise for his son to get involved in the "Irish brawls" of his home state. But O'Brien and O'Donnell reasoned that if Kennedy went to the 1956 Democratic convention as a member of the delegation instead of its leader, he would, in O'Donnell's words, "look silly." So they set about unseating the chairman of the State Committee, William Burke. They got a ruling that the chairman had to be a member of the State Committee, which Burke was not. Then they induced a man from Burke's home town of Hatfield to file against him for the State Committee. Burke, who was very big in Boston, was nobody in Hatfield, withdrew from the race, and the stage was set for the coup. The state convention convened in that atmosphere of mayhem and libel inevitable in gatherings of Bay State Democrats, and after fisticuffs and charges of betrayal had been exchanged, the Kennedy forces got the vote and John M. "Pat" Lynch was state chairman.

"If it hadn't come off, O'Brien and I would have been soup and nuts," says O'Donnell now.

In 1958, when Kennedy sought re-election to the Senate, the blueprints were refined to the point where they could serve for a national victory as well. Every one of Massachusetts' 39 cities and 208 towns was organized within an inch of its life. Kennedy won by 874,608 votes; he was in business as a national candidate.

In October 1959 O'Brien was one of half a dozen Kennedy men who was called to a six-hour strategy meeting at the Senator's home in Hyannis Port, Massachusetts. Soon after, O'Brien took off on what was to become a nonstop series of visits to states which held primary contests. "The thing about Larry is his durability," says David J. Powers, the Senator's personal aide in the campaign. "He went back to Indiana seven times."

The two greatest tests of O'Brien's organizing ability came in the hard-fought primaries in Wisconsin and West Virginia against Senator Hubert Humphrey. Wisconsin was so unorganized that the Kennedy forces had to import almost all their help. O'Brien set about winning Wisconsin with his usual care and attention to detail. He sat down with voting records and fresh statistics provided by Kennedy's private pollster, Louis Harris. He began making charts that showed patterns of weak spots and looked for the point he always seeks first: "Where do we start?"

Says his aide, Richard K. Donahue, "He did what he always does—he never gives up on anything and he never takes anything for granted."

Before he finished, he had Kennedy volunteers functioning all over the state. Kennedy eked out a narrow victory over Humphrey, and the Kennedy team decamped to West Virginia, where it was do or die. "He was good with the pols," said Powers. "He sold them the idea they could sell Kennedy the way we had sold him in Massachusetts. His big arguing point was not only that Jack could win, but that he *would* win, and that they were getting a chance to get in on the ground floor."

In West Virginia the religious issue emerged in uninhibited expressions of bigotry. The politicians told O'Brien that in their state a Catholic could not win. "Larry knew politicians never worry about substance," says Donahue. "A politician doesn't get worked up about issues, he gets worked up about votes. Larry never debated the theological aspects of it. He just kept insisting that Kennedy could win and they better get with it."

An admiring observer was Robert P. McDonough of Parkersburg, Kennedy's West Virginia campaign director. "Larry wasn't one of those outsiders who comes into a state and tells the insiders they are doing everything all wrong. He waited to see what they were doing before he said anything, and then he adapted his methods to ours."

The traditional method in West Virginia was simply to purchase an entire organization which on Election Day produced the votes, the voters, the checkers, and the drivers. O'Brien did it his way: He organized Kennedy committees, recruited telephone volunteers, supervised the distribution by hand of the Kennedy tabloids, leaned on laggards, and checked his men every day from his sixth-floor hideaway in the Kanawha Hotel in Charleston.

On the night of May 10 Kennedy flew back from Washington to claim the West Virginia victory. He called O'Brien "the best election man in the business." O'Brien had always considered him a miraculous candidate.

Despite their mutual admiration, curiously enough, Kennedy and O'Brien have never enjoyed a particularly warm or even easy relation. A local politician watching various aides report to Kennedy noticed that O'Brien always had proof for what he said and had arranged his presentation "like a step of stairs," whereas the others just stated flatly what they thought.

The difficulty seems to be that O'Brien, a rather sober fellow, was sometimes apt to take a gloomy view of things. The Kennedys like their helpers to be cheery, even if the facts don't entirely warrant it. Besides, President Kennedy has always felt that his judgment of any political situation was as good as any man's, and that if it was bad, he would be the first to know. And like most candidates he tends to look ahead rather than to brood about past errors.

O'Brien jokes a little ruefully about his status in the Kennedy entourage. "I don't know what I'm doing with this crowd. I didn't go to Harvard and I'm not athletic. I don't even play touch football."

But he continued to play the game of politics well on the Kennedy team, and in the spring of 1960, using a combination of bluff and pressure, he practically insured California's 81 delegates for the front runner. While the committee empowered to pick the delegates met in Carmel, O'Brien holed up at the Pine Inn four miles away. The selection committee felt O'Brien was breathing down its neck (he was), and that his presence was merely advertising the threat that if Kennedy didn't get a fair shake in the delegation he would enter the California primary against favorite son Edmund G. Brown, the governor. Various California delegates complained that O'Brien's methods were "crude and heavy-handed," but he has always been more interested in results.

In Los Angeles for the convention, he unveiled his "buddy" system, a device whereby every state delegation had an out-of-stater who lived with it and held its hand and said he wanted only to help it, but was actually keeping a gimlet eye on every quiver and change in the delegation. The "buddies" reported every morning to Bobby and Larry on the eleventh floor of the Biltmore. O'Brien guessed the Kennedy total within half a vote.

When he was made President Kennedy's liaison man with the Congress, O'Brien adapted his campaign tactics to a more static situation. Characteristically, he began to make charts of all major legislation. Even more characteristically, he started a card file of the entire Congress. On each card is shown a member's pet projects, his public statements, soft spots, friends, and prejudices.

He needed it right away, for the Administration was at once plunged into a fight for the life of its legislation. Howard W. Smith of Virginia, chairman of the Rules Committee, announced that he would resist the enlargement proposed by Speaker Sam Rayburn for the committee, which had become a graveyard for liberal measures. The Kennedy election team swung into action. Every day the Speaker, Representative McCormack, Whip Carl Albert of Oklahoma, and several interested congressmen met to go over the lists, rechecking the hopeless and the cinches, dividing up target areas, trying to reach agreement about whether someone from outside the group, a politician from a man's district, the governor of his state, the Speaker, or the President himself, was needed to reach a resister.

An hour before the vote Larry O'Brien informed the President that he would win with 216 votes. Actually, he was one short. "I think Larry's first-rate," says Representative Richard C. Bolling of Missouri, one of Speaker Rayburn's bright young men. "He's a close, hard counter, a checker, and rechecker."

On the Senate side O'Brien, a squarely built man of forty-three, with red hair cut like a brush and an air of guarded affability, is welcome. He is known approvingly as an organization man by the leadership, which knows he will work through channels and respect their wishes in all matters. It is a situation of infinite booby traps, rather like living with your in-laws. Larry bears up under it well, never forgets a face or to return a telephone call. He is not a student of legislation and does not pretend to be.

"Larry is not so foolish as to say to a congressman, 'Do this,' " says his friend and representative, Eddie Boland, who lends him his congressional office for lobbying. "He just lets them know he will remember whether they were 'on' or 'off' on a vote."

O'Brien's work is supposedly made easier by the fact that he has at his disposal both carrot and stick. That is, he has the job of dispensing patronage to congressmen. Officially, patronage for state jobs is in the hands of the chairman of the Democratic National Committee, John M. Bailey, of Connecticut. But obviously O'Brien has a great deal to say about jobs. So does Kenneth O'Donnell, and so does the President. Outsiders who have trouble unraveling the complexities of the situation think the ambiguity is purposeful, so that the buck never stops and the disappointed office seeker is never sure whether to blame Bailey or O'Brien.

O'Brien thinks that patronage is more than jobs anyway. There are bridges and roads and dams to be considered. There is also that great intangible, the President's favor. O'Brien, who regards his job as a perpetual convention, goes to great pains to bring the legislators and the President together. The President has received every House and Senate committee chairman alone for a half-hour interview. At O'Brien's suggestion he has entertained forty or fifty congressmen at a crack at a series of Thursday-afternoon coffee parties, where Kennedy campaigns all over again.

"We just have to exploit his charm and social grace," says O'Brien, a completely political animal who has found the ideal politician to exploit.

ALL THROUGH THE CAMPAIGN, BY DAY AND BY NIGHT, AT THE front of the press bus stood a dark-eyed man leaning over the railing, peering out into the crowd. Nobody knew whether he was counting the house or searching for bomb throwers. Sometimes he would mutter to the driver, hop out the door, shoulder his way through the crowd, and fling off the lead convertible anyone who got too close to or rough with the candidate or who in any way menaced the safety or well-being of John F. Kennedy.

If the man, whose name was Kenneth Philip O'Donnell, did anything else in the campaign, most of the reporters traveling with him for hundreds of thousands of miles had no idea what it was. It was typical of Kenny O'Donnell that he considered it no part of his function to enlighten them. His appearance added to the mystery. Light-footed, tight-lipped, low-voiced, black-haired, with high cheekbones and a small smile, he looked for all the world like someone right out of *The Informer* or some other drama of the "Troubles" of Ireland. He needed only a trench coat to complete the illusion. He laughed at any scribbler who asked him for any inside information.

When the candidate went to his suite, O'Donnell went, too. He always knew where he was and where he was going. He attended all the rallies, never volunteered any comment that anyone can remember about the performance of the candidate or the progress of the campaign. He was always there.

Actually, he was doing for the President what he does now. He was the doorkeeper and the schedule maker. During the campaign he put together the most ferocious itinerary in American political history. He wanted people to understand that Kennedy was an active man with an inexhaustible supply of energy. Luckily, one of the Kennedy campaign promises was to stay in Washington, so that O'Donnell's travel-agent chores, for the opening months of the Administration at least, were considerably lightened.

It seems that the President never specifically asked Kenny to be his appointments secretary. Kenny just went on doing it automatically. Actually, if Providence had tailor-made a confidential aide for John Kennedy, the product would have been very much like O'Donnell, who embodies the virtues that all Kennedys prize most highly: He is tough, terse, discreet, loyal, athletic, and funny.

The President says of Kenny, "He has good nerves and a good memory. He has a passion for anonymity. He is always optimistic."

Kenny says of the President, "He's a cold champion."

They have rapport.

The furthest from the public of the Kennedy technicians, Kenny is the closest to the President of the three. He is the White House staff member whom Kennedy sees most, first in the morning, last at night. Kennedy trusts Kenny completely.

Kenny, seeking to describe their relationship, says, "We're not friends. Bobby's my friend. It goes deeper than that." Nobody who knows Kenny doubts that he would die for the President if need be. Kenny says he would not do his present job for anyone else in the world. "It's not my cup of tea," he says. He would rather be in Defense or some department where he could initiate direct action.

But the President is delighted with the way he does his job. Kenny's "why?" can quickly dam up the torrent of self-seeking justification from a politician, eager to see the President, so that only a protesting trickle persists, and not for long. "When Kenny says no, it really takes," said a member of the intellectual branch of the official family. "And somehow it doesn't hurt either."

Kennedy finds Kenny both reliable and restful. Kenny never babbles like some of the academic types around the White House. "I don't care about the conversation," is an O'Donnellism. "What are we going to do?"

At the same time, Kenny is no Irish Calvin Coolidge, as has been suggested. His Harvard classmate, Bobby Kennedy, remembers him as "terribly gabby" in their college days. And today, over a drink or two, Kenny, who never goes in for small talk, can be extremely voluble on his two favorite subjects: politics and sports.

At the O'Donnell home, in Worcester, Massachusetts, these were the constant topics of conversation. Kenny's father, Cleo O'Donnell, was football coach and director of physical education at Holy Cross College. Kenny and his brother Cleo, Jr., played football at Classical High School. Kenny was captain of the team.

Kenny was born on March 4, 1924, and became involved in politics eight years later more or less involuntarily. He grew up in a ward that was Republican by eight to one. He fought with his playmates over Roosevelt as soon as he was big enough to put up his fists. Kenny's father, "the most literate man" he ever knew, was a Democrat. He also passed on to his son his interest in history and government. From his earliest school days Kenny was interested in leaders. His heroes at first were all generals: Alexander the Great, Robert E. Lee, and Caesar. Later he added Churchill, Roosevelt, and De Gaulle.

His father was an admirer of Harvard University, and both his sons went there. Kenny went to war first, however, and made a record that rivals President Kennedy's. He spent fourteen months overseas in the Army Air Force, as lead bombardier of the seventy-odd B-17's in the 490th Bomb Group. On his twenty-first birthday he was flying his thirtieth mission. Over the target he froze, forgetting which way to turn the lever on the bomb sight. He took a chance, guessed right, hit the target, and won the Distinguished Flying Cross.

Fletcher Knebel, who has described O'Donnell's wartime experiences, says they gave him "a distaste for the glory grabbers, the fakers, and the phonies," and also led him into politics because "he came to believe that an older generation must have made an epic botch of its job, since so many thousands of young men had been called upon to die."

Back from the wars Kenny began studying government at Harvard. He made a friend of a tousle-haired young man named Bobby Kennedy who was, like himself, slight but nevertheless played football. Kenny was captain of the team; he played right halfback. His greatest gridiron feat was to play in the Harvard-Yale game of 1948 with a broken leg. Harvard won 20–7, and O'Donnell, despite a plaster cast, scored the winning touchdown. Bobby remembers the times as "confused years," when grizzled veterans were thrown in with beardless prep-school grads and classes had no identity or personality. Bobby and Kenny hung around the Varsity Club, talking incessantly about religion, politics, and the Marshall Plan. Kenny was a savage, contrary debater, took the opposite side of any question. Kenny never went to class, as Bobby remembers, but was the best-informed man on history and politics of anyone around, read omnivorously, and never stopped talking.

After graduating from Harvard, about which he is not sentimental like his leader, Kenny went to Boston College Law School at night, enrolled in a paper company as a sales trainee, and married Helen Sullivan, a pretty, slim, gray-eyed Irish girl whom he met in Worcester through his sister Justine. On the side he took some part in Paul Dever's 1948 campaign. "I just hung around and listened," he said.

Bobby introduced him to his brother Jack. Kenny was impressed. He liked what Jack said about a housing bill then at issue. "He was a guy who said what we wanted to say," said Kenny. "We didn't fight the war for the real-estate lobby. I thought there was a touch of class in the way he did it." Both Kenny and his father who, like many Massachusetts Irish Catholics, were embarrassed by the antics of some of their own kind in politics, much admired Kennedy's 1947 refusal to sign a petition for the release of James Michael Curley from federal prison. "My father said Jack would be the first Catholic candidate for Vice-President," Kenny recalls. In 1951 Kenny's life took a new direction. His wife had twins, and Bobby asked him how he would like to come in on Jack's first statewide campaign. "It was like feeding a British soldier water in the Libyan Desert," says Kenny. "I was dying to get in." With Bobby and Larry O'Brien, and sometimes Jack, he began the work of organizing the state. He and O'Brien got on very well from the start. They shared each other's views on the subject of political organization: "It doesn't do any good to organize if you have a stiff for a candidate. But other things being equal, the organization can make the difference." Kenny is grateful to Larry for his political education. He thinks there's no one better in the business.

After Kennedy was safely in, Kenny came down to Washington to be Bobby's administrative assistant on the Senate Rackets Committee. He would have preferred to stay in Massachusetts and keep an eye on the ever-boiling pot there. Why did he come? "Because Bobby asked me to," he says.

Staff members came to marvel at O'Donnell's memory. He could recall a telephone slip or a bit of evidence that would tie up a whole case against a labor goon. He was unruffled and businesslike throughout the entire, sometimes melodramatic, proceedings.

In 1958 he gratefully went back to Massachusetts to help the Senator rack up his huge majority in a campaign against an unknown named Vincent Celeste. By this time the O'Donnells had four children. Helen O'Donnell was resigned to long separations. "I knew there was no other life for him. I'd rather have him interested than not liking his job—that's worse."

Kenny came in early on the drive for the Democratic nomination. He never panicked. On the Tuesday before the Kennedy nomination at Los Angeles, Adlai Stevenson made an unscheduled appearance at the Coliseum. The hall went wild. Kenny watched

the demonstrations lift Stevenson literally off his feet. His comment
was sardonic. "We never said he couldn't be elected mayor of
Los Angeles."

When the campaign for the presidency got under way, Kenny
went along. He and David J. Powers, a sweet-tempered Boston
baseball statistician, were Kennedy's handlers. Dave Powers could
make the candidate laugh. He also saw that Kennedy was up on
time. He learned to wake the candidate by saying, "What do you
suppose Nixon's doing while you're lying there?"

Kenny kept up Kennedy's spirits, too. He simply told the candidate every chance he got that he would bury Nixon. Before that,
in the primaries, he told him he would bury Humphrey, which was
slightly but not much more accurate. Kennedy still respects Kenny's
political judgment despite his own eyelash victory.

All through the campaign Kenny relentlessly filtered Kennedy's
visitors. He always wanted to know why they wanted to get in. If
he would not grant them access, he would at least see that their
messages got through. "They can knock me in other areas," says
Kenny, "but they can never say I didn't tell him exactly what they
told me."

It is the same today in the White House. A Cabinet officer who
wishes the President to know something but who does not wish to
take up his time will tell Kenny about a problem and what he has
done about it. Kenny tells the President, and he always gets it
straight. Vice-President Lyndon B. Johnson says approvingly of
Kenny, "He just says yes or no and gets it done."

Kenny doesn't think he should shield the President from people.
He couldn't if he wanted to, since the President is a notorious wan-
derer and people are always having unscheduled interviews with
him in White House corridors. Further, Kenny says he doesn't
think it's his job to keep divergent points of view away from the
President. "I'll let anyone in who knows anything I think he ought
to know," says Kenny. "I think all sides should get in and let the
President decide."

Kenny is helpful on patronage matters. He can remember exactly
what everyone did during the campaign, and there is, as he says,
"no point in trying to con me." If he doesn't know, he will find out.

He is perfectly capable of looking a senator in the eye and saying, "Where were you?"

He has not added materially to the ceremonial aspects of his job. "Hi, Governor," he said one morning, strolling into the anteroom. "Glad to see you." He insists, however, that he is very obsequious with foreign ministers. Nobody has seen it yet.

He arrives at work before the President, who comes at nine. Kenny has learned to read the papers before the President gets there, knowing that Kennedy will want to discuss any number of items before getting down to the day's work. Kenny has learned to keep the schedule open, because while the President is a reader he always has questions on the briefings which have been supplied to him. Kenny stands ready to call in anyone from any department who can supply further information.

The typed appointments schedule handed out to the press the night before bears scant resemblance to the log kept of the President's callers. As many as ten added starters find their way into the presidential office in the course of a day. Nor does the schedule show how often the President confers with his appointments secretary, who will be summoned in for a long talk on an average of once every three callers. In the daily round the Chief Executive probably sees Kenny O'Donnell more than anyone else in government. He never leaves before the President does. His wife holds supper for him until ten thirty or eleven at night. He shares the President's taste in food—meat and potatoes.

Few people get by him. Sometimes callers appeal to Kennedy's softhearted personal secretary for an audience. If she lets them in through the other door, Kenny knows about it. The next time the person calls, he may, says Kenny with his slight smile, "have a hard time getting in."

4.

THE MILD-EYED LIBERALS

David Bell
Walter Heller

By CHARLES B. SEIB

IF IT IS REASONABLE TO SAY THAT THE HEALTH OF THE NATIONAL economy and the way the federal government takes and uses its share of the national product are vital elements in determining the country's well-being, then it is also reasonable to say that two of the most important men in the Kennedy administration are a pair of lanky young economists still trailing academic ivy.

For David Elliot Bell, until recently chief administrator of the Littauer Center for Public Administration at Harvard, and Dr. Walter Wolfgang Heller, on leave from chairmanship of the Economics Department at the University of Minnesota, are clearly the ranking White House experts on just about everything concerned with the making, taking, and spending of money.

As director of the Bureau of the Budget, Bell has a dominant voice in all decisions affecting the way the Government spends more than $80 billion a year. As head of President Kennedy's three-man Council of Economic Advisers, Heller is the well-spring of the Administration's economic philosophy and policies. Each has the ear of the President and uses it frequently. And each is entering with zest and confidence into his role as a Washington mover and shaker.

It is easy to make too much of a point of the similarities of this pair. Both are outsize: Heller is a slender six feet, three and a half inches, Bell is an even slenderer six feet, four inches plus. Both are relaxed, sometimes even boyish, their intense drive cloaked in an easygoing manner. Both had earlier Washington careers as bright young men in government during World War II and the Truman years; they understand the workings of legislative and bureaucratic machinery and the arts of negotiation and compromise. Neither had known the President before his nomination; in fact, Bell didn't meet him until after joining the official family. Both are sharp, hard-working, extremely articulate mild-eyed liberals.

Further, and perhaps most important, both see the government as a perfectly respectable participant in the economic and social life of the country. From their high-ceilinged offices in the old State Department Building, next door to the White House, both reject, philosophically and emotionally, the argument that the best government is the least government. Each thinks the essential question to be considered by a President is what the government can do to maintain a secure, stable, healthy country. Each believes the President should seek by any constitutional means to achieve that end.

To stop there, though, would be to give a false picture. There are significant differences between the two men, in temperament and in function. Heller is bouncier, more voluble; Bell plays it in a lower key. Heller likes to spread the word; Bell likes to get the job done. A fellow economist who knows them both cast around for the essential difference and came up with this: "Walter Heller has the urge to mobilize public opinion. Dave Bell has the urge to mobilize administrative machinery. Each goes about it with terrific drive."

Either by coincidence or brilliant planning on the part of Kennedy and his recruiting team, these "urges" conform almost exactly to the tasks Bell and Heller were selected to perform. Heller's Council of Economic Advisers is just what its name implies, an advisory agency that can evolve, discuss, criticize, propose, propagandize, but cannot order or impose. It must work with opinion, first within the Administration, then among the public. Bell, on the other hand, is a man with great and specific powers. His job is to make the machinery of government function efficiently, economically, and to the desired ends. He and his staff dart into and around the government agencies, pecking away at a lagging or wasteful program here, pressing for more action on a desirable program there, resolving conflicts between projects and between the men who run them. At the moment it is anybody's guess as to which will have the more profound impact on the country. There can be no doubt, however, that each will leave his mark.

THE BUDGET BUREAU THAT DAVID BELL TOOK OVER FROM THE Eisenhower administration was a seat of negative power. The last Eisenhower director, Maurice Stans, a tough customer who hunted big game in Africa as a diversion, had a motto, "WHY?" that was hung in a place of honor at the head of the conference table in his office. Those who came to that table could expect to be asked WHY must a program be undertaken at all, WHY right now, WHY must it cost so much? No government agency was immune from his challenge. From the lowliest bureau to the Defense Department itself the Bureau's quest for programs that could be excised or trimmed went on relentlessly. Its role was that of a very crotchety bookkeeper who kept a tight hold on the cashbox with the full backing of the boss.

The Budget Bureau that Bell is trying to develop is a much different affair. It will, with his blessing, ask "Why not?" as often as it asks "Why?" He sees his agency as the conscience of the President, acting to achieve the national objectives as the Administration sees them. In some cases these actions will result in cutbacks and savings; probably more often they will result in new or increased spending.

The Bureau is up to the job. A comparatively new agency, dating back only to 1921, it has tremendous latent powers. It is the agency that, subject to the President's orders, sets the guide lines for each federal department and bureau to follow in drawing up its annual budget. This means, in effect, in planning its next year's activities. It investigates, studies, and, subject to rare appeals to the President himself, revises each agency's budget proposals, fitting them into the over-all Administration plan. And after Congress votes the funds for each agency, the Bureau steps in again to decide just how fast the money should be spent.

In announcing Bell's appointment early in December 1960, President Kennedy set the broadest possible scope for the Bureau. "The Budget Bureau's legitimate concerns go far beyond narrow accounting matters," he declared. "The preparation of the nation's budget is not just a mechanical task. It requires that the Bureau participate in the formulation of the President's program. It requires skillful examination of legislative proposals. And it requires the exercise of sound and imaginative judgment in recommending to the President how he can best integrate his policies with budgetary needs and considerations."

Bell agrees heartily. He wants the Bureau to be an idea factory, ranging all across the government. In his view, the ideal budget examiner is keenly and personally interested in the programs he oversees and wants to see them operating effectively. As a result, the examiner suggests ways to increase efficiency or bring about savings. He backs up administrators who must make the always-difficult decision to shut down an operation that has outlived its usefulness. He acts as a sort of people's defender, arguing against the special interests which sooner or later make their power felt within every agency. And he has the breadth and originality to propose or endorse ideas for new or expanded programs where there is a need.

Bell's Bureau has already shown how this new, positive approach works. When President Kennedy decided immediately after taking office that the economy was not coming out of its slump quickly enough, he ordered a speedup in government buying and building. It was the Budget Bureau that was given the job of riding herd on the other agencies to make certain they were spotting all the possibilities for accelerated anti-recession spending.

Outside the purely economic field Bell himself got the idea, after studying the Bureau analysis of military weapons, that the missile-firing Polaris submarine program should be stepped up. He found that Defense Secretary McNamara was arriving at the same conclusion and urged him to take the matter to the President immediately. Result: A speedup in the Polaris program was one of the first Administration actions in the defense field.

In still another field, some Bureau experts reported to Bell soon after he took over that career officials in the Department of Health, Education, and Welfare had developed some valuable ideas for federal aid to medical-research facilities. The ideas had been turned down by the Eisenhower administration, but the budget men still thought they were good. Bell encouraged the H.E.W. career men to take their plan to H.E.W. Secretary Ribicoff and it eventually became part of the Administration's health program.

Bell's idea of a powerful, far-ranging Bureau fits in well with the President's determination to hold down the size of his personal White House staff. During the Eisenhower administration the White House developed all sorts of bureaucratic closets where special assistants and substaffs with special areas of responsibility resided. Those responsibilities have, in large measure, been turned over to Bell and his people.

This broad view of the Bureau's functions and power is also in keeping with the recommendations of most recent students of the executive branch. A still-unpublished study which the Brookings Institution submitted to Kennedy soon after his election declared that "the history of the Presidency argues strongly that the President's responsibility is protected more effectively through the program, expenditure, and management controls available in the budgetary process than through any other single type of management operation. . . . For the purpose of making presidential power operative, and of safeguarding presidential responsibility, the controls provided by the budgetary process are the most effective and discriminating constantly available to the President's hand."

And, it might have added, the man who administers those controls is a very important man indeed.

To this position of power and trust David Bell brings both youth and experience. Only forty-two years old, he has been a key Budget Bureau and White House official under Harry Truman, a Stevenson speech writer in the hectic 1952 presidential campaign, a financial expert for the Pakistan government, and a Harvard economics lecturer and administrator.

Born January 21, 1919, in Jamestown, North Dakota, where his father was a Y.M.C.A. secretary, Bell spent his early childhood in California, where his family moved in search of a cure for his mother's painful sinus trouble. His parents still live in Colma, a suburb of San Francisco, and his father is dean of instruction at San Francisco State College.

Bell went to Pomona College at Claremont, California. He says his main claim to distinction there was the fact that on the varsity basketball team four of the five starters, including himself, were Phi Beta Kappas. He concedes that the fifth man was the best player.

A friend from those days offers this picture of the gangling young Bell: "He was a hardheaded guy, not a bookish type. He was always looking for the answers, and if he wasn't satisfied, he would dig deeper. He had the true inquiring mind."

Bell had gone to college pretty well settled on physics as a career, but midway through college he switched to economics because, as he remembers it, he decided its mysteries promised to be more fascinating than those he would encounter in the physics lab.

He claims no long-time dedication to the idea of public service. In fact, he isn't quite sure how he got interested in it. His parents give Senator Douglas of Illinois, a former economics professor himself, much of the credit for both the switch to economics and the interest in government work. They say that it was after hearing Douglas give a lecture at Pomona that their son, in a letter to them, first mentioned his interest in such matters.

A Bachelor of Arts degree in 1939 was quickly followed by a Master's degree from the Harvard Graduate School of Arts and Sciences. Bell was a fellow in the Department of Economics there, working on his Ph.D., when World War II began, and his deferment as a graduate student was canceled. Bell's first idea was to go to Washington and, as he wryly puts it, permit the government to take advantage of his brains and training. He hooked on at the Budget Bureau as an analyst in the burgeoning "War Organization Section," but it took only a few months in a desk job to convince him he had made a wrong decision. The place he really wanted to be, he decided, was in the fighting.

A walk to Fifteenth Street and Pennsylvania Avenue, where the Marines had a recruiting station, and a physical in which he had to scrunch down in order to get under the Corps' six-foot-four-inch height limit sent him off to Officers' Training School at Quantico, Virginia. He was thwarted in his desire to get into the fight, however. Completion of his training was followed by a tour of duty there as an instructor. His protest to his colonel that he had left a good job to get into the Marines and didn't want another one brought the cold response that "Marines serve where they are told to serve." Finally he was sent to intelligence duty at Pearl Harbor, and finished out the war there.

Upon leaving the Marines in 1945 Bell returned to the Budget Bureau and began a rapid rise, soon becoming the Bureau's top economist at the age of twenty-seven. It was in this job that he began to display the quality now commented upon by practically everyone who has had any dealings with him: an ability to take a mass of facts and ideas from different sources and synthesize them into a reasonable and coherent whole. This talent brought him to the attention of the White House, and he became a member of a special Budget Bureau crew assigned to help with presidential speeches and messages. In the atmosphere of crisis which surrounded the preparation of every Truman speech or message, Bell shone. Good use was made of his ability to listen, catch the essentials of a complicated situation, and express them in the kind of clear, unadorned prose Truman liked to deliver.

A former associate cites as an example the preparation of the President's 1947 veto message on the Taft-Hartley Labor Bill and the radio speech in which Truman explained his action to the public. With the deadline fast approaching, the staff men assigned to the project were getting nowhere. Their efforts had produced only chunks of heavy-handed prose with no beginning, no end, and no life. Along about midnight the night before the job was due Clark Clifford, one of Truman's top assistants, came into the workroom and read through what had been prepared with dismay and alarm. It just wouldn't do. After holding forth on what had to be said, Clifford announced he was going home to get some sleep. He'd be back at 6 A.M., he said, and the clear implication was that he wanted something usable waiting for him.

"Then," the former Bell associate went on, "Dave Bell took all the stuff, the material that the various staffs and departments had provided and what we had been working on, and sat down and pulled it all together in one expository statement. It wasn't a final draft, but at last we had something like what the President wanted to say. The rest of the job was mostly a matter of polishing."

By late 1947 Bell had become so valuable in this kind of work that he was transferred to the White House staff. Charles Murphy, then the President's Special Counsel and now Under Secretary of Agriculture, remembers that James Webb, then Budget Bureau director and now head of the National Aeronautics and Space Administration, first suggested that a member of the Bureau's staff be switched to the White House staff to help out on speeches and messages.

"He said we could have anybody we wanted," Murphy recalls, "and I said we'd take Dave Bell. Bell was then Webb's personal assistant, and Webb would have preferred to give us anyone else in the Bureau. But he had made his offer and he stuck by it, and Bell came over to the White House."

In 1948 Bell switched back to the Budget Bureau briefly, largely because the White House wanted him in a civil-service job he could keep if Truman should lose the election. He worked for several months on budget preparations in practically every area of government spending, including the military. According to a report in the Bureau, he so impressed his superiors that one rating in his file read, prophetically: "This is a man of exceptional ability. Should he ever return to the Bureau he should be given the highest post available."

After the 1948 Truman victory Bell returned to the White House staff, eventually becoming one of the anonymous special assistants to the President. He was in charge of preparing legislation and messages in a number of special areas, working with federal agencies to shepherd bills through Congress and helping to decide what the President should do about bills that had been passed.

As the 1952 elections approached, he took leave from the White House to plunge into the Stevenson campaign. All summer and fall he toiled on the top floor of the Elks Club in Springfield, Illinois, heading the Stevenson research staff and writing policy statements and speeches for the candidate. He had as cohorts such pros as historian Arthur Schlesinger, Jr., magazine writer John Bartlow Martin, White House aide David Lloyd, and labor expert Willard Wirtz. But one associate recalls Bell as the "steady one who always remembered that a speech was no good unless it was ready in time to be delivered. He ground out the stuff day after day while some of the others were searching for beautiful phrases and fancy metaphors."

The Eisenhower victory left him unemployed, but he was lucky enough to get a Rockefeller "distinguished public service award" —a grant to finance a year of leave for selected government workers—and he returned to Harvard to resume the doctorate work interrupted by the war. That was interrupted once again, however, in the fall of 1954, when the Ford Foundation put up funds to permit the Littauer School to send a team of experts to Pakistan to help the government there get its economic house in order. Bell was selected to head the mission and he spent three and one-half years in that country, returning to the United States only once for home leave.

The Pakistan experience was valuable in many ways. The American mission gave assistance to the Pakistan government in every area of planning—agriculture, transportation, industry, and the rest. Its members worked closely with the very top leaders of the government, many of whom took a dim view of the whole planning idea. It was an exercise in ingenuity, tact, persuasiveness, and, of course, technical skill. A fellow member of the mission said recently that Bell impressed him with the "absolutely masterful way he dealt with some of the most difficult personalities I've ever encountered. He was not harsh or tough, but he showed great strength, and his leadership was accepted."

In the fall of 1957 Bell returned to Harvard to teach economics, chiefly the economics of underdeveloped countries, and to continue in the supervisory end of the Pakistan project. In the fall of 1959, after a two-month assignment in Athens where he conducted a project similar to the one in Pakistan, he was named secretary of the Littauer School, becoming the school's chief executive officer.

One Budget Bureau colleague, who knew Bell well back in his Truman days, feels that the Pakistan experience had a profound influence. "Dave was always bright," he said. "Now he is seasoned. Of course, his experiences in the 1952 campaign and his doctorate work at Harvard had something to do with that, but, above all he was seasoned by the human, economic, and political experiences and problems he encountered in the Middle East."

The Pakistan experience has, for one thing, influenced Bell's whole approach to international problems. "He reacts to most things intellectually," the same associate explains, "but he reacts almost viscerally to problems involving the face we show the rest of the world—particularly that part of the world.

"Recently a foreign government asked us to release a member of our staff to work on a development program in that country. They said it was most urgent, but all of us here said we couldn't spare the man they wanted. Then Bell heard about it and sent the man on his way. He told us that our answer was the one he used to get when he was out on the combat line in Pakistan. 'It's the wrong answer,' he said. 'It will be a lot easier for us to find a replacement for the man here than for them to get along without him there.' "

During the 1960 presidential campaign Bell worked as part of the Kennedy "Cambridge brain trust." He prepared material on foreign aid, with particular attention to the Indian subcontinent. This did not become a hot campaign issue, however, and he and Kennedy never met until he was summoned to the President-elect's home in Georgetown the evening before his appointment to the Budget job was announced.

Clark Clifford and Richard Neustadt, another associate on the Truman staff, are generally credited with recommending Bell to Kennedy. Both were working for the President-elect on the prob-

lems of the transition period and both felt that a pressing need
was to get a top-notch man into the Budget Bureau post quickly
so he could work in December and early January with the group
preparing the final budget of the outgoing administration.

As for so many other New Frontiersmen, the twelve-hour day—
8:30 A.M. to 8:30 P.M.—is the norm for Bell. In addition, he is
always in the office on Saturdays, frequently on Sundays, and he
invariably takes work home with him. Nevertheless, he appears
neither driving nor driven. He wants deadlines met, but he doesn't
get frantic or irritable as they approach. Associates say he's generally calm and gentle, "a very light hand on the tiller," but he
has been known to explode when faced with carelessness or bad
judgment.

"I never saw a man so devoid of idiosyncrasy," one associate
asserts. "He is a solid worker, with infinite capacity, but never
erratic or splashy."

Bell is no playboy, but he enjoys a good time. He's not averse
to an evening of night-clubbing, particularly if a ringside table for
a performance by an authentic jazz artist is part of the program.
He has been known to jump into party song fests with very little
encouragement.

He's long since given up basketball for bowling, a sport he
shares with his wife, the former Mary Barry of Altoona, Pennsylvania, and their two children, Susan, fifteen, and Peter, twelve.
(Friends from the Truman days remember that the sure way to be
a winner in the volleyball games the younger White House staffers
played during the President's Key West vacations was to get on
the team Dave Bell was on.)

Bell's humor is the quiet, unexpected type. He endeared himself to reporters the day his appointment was announced when
photographers asked him to make believe he was talking. "Say
one, two, three, four," one photographer directed. "Forty-five
billion," Bell solemnly responded, proving he could talk Budget
Bureau language.

Bell has made comparatively few changes in the personnel of
the 450-man Bureau, and he plans few. Much to the surprise of
most observers and to the chagrin of some ultraliberal Democrats

in Congress, he kept Maurice Stans' deputy director, Elmer B. Staats, in that key post. Staats is a career man and an old friend of Bell. Another old friend, William D. Carey, was kept in his job as executive assistant to the director. Other major division heads have also been retained for the most part. Bell believes these men are outstanding career public servants, at least as ready to carry out the positive mission he had laid out for the Bureau as they were to carry out the more restricted mission of the Eisenhower days.

He does, however, plan slowly to expand the Bureau's total personnel. He feels that the Eisenhower team, determined to make the Bureau set an economy example for the rest of the government, cut too deeply into its personnel. His previous government service and more recent foreign and academic duty have given him a wide acquaintanceship among university and foundation people, and he has already begun to draw on these contacts to expand his staff.

Bell sees three broad problem areas before the Budget Bureau during the next few years. The first is to set the role of the budget in promoting sound national economic growth. As an economist, he is more aware than Stans appeared to be of the impact budgetary policy has on the economy. And as a liberal he is far more ready to take advantage of that impact. Like Stans and others in the Eisenhower administration, he believes budget surpluses are anti-inflationary and therefore desirable in good times. But he is far more receptive than Stans was to the idea of using budget deficits, which he likely will have at least through June of 1962, to stimulate a lagging economy. And he has few qualms about increasing the budget if he and others in the Administration feel the situation demanded it—for security abroad or for a fuller life at home.

A second question involves national-security policies. The Budget Bureau in recent years has been under fire for "setting military policy" and "running the State Department and the Pentagon." Such criticism doesn't bother Bell. He feels that the Bureau must have a role in synchronizing the military, space, atomic, foreign-aid, and other security activities and molding them into a coherent policy. Administrators of each of these programs tend to take a parochial view and Bell believes that the Bureau and its small but skilled staff of specialists can bring fresh insight and provide a desperately needed broader view.

Finally, Bell feels that the Bureau must do more to put budget decisions in long-term perspective. Nowadays there are few federal programs that are confined to one year. And programs have a habit of starting out small in the first year but mushrooming in the fourth or fifth year. Bell thinks that it would be more realistic to submit to Congress spending plans for four or five years ahead instead of the present one-year plans, always with the proviso, of course, that times and plans change and that the long-range estimates are necessarily rough.

In revitalizing the activities of the Budget Bureau Bell has continuous access to the White House. He sees the President several times a week, and other key White House officials more often. In the early days of the Administration, in fact, he was spending almost half his time at the White House with the President, Special Counsel Theodore C. Sorensen, and others. It was certainly a closer liaison with the top command than that enjoyed by any budget director in recent years.

"If the President decides that he will hold matters of fiscal program and management policy and control reasonably close to him, and that he will utilize the machinery of an integral Bureau of the Budget for this purpose, his personal relationship with the director of the budget becomes extremely important," the previously-mentioned Brookings study asserted. "In these circumstances the President needs a budget director whom he likes and finds compatible.

"He needs to like him because he will see more of him than of most other members of his team other than his immediate personal staff. He needs a Budget Director whom he trusts because he will have to take much advice from him mainly on faith, since there is not time enough in the President's day to explain every action which the Budget Director must take in the President's name. And he must trust the Budget Director because he is the central and pivotal figure around which many of the President's most delicate relations revolve. The President needs a Budget Director who is knowledgeable about the executive branch and about Congress, not primarily in respect of operations and procedures but in respect of people and values and interests. He needs a man of wisdom, but not an expert in accounting, auditing, program analysis, statistics, legislative reference, or any of the other technical skills which go into the budgetary process. Most of all, the President needs a man who is wholly and completely the President's man, with no other loyalties and no other interests."

The early months of the Kennedy administration argue strongly that the President has in fact found such a man in David Bell.

WHEREAS DAVID BELL'S BUDGET BUREAU CAN, THROUGH ITS control of the purse strings, match its power with that of any agency of the government, Walter Heller's Council of Economic Advisers must rely on its powers of persuasion and its influence with the President. But its impact can be just as striking.

Heller is well equipped to persuade. Ideas and convictions bubble from him in colorful and confident abundance. "He is not the greatest economist alive but he is probably the best salesman of economic ideas," one long-time associate has observed. He is the epitome of the forceful, articulate, intelligent teacher who knows his subject thoroughly and delights in that fact. And there is every evidence that he has found a responsive pupil in President Kennedy; there appears to be a mutual enthusiasm that bodes well for Heller's success.

Heller is politically in tune with Kennedy, as is Bell, in being a highly pragmatic liberal. This is no ivory-tower academician. Although never directly active in politics, he has been fascinated by it since his student days and understands well the rules and demands of the political life. He has doctrine, but he is not a doctrinaire. He believes he is right, but recognizes the need for compromise on occasion. He knows how to make his words cut, but he has learned that it is often more effective to make them soothe.

Heller is a member of a family with a public-service tradition. On both sides he comes from a line of lawyers, doctors, and town officials in Germany. His father's profession was civil engineering and mathematics, but Heller remembers him as an inexhaustible fount of information on government, politics, economics, and just about any other subject. "My father knew the answer to every damned question a kid could think of," he recalls.

This family public-service bent was fortified in his academic years. Born in Buffalo and reared in Milwaukee, Heller got his Bachelor's degree at Oberlin in 1935 and his Master's and Ph. D. in economics at the University of Wisconsin. Both schools put strong emphasis on public and social service. As to his interest in economics, Heller has given major credit to the depression. "Those of us who were growing up then saw the economy flat on its back. To explain why, and to try to do something about it, seemed a high calling."

Within the field of economics Heller selected public finance as his specialty. To him it seemed the root of government policies and problems. Also, at Wisconsin he studied under Harold M. Groves, professor of economics and public finance and the dean of experts in the field, who kindled his enthusiasm for the subject. It was during the years at Wisconsin that, under the sponsorship of the Social Science Research Council, he loaded himself and his baggage into a 1937 Plymouth and undertook a one-year tour of thirty-one states, Washington, D.C., and Canada to study state income-tax laws and their administration. Stop-offs varied from one night to one month, and by the time Heller was finished he unquestionably knew more about income-tax laws of the states than any other economist.

Heller was also provided by the tour with a graphic demonstration of inflation. When he was preparing to set out in the fall of 1939 he bought a 1937 Plymouth for $350. The car survived the tour and the war years, and he took it with him to Germany when he was sent there on a postwar mission. Finally, in 1948, he sold the eleven-year-old veteran, now with more than one hundred thousand miles under its belt, to a GI there for $700.

Ever since his school days Heller has shuttled happily between government service and teaching. Kept out of military service by poor eyesight (his thick, horn-rimmed glasses give him a slightly owlish look), he spent all four years of World War II in the Treasury Department in Washington, where he worked on wartime tax programs in general and, in particular, helped devise the withholding-tax system that is still in effect. An associate of those days remembers him as a man who excelled in reducing technical material to intelligible English and who, perhaps because of this skill, worked well with Congress. Although his job required him to appraise critically the work of other people, he is remembered as having been extremely popular with his colleagues.

After the war Heller joined the faculty of the University of Minnesota, but he maintained his interest in the practical side of public finance and also broadened into more general economic fields. For a year he went to Berlin to work with General Lucius Clay, the military governor, as chief of finance in the Allied government and Clay's top fiscal consultant. In that capacity he worked on such matters as currency reform, tax reform, banking reform, and the Berlin airlift.

There followed a dizzying string of other assignments: Back to Minnesota to resume teaching, then to Washington to help shepherd the Treasury's Korean War tax program through Congress, another mission to Germany to work on fiscal problems facing the West German government, intensive advisory work for the United Nations on policies by which underdeveloped nations can speed up their development, six years as chief tax adviser to Governor Orville L. Freeman of Minnesota, now Secretary of Agriculture, and, most recently, a trip to Jordan to help King Hussein devise a graduated income-tax system.

Midway in this round the strain took its toll. Soon after he had plunged into the Minnesota tax advisory job he developed a strep throat. He ignored it and, in the fall of 1955, came down with rheumatic fever, which kept him bedfast for six months. He says now that it was a stubborn case but not a serious one, so he was able to work from his bed, a telephone at one side and a dictating machine at the other. Because the Governor and others knew he could always be reached, the result of his illness was that he was more closely in touch with the legislative situation in the state than were the more active politicians.

The rheumatic fever left no heart damage or other aftereffects; in fact, two years after his recovery his life-insurance company rescinded the penalty premiums growing out of the attack. The only reminder now is the 250,000-unit penicillin pill he takes every morning.

Heller's capacity for great mountains of work is explained in part by his working habits. He likes to concentrate intensively on a project—working until 2 or 3 A.M. every day, including weekends, until a job is done, and then taking a long weekend during which he puts professional problems out of his mind and relaxes completely.

It was while he was doing his graduate work at the University of Wisconsin that Heller met his wife Emily, a professor's daughter who was taking her Ph. D. in physiology. They got their Doctor's degrees "about seven seconds apart," Heller recalls. For a time technical journals carried articles on endocrinology by "Heller and Heller." One was Walter's wife; the other his brother.

Slim and youthful despite his gray hair, Heller is no athlete. But he putters at golf, likes to chop wood for exercise, and enjoys canoe trips with his children. He is reputed to be a good poker player and a nonstop talker, a rather unusual combination. Heller proudly reports that he has the largest woodpile on the street back home in St. Paul. So addicted was he to maintaining and improving this pile when he was living there that a neighbor compared it to the tattered blanket that Linus, the wistful youngster in the "Peanuts" comic strip, carries to give him a feeling of security.

There are three Heller children—Walter, nineteen, a freshman at Oberlin; Eric, fifteen, and Kaaren, thirteen. Heller recalls that when Kaaren heard that the family would be moving to Washington, she was very unhappy at the thought of leaving her school and friends in Minnesota. He commented on this one day to the President, who pulled out a photograph of himself and inscribed it: "To Kaaren Heller, whose arrival on the New Frontier is most anxiously awaited by her friend, John F. Kennedy." Heller reports that this eased the pain considerably.

Heller's first meeting with John Kennedy was almost sheer happenstance. It occurred in Minnesota after the first Kennedy-Nixon television debate. Heller had passed up a chance to attend a dinner in Kennedy's honor because he was tired and his wife was ailing. But after dinner, on a whim—and because he wanted to advise Kennedy to hit the recession issue a little harder than he had in the debate—he wandered up to Kennedy's room at the Leamington Hotel in Minneapolis. In the hall he ran into Minnesota's Senator Hubert Humphrey, an old acquaintance, and the Senator bustled him into the room where Kennedy was changing his clothes for his next engagement.

Heller expected a few pleasant words and a request that he put his ideas in writing. Instead, he found Kennedy ready and eager to pick his brain then and there, exploring whether the nation could really achieve an economic growth rate of 5 per cent, just what economic indicators were most meaningful, the secret of West Germany's successful recovery, and so on. From that moment Heller was completely sold on Kennedy. And apparently Kennedy on him. The President-elect's talent scouts found Heller's name on practically every list they received of suggested economic advisers, and Kennedy was happy to go along. In mid-December Kennedy asked Heller to come to Washington for a talk and offered him the chairmanship of the C.E.A. A week later, just before Christmas, Heller flew to Palm Beach, where Kennedy was vacationing, and accepted.

The Council of Economic Advisers was set up by Congress in 1946 under the so-called Full Employment Act. Its job was to advise the President on ways the federal government could help bring about "maximum employment, production, and purchasing power." Under President Truman the C.E.A. had considerable influence on government economic policies although its work was frequently hampered by divisions among its three members. Under President Eisenhower, the Council's influence was diluted by the fact that the President maintained a personal economic adviser on the White House staff. In the latter days of that administration, particularly, the C.E.A. did little more than prepare the economic report that it was required by law to submit twice a year and pull together monthly economic statistics obtained from other government agencies.

Both Kennedy and Heller have plans for expanding the role of the Council. Announcing Heller's appointment, Kennedy said:

"I intend the economic reports to deal not only with the state of the economy but with our goals for economic progress." He made it clear that he wanted Heller to have an important voice in pointing out the economic impact of legislative proposals, to do long-range thinking on economic problems facing the country, and to enlist the cooperation and help of economists in foundations, universities, and private business.

Heller is more than ready to accept these tasks. And he has already embarked on a recruiting program to bolster his staff. He has always been a gregarious type, and he has built up a large circle of friends in the economics field. Now he's calling on these friends, enlisting as staff aides and consultants men no one ever believed would come to Washington.

A tribute to the Kennedy-Heller persuasiveness and to Heller's standing in his field is the caliber of the other two members of the Council. Each is an outstanding economist in his own right, easily qualified to be chairman of the Council. One is James Tobin, a forty-two-year-old professor of economics from Yale, who has been assigned chief responsibility for matters involving money and banking, international finance, and consumer buying. The other is Kermit Gordon, a forty-five-year-old economics professor from Williams College, who has been given responsibility over manpower, housing, foreign aid and foreign trade, natural resources, and wage-price relations. Heller himself takes prime responsibility for tax and budget matters, education, and welfare programs.

Recognizing the talents of his two colleagues, Heller has set out to make the Council more of a three-man affair than it has been. Often in the past the other members were completely overshadowed by the chairman. In contrast, Heller takes them with him when he goes to the White House to confer with the President, and he has indicated he would like all three members to testify before Congress whenever practical. Significantly, he has agreed that they should testify in open session as much as possible; in the Eisenhower years the Council insisted on testifying behind closed doors.

Besides giving President Kennedy day-to-day economic advice, Heller is launching the Council on many long-term projects: What should be the relative roles of public and private spending in the economy? Can we devise more scientific criteria for deciding how the highest rate of return on investment can be achieved? What kind of stimulus can government give private business? What are the most reliable indicators of business conditions? How can the Government accelerate technological change with the least economic dislocation?

Heller has long been an indefatigable speaker and writer on economic subjects, so his views are thoroughly on the record. They make it clear that he doesn't fit the liberal stereotype. For example, he is concerned about feather-bedding and overgenerous wage increases that push up prices. And he favors removal of the legal ceiling on interest rates on long-term government bonds, a view that puts him squarely in opposition to many liberals.

Generally speaking, he is a strong believer in the desirability of federal intervention in economic affairs. "I have the old Wisconsin belief," he told *Business Week* magazine soon after he took over his job, "in the importance of the public sector as a means for achieving welfare for the people." He would encourage full employment and a higher rate of economic growth, which is central to all of Kennedy's domestic and foreign programs, by a combination of low interest rates and government spending on needed national security and such vital domestic programs as education, housing, water-pollution control, resources development, and the like. He feels that these programs, neglected by the Eisenhower administration, are needed for their own specific ends as well as for the broader economic benefits.

To combat inflation Heller would place primary reliance on big federal budget surpluses, which he feels are better than high interest rates as a deflationary device. "We should switch emphasis from tight money to tight budget," he declares repeatedly. He is fascinated by, and frequently refers to, the argument that present tax rates are capable of producing a surplus of ten billion dollars or more if full employment can be achieved. He sees this surplus as a multipurpose weapon—possibly retained by the Government to soak up purchasing power and hold down prices, possibly spent on needed public programs, possibly used to trim the public debt. To combat a recession, however, and his early months on the job were concerned with that, Heller favors prompt and substantial deficit spending.

Over the years he has been a leading proponent, if not *the* leading proponent, of standby plans to raise or lower taxes to meet changing economic conditions. He would prefer to see this power to raise taxes to combat inflation or cut taxes to halt recessions in the hands of the President on a standby basis. But as an experienced tax man on Capitol Hill he recognizes the difficulties of getting Congress to turn its taxing powers over to the President. Accordingly he has come up with the idea of having Congress enact a number of different income-tax changes which it could then trigger by passage of a simple resolution when the emergency arose.

Heller's powers of persuasion bore impressive fruit early in 1961 when the Federal Reserve system abandoned a long-standing policy against buying government obligations of long maturities. This was needed help in the Administration's drive to push down long-term interest rates as an anti-recession measure. The Federal Reserve Board's chairman, William McChesney Martin, had been loudly proclaiming his opposition to such a step, and no one expected him to take it. Heller, Tobin, and Treasury officials began working on him. He was brought to the White House for two sessions with the President and his economic and Treasury advisers. And finally he went along. "Everyone working on the problem within the Administration deserves credit," one insider reported, "but if any man was to be singled out, it was Walt. He was at his most persuasive, and that's pretty damned persuasive!"

Heller is an ardent advocate of government spending in a wide variety of fields. But he becomes most eloquent when he is urging higher outlays on investment in what he calls "human capital"— education, science, and technology. He points to recent studies indicating that the return on such investments exceeds by wide margins returns realized on traditional capital investments in plants and machinery. He suggests that this calls for careful examination of many government policies. For example, he says, "the gain to be realized from giving up tax revenues in the form of liberalized depreciation allowances may not only be in considerable part the wrong kind of gains, but may be smaller than we could achieve by investing an equivalent amount in the education, training, health, and welfare of human beings, or in the advancement of knowledge through more liberal support of both basic and applied research."

Another pet subject is general tax reform. That, he maintains, is the "greatest single contribution Congress could make to the multiple objective of full employment, growth, and stability." He is a leading member of the school which holds that special tax privileges and advantages for particular groups have so reduced the yield of the tax system that across-the-board cuts in tax rates cannot be afforded. At the same time, he feels, inequities are destroying public confidence in the whole tax system.

Even though Heller favors a high-yielding tax system to cover spending or general anti-inflationary surpluses, he also believes that individual income-tax rates are generally too high, especially in the highest and lowest brackets. He would reduce these rates, but only if the over-all yield of the system could be preserved by reduction or removal of "loopholes" and special privileges that have been legislated or discovered by the tax lawyers over the years.

At one time or another he has proposed withholding taxes on dividends and interest; repeal of the special tax credit on dividend income; lower depletion allowances for oil, gas, and other minerals; higher tax rates on capital gains; less tax advantages for married couples, and ending the deductibility of many state and local taxes. Such changes, he suggests, would permit reducing individual income-tax rates from the present 20 per cent to 91 per cent range to a 14 per cent to 60 per cent range, and also permit substantial cuts in corporate and excise taxes.

Although the C.E.A. does not have primary responsibility for shaping the Administration's tax recommendations, Heller's reputation in this field undoubtedly will cause his voice to be heard when such recommendations are decided upon. Moreover, he has long seen eye to eye and worked closely with the two men who are directly concerned with tax policy: Assistant Secretary of the

Treasury Stanley Surrey, former Harvard University law professor and one-time Treasury colleague of Heller, and Internal Revenue Commissioner Mortimer Caplin.

When Heller takes a position, he states it with a bite that few members of his profession possess or see fit to use. Sometime back, when he was still a professor, he was holding forth at a National Tax Association session on the evils of the federal debt limit, a device Senator Harry Byrd of Virginia and other conservatives see as the last hope for the nation's fiscal integrity. After arguing that the debt limit had failed lamentably to curb federal spending and had, in fact, contributed to wasteful and perverse budgetary practices, Heller went on:

"Failing in its attempt to curb its own spending tendencies with the aid of one rigid rule or another, the Congress has, ironically, used the debt ceiling to harass and castigate the executive authorities for the deficits which congressional budgetary enactments have forced them to incur. In this sense the statutory limit has been an instrument of fiscal hypocrisy. . . .

"In the name of budgetary integrity, financial prudence, adequately financed national security, and aggressive policies to combat inflation and counter recession, in other words in the name of everything that is fiscally holy and wholesome, our anachronistic federal debt limit should be abolished."

And there was a Kennedian ring to the attack on what he called President Eisenhower's "preoccupation" with the problem of inflation and the goal of price stability in the President's 1959 Economic Report:

"The potential costs of a restrictive budgetary policy to promote price stability are great: Loss of production by slowing the pace of recovery; lower investment in public education and other public services that strengthen our long-run economic and military potential; attempts to push functions back on state and local budgets which are already under such extreme pressures, compounded by the adverse effects of recession . . . and perhaps, tragically, a laggard defense budget.

"To the extent that these results are risked in the name of price stability and balanced budgets, they represent as great a risk, calculated or otherwise, as this country has ever incurred in peacetime economic policy."

Heller is at his best when he is speaking with deep feeling and from deep conviction. His excursions in lighter discourse often have the chalk-and-eraser scent of the classroom. At his first Washington session with the press after taking over the C.E.A. job, a reporter objected to the lack of cost estimates on the Administration's anti-recession program. "The inference will be drawn," the reporter said, "that you don't care very much about how much they'll cost."

"That may be the inference," Heller snapped back happily, "but not the implication."

And like many academic types he has his pet gag lines. A warning he has been heard to issue to colleagues more than once is: "We have to approach this like porcupines making love—carefully."

When Heller first discussed the C.E.A. job with the President-elect, Kennedy assured him he would have direct access to the White House and the President himself. Heller says this promise has been kept. "I have had the feeling," he recently told a friend, "of wonderful acceptance across the street."

PART
II

The
Cabinet

5.

THE QUIET DIPLOMAT

Dean Rusk

By MICHAEL J. O'NEILL

ALTHOUGH HE HAD GIVEN THEM ELEVEN YEARS OF NOTABLE service, both as soldier and diplomat, Dean Rusk was a stranger to the American people when he was chosen as the nation's fifty-fourth Secretary of State, the heir of Thomas Jefferson, of Elihu Root, and Dean Acheson.

He was far less well known, in fact, than the men who were to be his principal subordinates—Adlai Stevenson, Chester Bowles, G. Mennen Williams, and Averell Harriman. Some of these, by their service to party and President, held greater claim than he to the "almost impossible" office; some, indeed, had aspired to the Presidency itself.

Rusk was not even personally acquainted with the young President-elect who had finally decided that he was the one best fitted to help him search for peace amid the temblors of a world in revolution. Their first meeting, in the living room of Kennedy's Georgetown home, came only four days before the appointment was announced.

Nor was there anything in the public record to give clear testimony to the qualifications of this tall, quiet man from Georgia. During five years' service in the State Department while Harry Truman was President, he had been immersed in the emotional crisis over Palestine. He had, in an act of courage, taken over the Bureau

109

of Far Eastern Affairs at a time when the national anguish over our China policy was at its height. And he had helped shape the historic decisions of the Korean War. But in all these things he was the professional diplomat, operating behind the scenes. He moved almost unseen in the shadow of another Secretary of State and another President. His achievements, and failures, were unpublished; the controversy that touched and hurt others largely passed him by.

Even after he had returned to private life, in December 1951, Rusk took surprisingly few public stands on the controversial issues of his time. He spoke often—to women's clubs, foreign-affairs councils, and student groups—because he has a strong sense of civic responsibility and an interest in youth stemming from his earlier days as a college professor. However, as president of the nonpolitical Rockefeller Foundation, he felt inhibited in what he said. Also, by inclination, he was less interested in commenting on policy than in making it, for he is more of a doer than a philosopher. Thus, except for a brilliant critique of summit diplomacy in 1960, none of his views attracted national attention.

But if Rusk's potential for high office had escaped the notice of the general public, and of the President-elect, it had not been missed by the men who knew him well, who had seen him in action during two wars and countless crises. To them—especially to Acheson and former Defense Secretary Robert A. Lovett—Rusk's extraordinary intelligence, his grasp of world affairs, his decisiveness and coolness under fire, his open-mindedness, his sense of history, and his moral conviction lifted him above most of the other men who might be considered for the critical foreign policy portfolio.

As Acheson remarked privately during the time of decision: "You are not picking God when you choose a Secretary of State. You are making a choice between alternatives; you are looking for a man with the greatest number of assets and the fewest liabilities." One monumental liability—public opposition to racial integration—proved fatal to the prospects of Democratic Senator William Fulbright of Arkansas, chairman of the Senate Foreign Relations Committee. This same issue was an asset for Rusk because, even though a soft, resonant drawl still betrays his southern boyhood, he has been a long-time critic of discrimination.

One night in 1941, when he was working late in the military intelligence section of the War Department, Rusk invited Ralph Bunche to join him for a snack in the officers' mess of the old Munitions Building. Bunche, then with the Office of Strategic Services and now a high United Nations official, protested that the mess was "notorious" for its policy of excluding Negroes. But the young Army captain brushed the objections aside, led Bunche into the crowded room, and sat him down at a table with white officers. "In that single act," Bunche recalls, "he broke the color line." Again in 1950, when he was an Assistant Secretary of State, Rusk complained that America's minority problem was doing more to "becloud" America's image in Asia than any enemy propaganda. One of his first moves as secretary was to order vigorous action to combat discriminatory housing practices which dangerously alienate newly-arriving African envoys.

Lovett, one of Kennedy's closest advisers during the preinaugural period, told the President-elect that Rusk had the makings of a "great Secretary of State." He cited his "high order of intelligence," his extensive experience both in diplomacy and military planning, and his unusually good "instincts and judgment." Among other things, Lovett remembered Rusk's superb staff work during the turmoil over the postwar disposition of Palestine. Even Bowles, who had hoped wistfully that he might be tapped himself, mentioned that Rusk would be a most satisfactory alternative. And Acheson added his strong recommendation. "This man," he told Kennedy, "has what I think is the most important quality—character. He is loyal, honorable, honest. He has courage. He is cool, intelligent, quite as capable of wrestling with the most complex problems as well as anybody else. And he is a team player, no prima donna."

As an example of Rusk's courage and team spirit, Acheson recalled a painful period in the winter of 1949–50 when a bewildered and troubled nation fell upon the State Department in its search for the cause of China's fall to communism. During the previous August the Department had issued a 1,054-page White Paper placing the blame chiefly on Chiang Kai-shek. But many congressmen, mostly Republican, charged that the principal fault lay with the anti-Chiang bias of the Truman administration, with Acheson and, most of all, with the old China hands in the State Department. By early 1950 the pressure was so great that Acheson feared his Assistant Secretary for Far Eastern Affairs, W. Walton Butterworth, would be destroyed; he desperately wanted a politically untarnished replacement.

Rusk was then Deputy Under Secretary of State, but he volunteered to step down to the far eastern affairs hot seat. "I like the job I have and I would just as soon keep it," he told Acheson, "but if you want to use me in another way, I don't want you to think about my personal preferences." Acheson gratefully accepted the offer, and Rusk took over officially on March 28, just three months before the outbreak of the Korean War.

As Kennedy weighed the advice of Acheson, Lovett, and others, he gradually narrowed his choices until by the end of November there were only two: Rusk and David K. E. Bruce, the former Ambassador to Paris. And of these he was leaning to Rusk because of his age (he was fifty-one while Bruce was sixty-two) and his extensive experience with Asia (Bruce's career was tied entirely to Europe). Finally, he telephoned Rusk, asking if he could see him in New York on December 5. The future Secretary said he couldn't make it because of a scheduled Rockefeller Foundation board meeting in Virginia's Colonial Williamsburg. He was convinced he was being sought for nothing more exciting than routine consultation.

But when Rusk arrived in Williamsburg, he found the air bristling with speculation. The Foundation board included no less than four rumored candidates: Rusk, Bowles, Douglas Dillon, and John J. McCloy—some of them more expectant than others but all very curious about what might happen. Every time one left the meeting to take a telephone call, the others followed him with suspicious glances and examined his expression closely when he returned. In due course Rusk departed, and when he rejoined his colleagues later, his face bore the telltale marks of preoccupation and puzzlement. After some hesitation, he passed a note to Bowles: "Kennedy wants to see me Thursday. What's it all about?" Bowles confessed he didn't know precisely but, characteristically, Rusk wanted to be prepared anyway. On the night before he was to see Kennedy, he spent hours in Bowles's Washington home quizzing him about the new President's views and operating style.

The next morning, a cold December 8, Rusk and Kennedy held their first meeting in the latter's tall red-brick home in Georgetown. For about half an hour they ranged generally over the challenges facing the Administration in the foreign field. They also touched lightly on some personalities, but never even mentioned the possibility of an appointment for Rusk. The newspapers turned their attention to another Georgetown caller that day, Stevenson, and Rusk telephoned his wife in Scarsdale, New York, to report that they had no decision to make. What he didn't know, however, was that Kennedy had been immensely impressed. Beneath Rusk's easy smile and genial manner he felt a toughness, an intelligence, a broad knowledge that he liked and wanted. And on Friday afternoon, December 9, he made his final decision: He would ask the one-time Rhodes scholar, the teacher, soldier, and diplomat to be his Secretary of State.

That same night at nine Kennedy telephoned Rusk in New York. Rusk knew instinctively the reason for the call, and asked the President-elect to postpone making his expected request until they had had a chance to confer again in more detail. It was then arranged that Rusk would fly to Palm Beach to see Kennedy on Sunday, December 11.

Rusk faced his decision with mixed feelings. More than most men, he understood the awesome responsibilities of the office, the frightening physical and mental burden of trying to simplify incredible complexity, of striving for stability in a world of conflict. Just a year earlier a study panel which he headed concluded somberly that the job had become "almost impossible."

Rusk was aware, too, of the personal sacrifices he would have to make. He liked his job at the Foundation; it had given him more security and, in many ways, more satisfaction than anything else he had done. Leaving it would also mean a financial loss, for he was not a wealthy man, and the $25,000 paid a Secretary of State would hardly cover the bare bones of his necessities.

Beyond these considerations Rusk was troubled by another seemingly trivial matter: He had supported Stevenson, rather than

Kennedy, for the Democratic presidential nomination. He had even gone so far as to wire his sentiments to the national convention in Los Angeles, to put himself on record even if he did not presume to tip the scales in Adlai's favor. He felt Kennedy should be aware of the incident, although he was prepared to add, in his own defense, that when the scales failed to tip he had joined wholeheartedly in the campaign to elect the party's official nominee.

As the head of a nonpolitical foundation, Rusk believed he could not properly take part in national politics. But he also insisted that no citizen should be denied the right to participate in the affairs of his own community. Because of this conviction, because of his allegiance to the Democratic party, and because he believed Washington urgently needed a "New Frontier," Rusk agreed to serve as the Kennedy campaign chairman in Republican-dominated Scarsdale.

This same sense of responsibility and duty compelled Rusk to set aside his misgivings about the President's offer. No man, he felt, could properly refuse so important a summons. On Saturday, the day after Kennedy's call, he took a physical to reassure himself of his good health. And then on Sunday he made his way to Palm Beach to see the man he would come to serve.

For long hours that night the two talked and planned for the future. They called Stevenson, obtained his consent to be Ambassador to the U.N.; they rang Bowles, got him to agree to be Under Secretary of State. And, exploring each other's minds, they discovered an amazing unity of viewpoint and approach. The next morning, December 12, Kennedy strode out onto the sun-flooded patio of his father's winter home and, while a palm tree stirred against the sky, made the announcement.

"Mr. Rusk will bring to this high office," he said, "the long view of the student of world affairs, the concern for peace shared by all those who have known war at firsthand, and a practical working experience in the conduct of our foreign relations." Standing at Kennedy's side, the new Secretary spoke confidently in reply: ". . . We are in a period of rapid and revolutionary change, as peoples in many parts of the world are striking out on new courses for themselves. But . . . we need not be afraid of changes which arise out of hopes and aspirations which we, ourselves, share with other peoples in many parts of the world. . . . Our enormous capacity to act imposes upon us a responsibility to make history, and to take a large part in the shaping of events."

The relationship between the President and his Secretary, two outwardly dissimilar men, began well during their first two meetings. And in the succeeding months, as they met continuously on the treadmill of crisis, their mutual respect grew slowly toward friendship. Kennedy confided that he was "tremendously impressed" by Rusk's detailed knowledge of foreign problems, by his excellent judgment, and toughness. Rusk was likewise impressed by his boss.

It is too early to pass judgment on the success of this relationship for it must still be tested in the crucible of time and adversity. But it can be said that it is essential to the successful prosecution of America's foreign policy. History has shown that defects in this vital human equation can lead to disaster. It was the source of great mischief when William Jennings Bryan served under Wilson, and when James G. Blaine served under Harrison. It was the reason for Cordell Hull's weakness under Roosevelt and Acheson's strength under Truman; for John Foster Dulles' extraordinary power under Eisenhower and Christian A. Herter's later relative ineffectiveness.

By chance, Rusk and other students of world affairs surveyed this very problem in a prophetic conference on "The Secretary of State" at Arden House in New York just a month before the presidential elections. In a memorandum to the still-unnamed President, they declared that the role of the secretary had become "central" to any successful administration. He not only has to carry the main burden of formulating foreign policy, but also must take the lead in coordinating all "military, economic, and cultural programs" so that they contribute to a coherent total national effort in the world. Clearly, the conferees agreed, this required a good relationship between secretary and President.

"It would be inadvisable to interpose any official between the President and the secretary in the field of international affairs,"

Rusk and his colleagues generally concluded. "The Secretary of State should have primacy in advising on international policy."

Quite early in the new Administration there were questions about whether the new secretary could maintain this primacy in the presence of such strong personalities as Stevenson, Bowles, and Williams. But during his nomination hearing before the Senate Foreign Relations Committee Rusk professed he could foresee little difficulty.

"I think it important when the President makes a decision," he testified, "that he know what the alternatives are and what major approaches there are to such questions, that he should not be confronted with simply a monolithic recommendation without knowing what diverse opinions there are from other departments of government and from whatever quarter." But he said confidently, "I expect to be the principal adviser to the President on foreign policy," and suggested that his celebrated subordinates would indeed be subordinates.

Less publicly there was also some concern that Rusk's position might be diluted by Harvard's McGeorge Bundy and Walt W. Rostow from the Massachusetts Institute of Technology. These two were installed next door to the White House as Kennedy's on-the-spot foreign-policy aides. They are strong-willed men and, as one presidential adviser put it privately, they would be quick to fill any vacuum that developed at the State Department. But this is the point: Rusk is no vacuum.

If he lacks the soaring eloquence and wit of Stevenson, he yields nothing to him in the force and clarity with which he can analyze and express complex problems. If he lacks some of the bubbling imagination of Bowles, he is still highly receptive to new ideas and can more than compete in the soundness and balance of his judgments. For sheer intelligence, Rusk yields nothing to any of the four. And equally important, he has had more experience, as well as broader experience, in foreign operations than all of them combined.

As Paul H. Nitze has observed, a modern Secretary of State must exercise vast responsibilities in the military, economic, and even scientific fields, not just in the purely diplomatic. Nearly every activity of a nation, even in the realm of art, has an important bearing on foreign relations. Rusk appreciates this more, perhaps, than most others because he not only knows intimately the techniques and machinery of diplomacy, but also has a good background in military affairs and at least a working knowledge of the main currents of modern science and economics.

Ever since he was an R.O.T.C. colonel at Boys' High in Atlanta, the Secretary has been intensely interested in military matters. During the war he served successively as an infantry officer, an intelligence analyst in Washington, a staff aide to General Joseph Stilwell in the China-Burma-India Theater, and finally as a political military adviser in the War Department. At one point, in 1946, he was on the verge of making the Army his career. And even though this didn't happen, he continued his education as he grappled with some of the perplexing, even unique, military problems of the Korean War.

The nearly nine years Rusk served as head of the Rockefeller Foundation were also a broadening experience, even though they drew him away from the front lines of foreign policy making. In presiding over the disbursement of $244 million for projects in the United States, Latin America, Africa, and Asia, he learned much about the role in foreign policy of science, medicine, agriculture, and economics. He also learned the value of "little things," something that has become a recurrent theme in his discussions at the State Department. He had seen how much good relatively small sums could do when they were spent training new envoys from underdeveloped countries, helping solve Indian farm problems, or even sponsoring an exile Hungarian orchestra in Austria. Now, even in United States-Soviet relations he feels "we have many smaller possibilities of working out a constructive relationship."

But it is more than broad experience, more than impressive intelligence and leadership, that tend to support Rusk's primacy over his better-known aides. It is also a quiet, resolute style—an unassuming manner, a clarity and decisiveness—that is more in tune with the President's own personality than Stevenson or the others. One suggestion of this harmony of style was Rusk's statement earlier this year that he and the President favored quiet diplomacy, emphasizing normal channels and barring "the immediate and full disclosure of every exchange."

But what of the possibility that Kennedy himself might become his own Secretary of State? One remembers what has been called the "Pooh-Bahism" of Franklin Roosevelt, who once complained, "I must be my own Secretary of State, War, and Navy." But Rusk himself is unconcerned. "Kennedy is not trying to be Secretary of State," he says. "He is just being President." And to Rusk's way of thinking, being President requires the most vigorous kind of leadership.

In a lecture before the Council on Foreign Relations in New York, published in the April 1960 issue of the quarterly *Foreign Affairs,* Rusk spoke of this need with unusual force and eloquence. Although much that he said was directed at former President Eisenhower, he officially—and ironically as it turned out—addressed himself "to the next administration."

"The crucial, indispensable contribution which the President can make to the conduct of our foreign affairs," he said, "is to enter fully into his office, to use its powers and accept its responsibilities, to lead a people who are capable of responding to the obligations of citizenship. . . . A presidential system cannot easily adjust to an interregnum; a nation moving with great mass and velocity needs the engineer at the throttle."

The statement was part of a longer argument attacking the idea of summit diplomacy, which Rusk called a method "to be approached with the wariness with which a prudent physician prescribes a habit-forming drug—a technique to be employed rarely and under the most exceptional circumstances, with rigorous safeguards against its becoming a debilitating or dangerous habit." Together, the definition of presidential leadership and the critique of the summit provided sound if unsolicited advice for the Secretary's future superior.

All of this isn't to say, however, that Rusk is invulnerable; he has his weaknesses. One of these is the fact that he lacks the political stature that commands attention and eases the task of leadership. It is an asset which gave Stevenson, even in defeat, a world-wide prestige that Rusk will find hard to equal. It is also an attribute that can facilitate a Secretary's always-difficult relations with Congress.

Initially, at least, the new Secretary has also been far less skillful in influencing public opinion to serve his policy than some of his predecessors, notably the late John Foster Dulles. He is articulate; he can fashion a pungent phrase, as when he pictured the American president as a leader "who, somewhat as a sheep dog, must round up a free people and persuade them to move in a given direction." He understands the theoretical role of public opinion, and yet he seems to shy away from putting it to its full use. Dulles employed his press conferences brilliantly to shift opinions, to float trial balloons, and even to make policy on the spot. Rusk instinctively holds policy within him until it has been finally shaped so that it must enter the world untested and without public preparation.

This goes to the heart of whether he will be able to achieve the prestige and national stature that will lift him above the level of the bureaucrat and technician which he was before. For next to the President, the Secretary of State is the chief spokesman of the American government to the world at large, and when he is silent, or indistinct, policy becomes blurred and the sense of direction is lost.

Another Rusk weakness, in the opinion of men who know him well, is that he is basically too decent. High office requires, at times, the capacity for ruthlessness—the ability to cut down those who would impede or impose—and Rusk does not have it. Although no one would accuse him of indecision, he can also be unduly deliberative because of his habit of careful analysis and logical policy development. When a chasm is opening, a leader often has to leap to conclusions, acting on nothing more secure than intuition or hunch.

Whatever Rusk's limitations are, however, he has been accepted eagerly by the thousands of American diplomats serving under him around the globe. For he is one of them, a professional whose competence inspires that rare degree of respect which engenders enthusiasm and even excitement.

Amid the paneled splendor of his State Department office and conference room, his voice seems as soft as the thick-piled carpeting. His round face breaks into a friendly smile almost as readily as a politician's will. His impish humor constantly bubbles to the surface, even in the most serious discussions. He seldom dresses down an errant subordinate, although they become uncomfortably aware of their misdeeds. He clothes himself in a reserve that partially shields him from even his closest advisers. And, unlike some of the administration's numerous Ivy League imports, he is modest to a fault. He shows little interest in being credited with a policy, only in making sure that it contributes to the President's program. As he puts it, he wants to reduce "the infant mortality rate of ideas," not to increase it.

He also has a way of packaging complex concepts in beguilingly simple, down-to-earth epigrams. "Perhaps," he says, "the United States has reached the point where we must not act like an old cow who is supposed simply to accept kicks in the flanks rather placidly, but rather we must begin to show our horns a bit. . . ." Or, on another occasion, "We can no longer afford merely to knock the tail feathers out of our problems as they pass by; delay or inaction should be intentional, not caused by neglect or entrenched bureaucratic habit."

But the genial surface of this unusual man is deceptive. It masks extraordinary intensity and drive, an understanding of power and how to use it, and a cool self-confidence born of ability and know-how. He works furiously and efficiently because he says a diplomat "has the hounds of time snapping at his heels." And he demands the same of his aides. At staff meetings, they know they are in trouble if they don't stick to the issues and carefully prepare their briefings. Rusk himself is so good at extemporaneous briefing that he never had to refer to any documents during the Macmillan and Adenauer talks, and he feels miserable when he has to make a set, formal address.

Because he encourages officials to accept more responsibility, he has been upgrading the role of the political officers in the State Department and of the ambassadors overseas. He says, "Power gravitates to those who are willing to make decisions and live with the results," and he set an example himself during the Laos crisis. He immediately decided that the West had to prevent a Communist

take-over even if it meant direct military intervention, and in Bang-
kok he pressured Britain and France into backing possible action
under the Southeast Asia treaty.

In terms of policy, Rusk, with Kennedy, is pressing for greater
American identification with national revolutionary movements
even though it means irritating old colonial allies. Thus, in a major
break with a previous Eisenhower decision, the new Administration
sided with the Afro-Asians in voting for a United Nations debate
on Portuguese Angola.

It is also championing the idea of tying foreign aid to social
reforms to assure genuine progress among the common people of
undeveloped countries and, in this way, to dampen the discontent
which fires communist movements. This was a key element in the
proposed ten-year aid program for Latin America.

Rusk is likewise urging greater tolerance toward so-called cold-
war neutrals in the conviction that their successful development as
free nations is more important than difficult or even dangerous
commitments to the West. This policy, to cite one example, was an
important factor in swinging Indian Prime Minister Nehru and
other powerful neutral forces behind the administration's effort to
win a cease-fire in Laos.

Like Kennedy, the Secretary also strongly advocates an increase
in the West's economic and military strength to give it a better
bargaining lever in negotiations with the Russians. He endorses the
idea of a sharp step-up in conventional arms, to reduce the need
for immediate atomic retaliation; he is pressing for greater economic and political integration in free Europe; he is struggling to
shore up the ramshackle NATO alliance which he calls the "key-
stone" of the free world's defenses. In all these things he is drawing
on a philosophy shaped by his years of diplomatic and military
service, his Rockefeller Foundation experience, and even his southern boyhood long ago.

David Dean Rusk, now a balding but still well-built man of
six feet one, weighed in at an impressive eleven pounds when
he entered the world on February 9, 1909, in Cherokee County,
north of Atlanta. The scene was a small farmhouse his father had

built on a plantation homesteaded by his great-grandfather when
southern aristocracy and slavery still flourished side by side. And
Dean—the Rusks called their children by their second name—was
the fourth family addition, following Mary Margaret, Hugh Parks,
and William Roger. Another sister, Helen Brooke, was born later.

Rusk's father, Robert Hugh Rusk, was a stern, disciplined man
of Scotch-Irish ancestry. He was a Presbyterian minister who had
studied at colleges and seminaries in three states. But he had been
forced by a throat ailment to give up full-time preaching and had
returned to Cherokee County to help his mother manage the family
farm, even though the work did not appeal to him. His preaching
then was limited to home Sunday-school services where Dean first
began learning his Bible verses and hymns.

Mrs. Rusk was the former Elizabeth Frances Clotfelter, of German and Dutch as well as Scotch-Irish descent. She was highly
intelligent and well educated, a teacher by training. She played a
decisive role in inspiring in Dean a great love for reading, learning,
and performing well in whatever he did. He was so inspired, in fact,
that when he was only five he had read all the schoolbooks of his
elder brother Robert. And when he was ready to enter school later
in Atlanta Mrs. Rusk suggested that he might as well start in
second grade instead of first. The teacher demurred, but finally
consented to test the young genius. He passed with flying colors,
even though he wrote "gal" for "girl," and was allowed to begin
his schooling one step ahead.

In 1913 the family moved to Atlanta where the father worked
as a postman (everyone had to be quiet after seven thirty every
night so that he could sleep). They settled down in a spacious six-
room house on Whitehall Street in the West End section. On one
side was a good residential subdivision and on the other a railroad
track that adjoined an industrial area. The children were installed
in the old Lee Street School where it was Dean's doubtful privilege
to participate in an open-air classroom experiment. This involved
hopping around in heavy canvas bags, jackets, and mittens while
simultaneously trying to absorb the day's lesson through the winter
cold.

Dean did well in school—his first teacher recalled he was both "brilliant" and "modest." He also sharpened his mind at home by reading and memorizing everything from Bible passages to poetry. In addition, he did odd jobs to help the family income. One summer he worked for an electrical supply firm. A year later he showed up at the same establishment, hung up his cap, and announced: "Here I am." The manager observed he had not been instructed to return the second summer. "But you didn't tell me not to, either," the boy replied brightly—and won a return engagement at $18.00 a week.

At Boys' High Rusk turned in his usual superior performance, winning honors, making the debating team, rising to colonel in the R.O.T.C., running on the track team, editing the school yearbook, helping to edit the newspaper, and presiding over the "School Page" in the Atlanta *Journal*. The *Journal* awarded him its annual cup for the Best All-Round student at Boys' High. A faded report card shows that in one semester Rusk averaged 90 in English, 92 in Latin, 90 in Greek, 95 in history, 90 in French, and 82 in algebra. One of his teachers said that he was "one of the few students I came across in forty-five years of teaching who seemed to be born mature and adequate to any situation."

After graduating from Boys' High in 1925, at the age of sixteen, Dean worked for two years in a small law office. With his savings and a quantum of blind faith he went on to Davidson (North Carolina) College where his father had studied. Again he was a standout. In between waiting on tables and clerking in a local bank he performed well enough (major: political science) to make Phi Beta Kappa. En route to his Bachelor of Arts degree (1931), he managed time to captain the school R.O.T.C., to head the student Y.M.C.A., and to play some tennis, baseball, basketball, and track. To top it off, he won a Rhodes scholarship to study ways of making peace.

The scholarship carried Rusk to St. John's College, Oxford, where he concentrated on politics, economics, and philosophy, winning another B.A., a Master of Arts, and the 1933 Cecil Peace Prize for an essay on "Relations Between the British Commonwealth and the League of Nations." More important than the formal studies, however, was the fact that Rusk was absorbing the exhilarating atmosphere of Europe, developing a feeling for its mood and problems. It was a time when Ramsay MacDonald was grappling with the depression in Britain and Hitler was on the rise in Germany. It was also a time, as he recalls, when some impressionable young undergraduates had an "unforgettable evening" with the "great spirit" of Gandhi.

During his spare time Rusk visited France (he still has a working knowledge of French) and studied in Germany, attending the University of Berlin in 1934. He developed a good facility in German but never completely shed his American accent. One time, after he had given a talk in German, a student inquired about the source of the accent. Rusk replied that it was Georgian. "Oh," replied the student, "I *knew* it was Russian." Although his vocabulary is now too weak for carrying on any negotiations in German, Rusk can still make out quite well. In one of his first speeches as Secretary he essayed a rather lengthy introduction in German for the benefit of an appreciative German audience.

While he was in Germany the future Secretary also learned a lesson he still relates frequently. "I was living in Neue Babelsberg and I had a canoe," he says. "One day I pulled the canoe up on the bank of the lake and went into a restaurant for lunch. When I came back, the canoe was gone. The police later said they had found the canoe and had caught the thief but 'you yourself will be fined five marks for tempting thieves.' The lesson has been worth many times more than the five marks to me because I believe that we in our democracies are confronted with the fundamental problem of how we avoid tempting thieves."

In 1934 Rusk returned to the United States to take a $2,000-a-year job teaching international relations and political theory at Mills Women's College in Oakland, California. Like most teachers, he took a special interest in his best students and particularly, as it happened, in a pretty coed from Seattle named Virginia Foisie. Her father was a well-known labor trouble shooter, but she was interested primarily in international affairs and assistant professors thereof. This, despite the fact that Rusk gave her the "worst grades" she received.

"He had such a personal way of teaching," she recalls. "He could talk about international problems in terms of his own experience in England and Germany. And he used to write very interesting and perceptive comments on our papers, often without bothering to add any grades." Other less prejudiced former students were similarly impressed, to judge by some of the letters they wrote Rusk after his appointment. One remembers his "smiling eyes" that "see a fresh challenge in each moment of living, that see the past, the present, and the future in all about them."

The man from Oxford and the coed from Seattle found themselves together often that first year, at seminars and world-affairs councils as well as in the classroom. Although it called for some discretion, in view of their disparate positions, the two began dating and soon became secretly engaged. The engagement was announced after Virginia graduated in 1936 and a year later, on June 19, 1937, they were married.

In December 1940 he was called to active duty as an Army captain when the nation hesitantly and reluctantly began preparing for possible war. He was put in charge of a crack infantry company and, to keep ahead of his men, he used to take machine guns apart and put them back together again in the family living room. Eleven months later, just before Pearl Harbor, his Oxford background brought a summons to Washington to run the almost non-existent intelligence section on British-held Southeast Asia. And he was on duty there December 7 when the first flashes came in on the Japanese attacks at Pearl Harbor.

Rusk had some narrow escapes during the war. In the winter of 1943, Lieutenant Colonel Rusk was named a deputy chief of staff to General Stilwell in the China-Burma-India Theater. As he and Stillwell prepared to fly to the theater, Rusk recalls, they changed their flight plans for the European leg at the last minute. If they had not, the German fighters that shot down the plane on which British actor Leslie Howard was flying would have hit them.

Rusk spent most of his time in New Delhi, pursuing the delicate mission of encouraging the Indian contribution to the Burma fighting. But he also flew the famous Himalayan "hump" fourteen times. On one occasion a Jap plane swooped in on an airport near the front just as his plane and another were taking off. The Zero elected to concentrate on the other plane, shooting it down, while Rusk and his plane were allowed to escape.

In the summer of 1945 Rusk and another officer flipped a coin to see who would get a single open space on a ship returning to the States. Rusk lost, and the ship was sunk with a heavy loss of life. He later returned safely, reporting to the War Department on August 1, just in time to experience the furor over the dropping of the first atom bomb on Japan.

Rusk's new assignment was to the political-military survey section of the general staff where he worked closely with the State Department on military details of the U.N. Charter. His performance immediately attracted the attention of the State Department official in charge, Joseph E. Johnson, now president of the Carnegie Endowment for International Peace. In February 1946 he lured Rusk to his division, to be assistant chief of International Security Affairs. But this wasn't enough of a challenge for Rusk; he was unhappy and decided to sign up as a regular officer in the Army.

At this critical point he was summoned back to the War Department to be a civilian assistant to Secretary Robert P. Patterson. But he had hardly hung up his hat, when in March 1947 he was called by Secretary of State George C. Marshall to take over Alger Hiss' old post as director of Special Political Affairs. One of his strong boosters at the time was his former chief, Johnson. "You don't hire a man," Johnson recalls, "and then recommend him to be your boss unless you think he's pretty good."

Rusk's new job put him in charge of mapping United States policy in the U.N. It plunged him into one of the most mentally agonizing periods of his life, the great postwar conflict over the disposition of Palestine after the British withdrawal. The fear of religious war in the Middle East filled the atmosphere. Emotions were high, nerves raw. Rusk, the diplomat, had to walk a taut wire between Arab and Jew, speaking to both, negotiating with both, but straining not to appear to take sides. He was also striving, with the whole State Department, to develop a pattern for peace at a time when domestic politics clouded, complicated, and frustrated.

"In the background of our thinking at the time," the Secretary recalls, "was an overestimate of Arab military strength and an underestimate of Israeli power. Our worry was that there would be war and, moreover, that the Jews, after all they had suffered in Europe, might be pushed into the sea." Rusk, working under the immediate command of then Under Secretary of State Lovett, bent his effort to developing ways of promoting a military and political stalemate to provide time for efforts toward a long-range solution. (He also worked particularly hard, though in vain, to have Jerusalem internationalized as a religious shrine.)

The U.N. General Assembly began its historic special session on Palestine on April 28, 1947. The chief issue: whether to support partition of the zone into Arab and Jewish states. Rusk and others in the State Department would have preferred to deal with the problem in terms of foreign policy alone—to be fair to the Jews but still avoid action "which would leave deep gashes in America's relations with the Arab and Muslim worlds." But as Rusk is the first to recognize, foreign policy cannot be compartmentalized. "There are times when it cannot be separated from domestic policy." And this was one of them; rather than risk offending Jewish voters, President Truman personally ordered United States support for partition.

During the height of the maneuvering over the partition resolution, Congressman Emanuel Celler, a New York Democrat, charged that Lovett and his aides were failing to put the heat on other delegations for support. This was true. As Rusk confided later, the American delegation "never exerted pressure on countries of the U.N. in behalf of one side or another," although "certain unauthorized officials and private persons violated propriety and went beyond the law" to do it.

Partition passed the Assembly but proved impossible to enforce. In the dangerous no-man's land that followed Rusk and the Department fought to patch together a resolution that would, at least, prevent fighting. This led to United States support for a U.N. trusteeship which implied at least temporary abandonment of partition. Rusk and the United States delegation were still pushing this plan in the Assembly when American policy took another dramatic turn.

At about 5:45 P.M. on May 14, 1948, Rusk recalls, he got a telephone call from the White House informing him that President

Truman would recognize Israel as a new state just fifteen minutes later. The British mandate was due to expire at that hour. Rusk protested that this conflicted with the policy the American delegation was pursuing at that very moment in the Assembly, that it would appear that the United States had been double-dealing. But a presidential election loomed, and there was no turning back; Rusk called U.N. Ambassador Warren Austin in New York to relay the word.

"Austin," the Secretary recalls, "made a personal decision which I think was right. He felt it would be better for the prestige of the United States to make it perfectly clear that this was a personal action of the President's, that the delegation had not been negotiating in bad faith. He decided against telling his fellow delegates in the Assembly hall."

Consequently, when the news bulletin came over the wires shortly after 6 P.M. the acting United States representative, Francis B. Sayre, could honestly confess he had no official confirmation. Later, after checking with Washington, Philip C. Jessup limply provided the confirmation, reading the White House announcement from a wire-service dispatch.

During this period Rusk put in killing hours. He served on the State Department team to the General Assembly meeting in Paris in 1948, and as an alternate delegate to the 1949 session. In February 1949 his title was changed to Assistant Secretary of State for U.N. Affairs, but only a month later he was promoted to Deputy Under Secretary of State. Although Rusk is able to shed his problems at the office—to make decisions and not worry about them afterward—he spent most of his time at the office. And this proved hard on his family. Mrs. Rusk recalls that once she had to delay a birthday party for her eldest son, David, for two months so that the father could fit it into his schedule.

From the troubled Levant Rusk moved to the equally troubled Orient, taking over as Assistant Secretary of State for Far Eastern Affairs on March 28, 1950. It was a time when the Bureau was still reeling from the storm that had broken over the loss of China. But still another crisis descended when, at 9:26 P.M. E.D.T., June 24,

Ambassador John Muccio messaged from Seoul that an "all-out offensive" had been sprung against South Korea.

Rusk and Army Secretary Frank Pace were dining at the Georgetown home of columnist Joseph Alsop. When they got the call from the State Department, they departed hurriedly, leaving their wives, hosts, and other guests in the dark as to what was afoot. Even as he rode to the State Department, Rusk realized it was imperative to get the issue before the U.N. Security Council at once, while the Russians were still boycotting it and could not wield their veto. Assistant Secretary of State John Hickerson, then in charge of U.N. affairs, agreed and Acheson, still at his suburban Maryland farm, obtained the approval of President Truman who was then in Kansas. That very night the alert went out to the Security Council, a speed record that has seldom been matched in diplomacy.

"Had the series of decisions been postponed on a scale of say twenty-four hours," Rusk recalls, "we should have faced a wholly different situation on the Korean peninsula."

During the first night and the following days Rusk played a major role in drafting the historic recommendations for mobilizing the nation to meet the emergency: to evacuate Americans from Korea, to rush ammunition and supplies to the Republic of Korea's forces, to throw the Seventh Fleet between Formosa and the mainland to guard against a second front, and to provide air cover for the supply and evacuation operations. He also took part in the secret meetings at Blair House where Truman approved the proposals.

"There was very little neutralism that week," Rusk recalls. "The decision to intervene had been shaping up in people's minds for twenty years. Everyone at Blair House remembered Manchuria, the Rhineland, Ethiopia, and Czechoslovakia. If there was aggression, it had to be resisted. Even so-called neutral countries made it clear they were pleased that the United States had taken the lead. One ambassador told me, 'I feel so much better in the pit of my stomach than I did yesterday.' "

During the first moments of the war the Chiang Kai-shek government formally offered 33,000 troops to help the embattled South Koreans. President Truman wanted to accept, but he was dissuaded by Acheson and Rusk. Although Rusk came under fire for the decision, at least one argument he made at the time was persuasive: It was quite possible that the attack on Korea was a decoy for a major Chinese communist assault on Formosa. It would be folly, under the circumstances, to weaken the Nationalist defenses.

On an even more critical issue, full American military intervention under the U.N. flag, Rusk was a powerful and resourceful advocate. The Defense Department recoiled at the thought of getting bogged down on the rugged little peninsula and hung back at recommending the use of American troops. But Rusk, with the State Department, insisted that the aggression had to be resisted and that this urgently required United States forces. The view prevailed.

Rusk contributed to another fateful Korean War decision, the order to MacArthur to cross the 38th parallel during his great counterattack of 1951. The Indian Ambassador to Peiping had already relayed a warning from the Chinese Communists that they would not stand idly by if the parallel were crossed. But Rusk was among those who did not take the warning seriously, who mistakenly believed the Chinese would not intervene in force. Although the issues were not very clear at the time, Rusk says candidly, "I was wrong." The attack north of the 38th did indeed bring the Chinese into the war.

At another critical juncture Rusk again took a strong stand for which he was later criticized: He vigorously opposed MacArthur's demand for authority to bomb targets across the Yalu River. Weighed against the possibility that the action would trigger a general war, it was totally unjustified, Rusk felt. "What we are trying to do," he explained in a TV address on April 15, 1951, "is to maintain peace and security without a general war. We are saying to the aggressors, 'You will not be allowed to get away with your crime; you must stop it.' At the same time, we are trying to prevent a general conflagration which would consume the very things we are now trying to defend."

During the MacArthur hearings a few weeks later Senator Leverett Saltonstall, Massachusetts Republican, read the excerpt to the General and asked him for his assessment. "That policy, as you have read it," he replied, "seems to me to introduce a new concept into military operations—the concept of appeasement, the concept that when you use force you can limit that force." His own view, he added, was that "when you go into war, you have exhausted all the other potentialities of bringing the disagreements to an end." But it was Rusk's position, shared by his superiors, that prevailed. (The future Secretary, as a military hand himself, also shared the opinion of many of his colleagues that MacArthur's relief by Truman was required.)

Acheson, who considered Rusk a "pillar of strength" during the Korean War, says there are many examples of his toughness and conviction. But one that impressed him especially was Rusk's handling of the clash within the administration over the treatment of Chinese and North Korean prisoners of war. Thousands of these, it turned out, did not want to return to communist rule. The Pentagon, understandably preoccupied with getting American prisoners returned, pressed for a simple man-for-man exchange. But Rusk insisted it would be inhuman, a violation of everything Americans stood for, to force soldiers back to communism against their will. In endless debates within the government he stuck to his guns, and the military finally was forced to yield; voluntary repatriation became the pattern.

Meanwhile, under the impact of the Korean War, American policy toward Nationalist China was rapidly changing. Like most other State Department experts, Rusk felt that the failures of Chiang's Kuomintang government contributed to the Nationalist defeat on the mainland; he believed that there was wide grass-roots support for the revolt, even if it was communist controlled at the top. In an address in June 1950 he compared the revolution to "the American revolt against the British." But on May 18, 1951, in a slashing attack on the Peiping regime, he declared America's support for the Chiang Kai-shek government in stronger terms than any other administration leader had used.

"We do not recognize the authorities in Peiping for what they pretend to be," he said, speaking off the cuff to the China Institute in New York. "The Peiping regime may be a colonial Russian government—a Slavic Manchukuo on a larger scale. It is not the government of China. It does not pass the first test. It is not Chinese. It is not entitled to speak for China in the community of nations. It is entitled only to the fruits of its own conduct—the fruits of aggression upon which it is so wilfully, openly, and senselessly embarked.

"We recognize the National Government of the Republic of China, even though the territory under its control is severely restricted. We believe it more authentically represents the views of the great body of the people of China, particularly their historic demand for independence from foreign control. That government will continue to receive important aid and assistance from the United States."

The speech was an immediate sensation; it was hailed as a major shift in American policy, although it had merely synthesized and dramatized a process that had been in quiet progress for some months. The speech had been cleared, but only by Rusk himself who happened to be the department's clearance officer. And Acheson was compelled to issue a statement disclaiming any major policy change. What was unknown to most at the time was that the speech was not only a forceful and succinct statement of the newly-hardened China policy, but also a secretly-planned effort to stir anti-Korean war feelings among the mainland Chinese.

Months later, in December 1951, Rusk followed through on this speech by arguing strongly against Red China's admission to the U.N. as Britain's Clement Attlee was then suggesting in conferences with Truman. In his *Memoirs,* the former President wrote that Rusk insisted there was "no reason why we should have to prove our good will by agreeing to the seating of the Chinese Reds" to promote a settlement of the war. Nine years later, after his appointment, the same theme was heard again: "I see no prospect at the present time that normal relations could be established with the authorities in Peiping because they seem to feel that the abandonment of the government and people on Formosa would be a prerequisite to any such normal relations."

Amid the hubbub of Korea and China Rusk was also serving, as he has put it, as the "principal backstop" for the late John Foster Dulles who was then negotiating the Japanese Peace Treaty. In fact, he personally negotiated an administrative agreement which set the terms under which United States forces and bases would be permitted in the freed nation. Under the impact of their association, the two men developed a great personal respect for each other. Rusk has said that Dulles' performance was one of three major achievements of diplomacy in the postwar period. (The other two: the handling of the Berlin blockade and negotiation of the Austrian Peace Treaty.) For his part, Dulles was so impressed that he recommended his State Department colleague for the presidency of the Rockefeller Foundation of which he was then board chairman. It was this circumstance which finally led Rusk to leave the government in December 1951, after eleven years of eventful service.

If Rusk had any idea that the Foundation would be a quiet eddy, he was quickly disillusioned. At the time he took formal command, in July 1952, the tax-exempt foundations of the nation were coming under heavy attack in Congress. In a matter of weeks he had to master the vast operations of a $518 million organization with a thirty-nine-year history and inquire into the myriad details of the charges which had been leveled against it.

Day and night Rusk tackled his problem, soaking up facts like an electronic brain, and rattling out memos and drafts of testimony on his own small typewriter. His performance, when he finally appeared before a House Committee in December, was almost flawless. When Rockefeller grants for Russian studies came under fire, for example, he adroitly quoted the views of a politically invulnerable authority: Dwight D. Eisenhower, then president of Columbia University. He also added his personal opinion: "If we are to have a reasonable chance to survive, if we are to put ourselves in position to meet their [Soviet] propaganda among the peoples of the world, it is of the utmost importance that we understand not only what they are saying to the rest of the world but what their institutions are like and what they are saying to themselves in Russia."

In 1954, when the investigation was resumed, Rusk declared that the Foundation had never issued a grant to anyone on the Attorney General's list of subversives. But he said it also recognized the "importance of the nonconformist in the advancement of human thought" and called this "the antithesis of communism." He also denied that there was anything "mysterious or sinister" about the organization's interest in international affairs. Indeed at the Foundation Rusk spurred an even deeper involvement in international programs.

"The world during the next quarter century can be decisively affected by what happens in the independent nations of Africa, the Middle East, and Asia," he said. "If they succeed in establishing constitutional systems with friendly and easy exchange with the rest of the world, increasingly productive economies . . . and educational systems which can train their leadership, then peace and stability will have gained tremendous support." He felt so strongly about the need for helping meet this challenge that he persuaded the Board to increase the Foundation's overseas grants sharply, even though it meant dipping into capital reserves. One of his pet projects was financing diplomatic training for the novice foreign services of new nations.

During his service with the Foundation Rusk managed to work in trips to projects in Europe, Latin America, and Asia. But he is not a compulsive traveler, like Dulles, and he concentrated on running the big organization from New York. Although this was a full-time job, he also managed to keep in touch with general foreign-policy problems by regular attendance at meetings of the Council on Foreign Affairs and similar groups. He even did a good deal of speaking around the country to school groups, women's clubs, and study organizations. (He was surprised when many of those who heard him wrote him at the time of his appointment.)

For the few hours he had left over each week Rusk retired to his comfortable big brick home on Fenimore Road in Scarsdale and his wife and three children, David, now twenty, Richard, fifteen, and Margaret, twelve. He liked to read—everything in the way of world affairs and politics, as well as biography and, for real relaxation, good mysteries. He also had a fondness for TV westerns and he became proficient at doing double-crostic cross-word puzzles. He occasionally tried helping Richard with his woodworking hobby but, as Mrs. Rusk puts it, her husband "couldn't even make second-class scout." Although he retained his interest in sports, he only infrequently had a chance to play golf or tennis. And a fishing trip was even rarer.

During his nine years in New York the onetime Rhodes scholar continued shaping and refining his ideas, laying the philosophical bedrock upon which he would build later as Secretary of State. One of the convictions, fundamental to his thinking, is that it is possible, however difficult it may be, to influence the tides of his-tory; they are not wholly determined by forces and environment over which man has no control.

"The United States, in this second half of the twentieth century, is not a raft tossed by the winds and waves of historical forces over which it has little control," he declared in his essay on presidential leadership. "Its dynamic power, physical and ideological, generates historical forces; what it does or does not do makes a great deal of difference to the history of man in this epoch. If realism re-quires us to avoid illusions of omnipotence, it is just as important that we not underestimate the opportunity and the responsibility which flow from our capacity to act and to influence and shape the course of events. . . . The range within which the nation can make deliberate choices is wide; if we do not make them delib-erately, we shall make them by negligence or yield the decisions to others, who will not be mindful of our interests."

Another key to Rusk's basic thinking is the belief that it is the totality of America—its every act and its every failure—that will determine its success in foreign affairs. "Our way of life was born in struggle," he says. "It has survived appalling events and has been strengthened by them; it demands no less of us today than when we ourselves were throwing off our own forms of tyranny.

Those who would bury us are moving with energy, speed, and sophistication. We cannot compete by consulting our comforts nor by nourishing our illusions. The contest in which we are engaged will involve every aspect of our national life; our readiness to look to our arms, the development of our talents, the productivity of our economy, our competitive position in the world." Among other things, he feels this demands action to meet "our desperate needs in education," and "the acceptance of our minorities as full-fledged citizens."

It is also a Rusk conviction that American leadership should not be wholly—or even principally—preoccupied with the day-to-day clashes with the Soviet Union. It must act beyond these to provide drive and leadership for the positive programs which will hurry the development of strong nations and societies which will be naturally resistant to communism.

"I don't know whether any of you grew up in our Southland and recall some of the early days of development there," he told a press conference. "Development requires advance on a broad front; education, health, increased productivity, capital investment. Obviously, these are not things which can be brought in from the outside and given to people. They have to be part of a total national effort under vigorous leadership." Thus he put the principal blame for Cuba's "tragedy" on its own leaders; but he also asserted that the United States and other countries might have exercised more influence. "Our need," he says, "is to find those particular points, sometimes relatively minor points, where our contribution can be critical, whether it's in assisting in the development of new varieties of basic food crops or whether it's training individuals in public administration."

In line with this thinking the Secretary feels that the United States must establish closer contact with the nationalistic movements sweeping the world. And it should not try to polarize them into East and West. "I do not believe that we ourselves should be unduly concerned about what might be called genuine neutralism," he says, "because if a new nation is internally vigorous, viable, strong, progressive, its orientation in foreign policy is not so important as its health and strength. . . . I do not believe we ought to ask commitments of a sort that would make it difficult for them to lead their own peoples in development. . . ." At the same time, he recognized that the free world had to guard against neutrals being subverted so that they become committed to the other side.

Rusk also believes that method, as well as substance, is vital to the success of a foreign policy. As he put it in his foreign-affairs article, "We are not likely to achieve significant improvement in the conduct of our foreign relations simply by thinking up new ideas but rather by serious attention to the manner in which we make policy and translate it into action."

After he became secretary, Rusk sought to temper his harsh criticism of summit diplomacy. He said "it would be wrong to be dogmatic" about summits, and insisted that the Administration could feel free to use any method that seemed fitted to a particular problem, for "method is the handmaiden of policy." But one of the first acts of the Administration was to go to unusual lengths to give special status to our ambassador in Moscow, Llewellyn Thompson, so that there might be less need for direct talks between Kennedy and Premier Khrushchev.

Certainly Rusk's preference is for quiet diplomacy, through normal channels. Only a full-time diplomat, he suggests, can devote enough time and attention to complex foreign problems to be an effective negotiator. In an apt description of his own method Rusk characterized the ideal principal negotiator: "He must understand the full scope of the issues and their innermost detail. He must gnaw at his own position and become familiar with its strengths and weaknesses. . . . He must know intimately the positions of others. . . . He must be aware of the impact of the issues upon nations not present at the table and upon American interests in all parts of the world. . . . He [anticipates] as best he can the most probable attitude of his principal adversary, and the range of alternatives with which his opponent might confront him." He must ever be careful, Rusk added, about little things, social arrangements, casual conversations, and relations with public and press.

Taken together, these bits and pieces of Rusk's mind and life form an intelligent whole—a philosophy, a mood, a viewpoint. But

what can they say of the future? What can the tracings of the past
tell when a man has crossed the frontier into the lonely realm of
momentous decision? Little, really. For perhaps no other office,
except the Presidency itself, carries greater responsibility for the
world's destiny. And only adversity and history and time will decide whether David Dean Rusk will fill it well—or greatly.

6.

RICH BOY MAKES GOOD

Douglas Dillon

By THOMAS B. ROSS

"MAN, I'M BUSTED," MOANED DOUGLAS DILLON OF THE TREASURY. "When I tried my Diners' Club card at the bar, I got the bounce. What I need is gold, gold, gold."

"No," replied German Chancellor Konrad Adenauer with a shake of his head, "I never forgive anyone who does me a favor."

This irreverent impersonation took place during the 1961 version of the Gridiron Club's annual spoof of the folk and folkways of Washington's high officialdom. Both Dillon and President Kennedy were in the audience and they threw back their heads and guffawed as "Adenauer" put his own words to "Take Back Your Mink."

> *Take back your gold,*
> *Don't do-re-mi,*
> *Time you were told,*
> *You've lost your mortgage on me.*
> *Take back your dough,*
> *Your banknotes and such*
> *Who'd ever know*
> *That you'd be making a touch?*
> *You've got a lousy deficit that you hate in*
> *   your balance of trade,*

139

And now you've called the cops because your
    old pal has it made.
Take back your gold,
Your poor, tired pelf,
And sock it right in the kitty,
To spend on yourself.

The humor was broad but pertinent. And no one in that gold-plated audience knew it better than Kennedy and Dillon. Much has been written and much has been whispered about why Kennedy picked a Republican from Wall Street to be the keeper of his treasury. Some said it was a canny political maneuver to create the mandate that failed to materialize on election day; some that it was a triumph of Dillon's ambition over his fiscal principle; some that the Democrats were stealing the Republicans' economic thunder in 1964. But the main reason was that Kennedy wanted as his Secretary of the Treasury a man who could come immediately to grips with America's foreign economic problems. And Dillon happened to have had more experience in international economics and to have known more of the world's financial leaders than anyone else.

These facts were no secret to Kennedy, and Dillon had the inside track all along. Kennedy first met Dillon at Harvard in 1956. Kennedy was there to receive an honorary degree and Dillon was serving as first marshal of his class's twenty-fifth reunion. They were introduced at the Spee Club, of which both are members, and they impressed each other immediately, although neither can now recall what was discussed.

During the next few years they talked at great length on several occasions, Dillon as the State Department's chief economic official and the most knowledgeable, persuasive spokesman for foreign aid in the Eisenhower administration; Kennedy as a bright young member of the Senate Foreign Relations Committee. The two men had a common patrician reserve and an almost British sense of understatement. They also had a community of intellectual interests and tended to view economic problems in international terms; their concern with India was a common thread of their talks. From Congress the relationship broadened to an occasional social meeting. Once Kennedy went to dinner at Dillon's exquisite $150,000 house on Embassy Row.

It was no great surprise to Dillon, then, when Pierre Salinger, Kennedy's press secretary, called him December 8 and said that the President-elect wanted to sneak away to his home for another quiet chat that night. Predictably the forty-five-minute conversation centered almost exclusively on foreign economic policy. There was no job offer at that time, but Dillon knew what was on Kennedy's mind. With great delicacy and indirection the two men gingerly alluded to the domestic political implications involved in naming a big Republican to a Democratic administration. Kennedy obviously wanted to be sure Dillon would go quietly, if a difference arose. Eugene Black, president of the World Bank, would be retiring in 1962, Kennedy recalled, with the clear implication that the opening would provide a mutually happy escape hatch in event of political trouble. It was pure Kennedy. Dillon got the word even though nothing was really promised.

Dillon flew to Paris the next day as United States delegate to the meeting of the Organization for Economic Cooperation and Development, his plan for a coordination of Western effort to stimulate the free world's economy and raise living standards in the world's poorer nations. He returned the following Thursday night and Kennedy phoned him Friday morning. He was wanted right away at the President-elect's house in Georgetown. Dillon promised to go as soon as he could, but said he first had to report to President Eisenhower on the Paris meeting.

Dillon had talked to Eisenhower a few weeks earlier when the press began to speculate about the appointment. The President then raised no objections. Now Dillon wanted to make sure he was still open-minded. As hoped, the White House meeting was frank and cordial. "Doug," Eisenhower said, "if the President-elect asks you to serve, you have no choice but to serve."

Later several newspapers carried stories that Eisenhower and Nixon told Dillon they were annoyed at his joining the Democrats. But Dillon is convinced that the stories were planted by "over-eager" White House assistants, still rankling from the election returns, still caught up in campaign extremism. Dillon's aides blame Eisenhower's special assistant, General Wilton B. Persons, and his press secretary, James Hagerty.

But if reports of Eisenhower's admonition to Dillon had been exaggerated, there is no doubt that the President relieved himself of strong sentiments on the subject to others. During a meeting with congressional leaders shortly before he left the White House, Eisenhower bitterly criticized Republicans who were abandoning his anti-inflation crusade. He made it clear he was talking about Dillon. But perhaps because of his awe of rich men, perhaps because of Dillon's diplomatic finesse, Eisenhower never conveyed the depths of his discontent to Dillon himself.

Nixon's reaction, Dillon says, was one of incredulity, not bitterness. During the Vice President's meeting with Kennedy at Key Biscayne, Florida, just after the election, the President-elect had mentioned Dillon as a Republican who might fit into the New Frontier. But Nixon got the impression that he was thinking about a lesser post such as Ambassador to NATO. He could not believe that Kennedy would give such an important and prestigious job as the Treasury to a man whose family had given hundreds of thousands of dollars to the Republicans over the years.

"I don't think it will ever happen," Nixon told the man he probably would have named Secretary of State. "But if you think you can contribute and live with his policies, it will be hard to refuse."

Dillon had no intention of refusing. He had already been approached during the interregnum by high Republican officials who wanted him to run for governor of New Jersey in 1961. He was interested but, with the idea he would be tapped by Kennedy, he said his answer would have to depend on the job he was holding when it came time to run. The Treasury would rule out a try for the governorship, at least the next time around.

Dillon had read all of Kennedy's major pronouncements during the campaign, particularly his economic speeches. Unlike many militant Republican editorialists, he could find no grounds for the vague suspicion that Kennedy was an economic radical. In fact, Dillon was convinced that Kennedy the man, as opposed to the official defender of the ambiguously liberal Democratic platform, "believes the same things I have always believed in." With his flexible attitude toward government's role in the economy, Dillon was described by associates as closer to Kennedy's thinking than to Eisenhower's.

Even during the campaign Dillon suspected that Kennedy might offer him something if he won. When post-election speculation indicated it would be Treasury, there was no doubt in his mind. Kennedy popped the question as soon as he arrived at the Georgetown house that Friday morning, December 16, and Dillon accepted without hesitation. Bobby Kennedy was also there—"shifting from one foot to the other like me," Dillon recalls—to accept the Attorney Generalship. Dillon went along with a joint announcement covering both appointments, a tactic designed to take some of the glare of publicity off Bobby and perhaps partially blunt the nepotism charge.

Dillon has been a willing member of the New Frontier ever since. He often stops at the White House on the way to the Treasury each morning, and he and the President have developed an easy relationship centered about a bit of governmentship. Both are marvels at the minutiae of the bureaucratic process and vie with each other in their expertise.

Dillon and Kennedy have much in common. Both are of immigrant stock. Both inherited millions from fabulously rich fathers who made it all themselves. Dillon's paternal grandfather was Sam Lapowski, son of a Polish Jew and a French Catholic (Dillon himself is an Episcopalian). He emigrated from Poland to Texas just after the Civil War, adopted his mother's maiden name of Dillon, and became a prosperous clothing merchant in San Antonio and Abilene. Later he moved to Milwaukee and entered the machine-manufacturing business.

Sam's son Clarence went to Worcester Academy in Massachusetts and on to Harvard. His family credentials were inadequate for an invitation to one of the family-tree-conscious social clubs. By senior year, however, Clarence was deemed proper enough for the less exclusive Hasty Pudding. Son Douglas, like Kennedy, made Spee, a step up the ladder but by no means the top. Clarence was only a fair student and he flunked the debating team, but he earned a considerable reputation as an abstemious (no tobacco, no beer) gambler. They called him "Baron" and he took all their money at no-limit, all-night poker. Before making a final raise he would ask, "Do you think I'm strong enough?", expose his hand, and study the expressions around the table. Like the men who were to face him later on the stock market, they were hard put to bluff him.

After graduating from Harvard in 1905 Clarence returned to Milwaukee and entered business. One Monday morning in the summer of 1907, after a weekend in the suburbs, he was standing on a train platform waiting for the local back to town. A big Newfoundland dog wandered onto the tracks, was hit by an onrushing express, and was hurled dead against Clarence. He fell unconscious and was rushed back to the home of his wealthy and prominent weekend host. Desperately ill for three weeks, he was nursed back to health by the daughter of the house, Anne McEldin Douglass. They were married the next year and went to Europe for a two-year honeymoon.

They painted, sketched, dabbled in the arts, mainly in France. And Clarence established a lifetime pattern of periodic residence in his grandmother's homeland. Later, after his big success on Wall Street, he was to buy Château Haut-Brion, south of Bordeaux, which produces one of the world's five best clarets.

Back in Milwaukee, Clarence entered the machine-tool business with his brother-in-law and prospered rapidly before heading for New York in 1915. Within five years he had forced his way to the top of William A. Read & Company and changed the name to Dillon, Read. It was a hidebound concern, and he revolutionized it with the calculated flamboyance he had shown at the poker tables of Harvard. In one of the expansively grand gestures of that giddy period he once wrote out a personal check for $146 million and bought the Dodge Brothers Auto Company for a syndicate which he headed.

Clarence Douglas, the elder of his two children, had been born in Geneva on August 21, 1909. (Young Dillon shortened the name to C. Douglas, and recently dropped the first initial entirely.) The young heir was raised in the glare of his father's financial brilliance and tended to recoil from it. He was a shy, sickly, and dominated boy. Even now, though a tall (six foot one inch, one hundred and eighty-five pounds), handsome man, he is still somewhat awkward. He has a nervous giggle and a squeaky voice. His public speaking is dull and tortured.

Young Dillon's boyhood was outwardly conventional in the manner of the very rich of the eastern seaboard. But he had few of the carefree days of his wealthy contemporaries. Largely because of ill-health, he was a bad athlete. And in the home his father exercised an iron rule. The intellectual regimen was exacting. He was taught to read two years before he entered grammar school and learned so well that he devours whole pages at a time with total recall. From his earliest school days he shrugged off his unvaryingly superior grades and attributed it all to his fast reading.

At Groton he devoted himself almost exclusively to his studies. But he also made his first plunge into the competitive world. The manager of the football team was an important man at the school and the job was much coveted by those who could not prove their manhood at sports. Dillon thrust himself into the stiff three-year competition with a single-mindedness previously undetected. He was the unquestioned winner when it was over. His classmates and friends mark it as the first step in his emancipation from a domineering father, who kept close touch by taking the boy out of school for an occasional week of fishing.

The pattern was somewhat the same at Harvard. Again he was an exceptional student (he was graduated *magna cum laude* in 1931). Again he determined to become manager of the football team, and was successful after an even tougher competition. His biggest conquest was Phyllis Chess Ellsworth, a Back Bay Bostonian, whom he married just after graduation. She is a very pretty woman of great good taste and her friends regard her as a wife of deep tenderness and love and great ambition for Dillon.

Although as shy as her husband, she has always been a magnificently efficient hostess at the six Dillon residences—Washington, Château Haut-Brion, a winter place at Hobe Sound, Florida, a summer "cottage" at Dark Harbor, Maine, an apartment in New York, and the old family home in Far Hills, New Jersey. Together they have amassed a brilliant collection of Italian statuary, impressionist paintings, and *objets d'art,* including the eight French crystal chandeliers they provided for the new State Department annex (at a cost of $40,000) when Congress refused the money. The Dillons have two grown daughters, one of whom is on the staff of the *avant-garde Paris Review.*

Groton and Harvard had been a brief interlude of independence for Dillon, but now he was back on Wall Street under his father's firm hand. A $185,000 seat was purchased for him on the stock exchange and he settled somewhat uneasily into the straight and conventional path his father had marked for him. He was still sickly. He was always watching his strength. He worked set and limited hours. His social life was restricted, and he went to bed early. He tried a little golf, but it was not unusual for him to quit after seven holes and return to the locker room for a rest. He was considered a competent investment banker, largely because of his quick mind and powerful memory, but it was not difficult to make invidious comparisons with his spectacular father.

As it was for Kennedy, only in a less dramatic way, the Navy was the turning point for Dillon. He enlisted just after France fell and finished at the top of his officer training class at Quonset, Rhode Island. He was assigned as an air operations officer with the Seventh Fleet in the Pacific, and saw action in Black Cat bombers at Guam, Saipan, and the Philippines. He was under fire several times ("It wouldn't make much copy," he says), rose to the rank of lieutenant commander, and won the Air Medal and the Legion of Merit.

The war provided Dillon's first complete separation from his father, and he returned sturdier, more mature and independent. For the first time in his life he had proved to himself that he could survive and succeed on his own. The change was immediately evident to his friends and associates. His old ailments seemed to have slipped away. He was more robust. He was able to put in more time at the office. He lasted a good eighteen holes and proved to be a fine club tennis player.

He was also more assertive in his father's firm. He was made chairman of Dillon, Read in 1946 and took a good grip on its multimillion-dollar holdings in chemicals, metals, natural gas, oil, and public utilities. (He doubled the portfolio by 1952.) But he was still reaching for independent achievement. He had tried his hand tentatively in Republican affairs during the thirties. Now he began to engage himself more vigorously. He helped John Foster Dulles in the Dewey campaign in 1948. He led the draft-Eisenhower movement in New Jersey, and went to the Republican convention as a delegate in 1952.

His contributions, in talent and money, had been big, and President Eisenhower named him Ambassador to France in 1953. The French were not at all pleased. They considered his appointment a political payoff and took his shyness for mediocrity. Although he had spent much time in France, his French was bad.

But Dillon considered Paris his critical test. Now, in a major enterprise, he could match his own talents against his father's reputation. He polished his French with daily tutoring. He mastered the intricacies of French politics. He displayed his expertise in matters of international finance. And, rare for a cloistered businessman, he knew how to handle the press.

Five days after he arrived he called in a dozen of the leading editors in Paris, poured them some Haut-Brion, and talked freely about policy and wine. "I can tell the year of a given Bordeaux or the district it comes from," he says, "but I can't spot both the year and the vineyard as some profess to do."

Except for times of unusual tension between the United States and France, Dillon had an invariably good press thereafter. Much of it undoubtedly can be attributed to a flexible approach and his quick perception of character. Shortly after he arrived, Dillon entered into a long dialogue with Stanislaw Gayewsky, Polish Ambassador to France. It was hardly fashionable then, particularly for a man from Wall Street, to associate with an emissary of a communist state. But Dillon perceived, long before it became a cliché of American foreign policy, that Poland might provide an opening in the Iron Curtain. His conversations with Gayewsky are now generally credited with creating the atmosphere for the first United States loan to Poland, which Dillon won from Congress in 1957.

Dillon also showed a remarkable resistance to McCarthyism, which had reduced many supposedly tougher and more experienced diplomats to abject servility. Six weeks after Dillon's arrival Theodore White's *Thunder Out of China* was banned from United States Information Agency libraries in Germany. White, a gentle journalist with a brilliant record as a reporter, analyst, and writer, was then in Paris and had chatted briefly with Dillon a short time before. His latest book, *Fire in the Ashes,* was under consideration by the Book-of-the-Month Club, and he feared the U.S.I.A. order would destroy its chances.

White related his plight to Benjamin Bradlee, then Dillon's press officer and now a *Newsweek* correspondent in Washington, and Bradlee prepared a strong cable to the State Department demanding that the ban be lifted immediately. White was known favorably by United States ambassadors throughout the world, Bradlee wrote, and his reputation as a loyal American was unimpeachable. The cable required a top-secret classification and had to be cleared by the Ambassador. Without hesitation Dillon strengthened the language and upgraded it to "eyes only Secretary of State." The ban was lifted in three days and White's work was chosen by the Book-of-the-Month Club.

Dillon's stickiest problems in Paris were the Algerian war, the Suez crisis, and a serious disc operation which forced him to work in great pain at a chest-high desk.

He took a bold position in April 1956 by declaring that "the United States stands solidly behind France in her search for a liberal and equitable solution of the problems of Algeria.

"My countrymen have always been shocked by blind acts of terrorism," Dillon said, "and those who take part in such activity should not for one moment imagine that they have the support of my government or any segment of our public opinion. . . .

"We believe the less-favored people of the world should be brought forward as rapidly as possible to a state of freedom in which they can freely and rationally choose their own destiny. Such freedom can take many forms. It by no means requires a rupture between the peoples that have acquired their freedom and those who have led them along the path to this freedom."

His words were not calculated to please the North African nationalists, and they did not, but Dillon felt the time had come for him to speak his mind. This very undiplomatic urge for periodic truth saying provoked a mild international crisis in December of 1956 when he made a very frank analysis of the Suez situation during a radio interview in Washington.

It wasn't "moral suasion" that induced the British and the French to stop their advance into Egypt, Dillon said. It was the Soviet threat of armed intervention. Dillon's remarks ran against the Dulles line that it was the moral force of the United States that had ended the hostilities. Considerable pressure was brought to bear for a retraction through qualification. Dillon agreed to retrieve the statement to some extent, but he refused to deny flatly what was to him only the simple truth.

Despite his assertions of independence or, perhaps, because of them, Dillon was called back to Washington in 1957 to become Deputy Under Secretary of State for Economic Affairs. During the ensuing years he became a familiar figure on Capitol Hill. He was the Administration's most persuasive champion of foreign aid. He advanced his facts and arguments with rare finesse. Even the most bitter opponents of foreign spending were impressed.

Senator Russell Long, Democrat of Louisiana, decided to wage a one-man campaign against Dillon's nomination as Under Secretary of State for Economic Affairs. For close to a month in the spring of 1959 Long addressed a nearly-empty Senate chamber about the damning secrets in his possession. The oratory evoked memories of his spellbinding father, Huey. But few were listening. On June 9, 1959, after another Long attack on Dillon for "mismanaging the foreign-aid program," the nomination was confirmed by voice vote with only one shout in dissent.

Dulles had died the previous month and Dillon was now State's Number 2 man behind Christian Herter. He was undisputed negotiator for the Department's viewpoint on foreign aid with Congress, the Treasury, and the world. He was largely responsible for having the resources of the International Monetary Fund increased by 50 per cent. He recommended the changes that raised India's share of foreign aid and Development Loan Fund money in 1960.

He was also assuming much of Dulles' world traveling. Dillon
went to New Zealand in the spring of 1959 as United States delegate to the Southeast Asia Treaty Organization. Late that year he
flew to Tokyo to warn an international economic meeting that the
world's newly prosperous nations must now assume their fair share
of foreign aid.

In the fall of 1960 he went to Bogotá, Colombia, to sell Eisenhower's $500-million "first-step" installment on a new program
for improving social conditions in Latin America. Despite Castro
demonstrations and anti-Yankee sentiment, he won general approval for the plan by persuasive arguments and a new-found
heartiness. Shucking his shyness, he swooped across the conference
room and grasped Augusto Federico Schmidt, chief Brazilian delegate, in a warm *abrazo*. He understood no Spanish when he arrived
but within a few days he was nodding agreement before his inter-
preter could start the English translation.

In Quito, Ecuador, on a stopover, he fielded questions for an
hour and a half at a labor school and later was swamped with
congratulations by unionists, amazed that "a man from Wall Street
could speak in such human terms."

During the great flurry of personal diplomacy in 1960 Dillon
was involved in the Ben-Gurion and Macmillan talks in Washington, and escorted De Gaulle on his tour of the United States.

His most controversial mission was to accompany Robert H.
Anderson, his predecessor as Secretary of the Treasury, on their
embarrassing post-election trip to Bonn in November of 1960.
Dillon agreed with Anderson and Eisenhower that the gold outflow
was serious. But he questioned the timing of the trip and the style
of the approach.

He found it difficult to accept the problem as one of such immediate urgency that it required frantic efforts by a lame-duck administration whose policies could be overturned in a few weeks by a
new President. But, then, he was inclined toward the State Department's calmer view of the situation. Eisenhower's and Anderson's
morbid fears of the "radical" Democrats did not seem very real to
him.

"We can handle this problem," Dillon said, "but it can't be done overnight. As a matter of fact, the balance-of-payments problem will be with us forever. It is going to fluctuate one way or the other, and some years we may be troubled by a surplus."

The United States has been running a $3.5 to $4 billion a year deficit in its balance of payments (exports minus imports, foreign aid, and business investments overseas), a situation that tends to decrease confidence in the stability of the dollar. The deficit is cutting into the United States gold reserve, down from $22 billion in 1956 to $18.4 billion in 1960, because international creditors have been demanding gold for their dollars to buy more attractive currencies.

Dillon felt half the surplus was the result of curable, short-term complications. He believed a concentrated but undramatic policy could steer the nation toward a balance in a year or two. But Anderson thought the situation bleak enough to demand some immediate help from the West German Republic which has been running a $2 billion surplus. He asked the Germans to cover the $600-million-a-year cost of stationing United States troops in their country.

Dillon disagreed with the approach. He thought it gave the reluctant German government an opportunity to portray the mission to the German people as a demand for more war reparations. Anderson's problems were complicated, Dillon feels, by his refusal to see the press under any conditions. Generally, reporters are invited to "background" sessions in which government officials explain their point of view with the agreement that they will not be quoted. Dillon was a successful exponent of the technique at the State Department. But Anderson, a less flexible, less articulate banker, refused to run the risk.

Excluded from any information about the United States position, the press was forced to turn to German officials who obliged to their own purposes. A rash of stories began to appear about Anderson's heavy-handed tactics at the bargaining table, his impolitic outbursts, and his tiffs with Dillon. They were greatly exaggerated, Dillon contends, but they had their intended effect on the German people. The highly-publicized mission was a failure.

Although Dillon had not yet been named Kennedy's treasury secretary, the Germans were already sure he was headed for a major role in the new Administration. Several of the negotiators approached Dillon privately, when Anderson wasn't around, and gave him the assurances they had held back in the meeting room that Germany was willing enough to make significant concessions on the balance-of-payments problem but wanted to get the most out of it by making the concessions to the new Administration, not the lame-duck Eisenhower regime. Shortly after Kennedy took over the Germans agreed to extend $1 billion of foreign aid annually to poorer nations, prepay part of their debts to the United States, and speed up ordering of American goods.

America's gold is now a matter for the "quiet diplomacy" of the New Frontier. And that is just fine with Dillon. He is a preternaturally quiet man and has a deft way of tiptoeing through the raucous controversies that afflict every high government official.

Early in 1959, for example, Republican National Chairman Meade Alcorn kicked up a big fuss over the nomination of a Democrat, Henry R. Labouisse, to be director of the International Cooperation Administration. The dispute ran its nasty course and the nomination was pulled back by Eisenhower without any real public awareness that the man in the middle was Dillon, who had been Labouisse's chief backer. Two years later Labouisse became I.C.A. director in the Kennedy administration.

In August of 1960 Dillon was the quiet man in the middle again. Senator Hugh Scott of Pennsylvania, a charter member of the Republican "truth squad," wondered out loud on the Senate floor if Kennedy was trying to "buy votes" by paying for the transportation of African students to the United States. The Joseph P. Kennedy, Jr., Foundation had offered $100,000, after the State Department refused to do so on four occasions.

James Shepley, a Nixon lieutenant, thought his man might be hurt and put the heat on the State Department to reverse its stand and provide the money in the name of the Republican administration. He contacted William B. Macomber, Jr., assistant secretary for congressional affairs, and Macomber contacted Dillon. The next day Dillon phoned Shepley and said he was now prepared to authorize the funds. Shepley, in turn, called the African-American Students Federation and told them the Administration would produce the money. Nixon was to get the credit.

Kennedy denounced the intrigue as the "most unfair, distorted, malignant attack I have heard in fourteen years of politics." His wrath seared Scott, Shepley, and Nixon, but Dillon got away unburned.

Two months earlier he had extricated himself unscathed from an even touchier incident. More than most of the publicized participants, Dillon was a key figure in the U-2 debacle. Herter was at a meeting in Turkey when Khrushchev proclaimed that the spy plane had been shot down on May Day over the Soviet Union. Dillon was serving as acting Secretary of State and made the initial incriminating decisions to issue the "cover" story that the U-2 was a civilian weather plane, to imply at first that Eisenhower knew nothing about it, and to keep the truth from the government spokesmen who were making the official statements to the press and to the world.

On May 5, four days after the plane went down, Dillon was informed, much to his surprise, that the pilot was probably alive and had not been killed in the crash or committed suicide. The American embassy in Moscow reported that foreign diplomats were being so informed by Soviet officials on the cocktail circuit. The next morning Dillon received rather conclusive evidence that the Russians had been publishing a phony picture of the U-2 wreckage. His immediate and correct assumption was that the plane had fallen into Russian hands essentially intact.

Still, Dillon made no effort to readjust the cover story or advise Lincoln White, the State Department spokesman, of the hazards involved in pushing it too hard. "I don't even know if the Secretary of State was allowed to let him know," Dillon said. "It was standard operating procedure. We were all brought up with it."

At the regular afternoon press briefing on March 6 White was subjected to stiff questioning. Finally, somewhat in exasperation, he declared flatly and innocently: "There was absolutely no, N-O,

deliberate attempt to violate the Soviet airspace and there has never
been."

The next day Khrushchev sprang the trap. He announced that
the U-2 pilot was alive and his espionage equipment was intact.
The Americans, he declared, had been exposed before all the world
as colossal liars. That afternoon the United States confessed that
it had, indeed, been spying. But in one last effort to save the forthcoming summit conference, the State Department reached for an
out for Eisenhower. "It has been established," the State Department declared, "that in so far as the authorities in Washington
are concerned there was no authorization for any such flights as
described by Mr. Khrushchev."

By this time Herter had returned to the capital and Dillon had
been relieved of the command decisions. He remained on, however,
as an intimate observer of the policy flip-flops which ensued.
Charles Bohlen, the State Department's principal Russian expert,
was advising against any acceptance of responsibility by the President. Spying was always blamed on underlings, he argued, and
that was the way Khrushchev wanted it. Blame the Pentagon,
blame the C.I.A., blame some obscure colonel, and the summit
could be saved.

But Hagerty, who was intensely jealous of his boss's reputation,
argued that Bohlen's plan would tend to bolster Democratic criticism that "Ike wasn't minding the store." He recommended that
Eisenhower assume full responsibility for the flights. The President
accepted the advice but not, Dillon insists, for Hagerty's reasons.
Eisenhower was touchy about charges of being a "part-time President," Dillon concedes, but his main concern was to protect his
subordinates.

Allen Dulles, director of the Central Intelligence Agency, offered
to resign as a scapegoat, but Eisenhower would have none of it.
His Kansas boyhood and his Army career had trained him to a
strict loyalty, Dillon says, and if the summit could be saved only at
Dulles' expense, it would not be saved.

Dillon was later called behind closed doors to explain his part
in the affair to the Senate Foreign Relations Committee. With
characteristic candor, he confessed all. But he was held in such

high esteem by the Committee, particularly by Chairman J. William Fulbright, a regular golfing companion, that he escaped with not so much as a wrist slap.

Despite serious misgivings over his appointment by many liberal Democrats (one towering economic expert in the Senate fired off a secret telegram of protest to Kennedy), Dillon has enjoyed equally good relations with Congress since he joined the New Frontier. He has managed the seemingly impossible task of convincing both the right and the left that he is one of them.

"He assured me," said Senator Harry Byrd, the impeccable Virginia conservative, "that he stands very stanchly for sound monetary policies, for a balanced budget, and for a sound dollar."

"I accept him," said Representative Wright Patman, the uncompromising easy-money Texan, "as a flexible man who will cooperate with Congress and President Kennedy. He will adjust his thinking."

Dillon's technique for corraling both a Byrd and a Patman is to avoid abstract, doctrinaire statements ("I'm not an economist"). He tries to skirt sweeping judgments and to concentrate on specific problems. Some of his basic convictions have, nonetheless, seeped out over the years.

For example, he was one of the original exponents of "growthmanship." In 1959, at a time when only the more vocal liberal economists were saying such things, he told the Harvard Alumni Association: "It is imperative that the United States find ways of accelerating its own economic growth while always maintaining the stability of our currency. The 5 per cent annual increase recommended as a goal in recent studies would seem to be an absolute minimum." In this he finds himself in complete agreement with Kennedy and his chief economic adviser, Walter Heller.

Privately, Dillon has been critical of the Eisenhower administration for failing to perceive the need for a steeper, prolonged rate of economic growth. "It hasn't been as much concerned with fundamental trends in our economy" as the New Frontier will be, he once told friends. Dillon was upset when Nixon mocked the supporters of "growthmanship" during the 1960 campaign, regarding the speech as one of the former Vice-President's most serious mistakes.

"We haven't been growing fast enough," Dillon says. "I look on growth as the outer sign of economic health. We have to get to work here at home to show the success of the private-enterprise system."

At heart Dillon is an economic middle-of-the-roader. "Everything we do," he has said, "depends on the maintenance of a strong and sound economy." But he is convinced, as is Kennedy, that the private-enterprise system can prosper and triumph only if the Government plays a bigger role in economic policy and planning than it did in the Eisenhower administration. He is not intimidated by the gold problem and is prepared to experiment with new ideas.

"Banker" is an epithet widely used to describe Dillon. But it is well to remember there are different kinds of bankers. One type that comes quickly to mind is the man who runs a bank, lends money, and is, by nature, extremely conservative. But Dillon is another kind, an investment banker who deals in securities and capital appreciation. He is thus concerned with economic growth. He isn't frightened by inflation, though he may fight it. He isn't bound by economic orthodoxy.

"I believe in doing things the orthodox way," Dillon once said, "so long as the orthodox way works. When you run into places where the orthodox won't work, then you try something new." Dillon's remarks came in answer to criticism of the un-bankerlike approach of foreign aid. But the philosophy therein remains the key to his approach to his job as Secretary of the Treasury.

Soon after he took over the assignment the Treasury undertook the unorthodox task, in cooperation with the Federal Reserve Board, of trying to hold up short-term interest rates while simultaneously bringing down long-term rates. The idea was to encourage long-term borrowing by business to stimulate the economy, while at the same time stemming the exodus of short-term funds looking for more profitable returns overseas.

Dillon is planning a more active use of tax and debt-management policies to achieve his economic goals. Rather than trying to balance the budget each year, he talks of an equilibrium over a longer period, with surpluses some years offsetting deficits in others. He doesn't shrink from the idea of running temporary deficits to spur business, and he was willing to accept a deficit in the 1960–61 recession. But he wants to achieve a greater "control" over the ups and downs, cutting deficits during hard times, increasing surpluses during prosperity.

The latest recession never did become serious enough for the Kennedy administration to propose a temporary tax cut to bail out the economy. But Dillon has made it clear that, in seriously bad times, he favors a tax cut over increased government spending. Big, new federal programs set in motion spending that is far more difficult to control, he feels, than a temporary cutback in revenues.

As for long-term tax policy, Dillon claims no superior knowledge in matters of tax reform, but he has promised to go along with many of Heller's efforts to close some loopholes and thereby permit a lowering of tax rates. He favors new tax incentives to encourage business to sink more money in new plants and equipment.

Dillon is a stern taskmaster and an empire builder of sorts. On taking over the Treasury, he felt the various sections of the department were operating too much on their own. He established a new system of coordination and set out to impress his will on all segments of the operation. He gathered a staff which many believe to be one of the best in Treasury's long history. He has always relied heavily on specialists but refuses to become their captive.

Dillon feels the Treasury had been suffering from a lack of brain power in many areas. He is trying to bolster the quality as well as the size of the staff to give the Treasury equal footing with Walter Heller's Council of Economic Advisers, and give it more weight in dealing with other departments and with foreign governments.

He does his homework thoroughly and expects those who work for him to do the same. He is intolerant of poor performances. Once, while he was a sub-Cabinet member in the Eisenhower administration, he attended a dull, bumbling press briefing by a Cabinet official. Although the Cabinet officer was his superior, Dillon showed his disdain by casually reading a newspaper.

The new Secretary of the Treasury has an orderly, logical mind, not hobbled by an unruly imagination. He likes to tackle one problem at a time, getting all the relevant details, then make up his mind. Decision making is thus often a time-consuming process for Dillon, but he does take great relish in finally choosing his course.

Perhaps because he is so self-effacing and reserved, Dillon's friends and subordinates take a special interest in analyzing his talents and his personality.

"If everybody waited to sound off on a subject until he understood it as well as Dillon does," one of them said, "the world would be full of people going around saying nothing."

"Dillon can get a lot out of you," another observed, "because he has respect for specialists without being in awe of them. He is not afraid to delegate authority as long as you realize he is ultimately responsible."

"He has a happy faculty," said an observer on Capitol Hill, "for listening to what congressmen say, and treating a silly question as if it were important."

"Dillon," a foreign diplomat remarked, "reminds me of some English aristocrat who likes others to think of him as a dilettante. But once you get down to the question at hand, you find he knows more about it than you do."

The key to it all is unremitting hard work. Although he can discourse competently on art, politics, and other weighty topics, he rarely has time in the evening for "fun." He is too busy boning up on his work. Since his return from the Navy his vigor has advanced with the growing challenges. It is not unusual for him to put in an eighteen-hour day. He is much less solicitous of his health than he was in his twenties and he plays golf well enough (in the eighties) to make him a sporting as well as an intellectual companion to the President.

Like Kennedy, he has a strong hunger for service and a great ambition to do things that will influence the course of history. Perhaps because both are sensitive to their immigrant lineage, they are restless and find it difficult to accept what they own or what they have already done as an assurance of their good name and enduring repute. They still retain something of the uneasiness of the upward mobile.

Dillon has an almost Calvinistic devotion to his work and a deep loyalty to his superiors, which might account for the high esteem in which he was held by Dulles. The late Secretary of State had a stern sense of self-control and rarely allowed himself a public display of emotion. But one of his closest assistants recalls he always had great difficulty refraining from throwing his arm around Dillon.

Those who have watched closely at the White House say a similar rapport is growing between Kennedy and Dillon. No one expects Kennedy to be quite so demonstrative—although pure Irish, he is in many ways more English than the English. But it would come as no great surprise to them if the truest intellectual embrace of the Cabinet involved these two rich immigrants' sons.

7.

THE THINKING MAN'S
BUSINESS EXECUTIVE

Robert McNamara

By ELIE ABEL

ROBERT STRANGE MCNAMARA, A YOUNG TYCOON OF SOBER MIEN and bookish habits, took five days to decide that he was not unqualified for the job of Defense Secretary. It was the hardest decision of his life, not because joining the New Frontier meant the loss of millions; by his own standards, Bob McNamara was already a rich man—rich enough to quit making money for as long as President Kennedy wanted him in Washington. The reason he hesitated was that he had honest doubts about his own ability to handle the job. He needed reassurance—and he got it from the President-elect at their first meeting. He also received an authoritative answer to another question that had long troubled him: Did John F. Kennedy write *Profiles in Courage* himself?

McNamara had bought the Kennedy book at home in Ann Arbor, Michigan, when it was first published. He found in its pages a moving statement of the age-old dilemma between principle and compromise, the same dilemma he faced time and again in his own life. In fact, he was so moved by the book that he read sections of it aloud to his children. Then he started hearing gossip that *Profiles* was the work of a ghostly hand. Some said it was written by Arthur Schlesinger, Jr.; others credited the book to Theodore Sorensen.

It was a measure of McNamara's own quiet courage that the first time he met the President-elect—on December 8, 1960, in the Kennedy house in Georgetown—he put the question bluntly: "Did you write *Profiles in Courage*?" Kennedy replied that others had helped with the basic research, because he was gravely ill at the time, but the writing was his. McNamara flew home to Michigan twice reassured. On December 13 he was back at 3307 N Street, Northwest, standing beside Kennedy on the front stoop as the news of his appointment was published and broadcast around the world.

His arrival on the New Frontier, in a position of vast power and influence, was anything but fortuitous. McNamara had no political ambitions or connections. At the age of forty-four he had just been chosen president of the Ford Motor Company, the first president who was not a member of the Ford family. There was every reason to expect that he would devote the rest of his working life to the automobile industry, picking up enough stock options and bonuses along the way to make him a multimillionaire before he was fifty.

The company's line of command had been recharted to fit McNamara as president and Henry Ford II as chairman of the board. In the upper reaches of American industry such changes are not made on the spur of the moment; they are meant to endure. Ford had the benefits of McNamara's leadership for exactly thirty-four days. What deflected him from his predestined course was Kennedy's determination to seek out men of extraordinary talent and toughness who could help manage the nation's business with the same professional skill they brought to industry, teaching, or politics. Sargent Shriver, the President's brother-in-law, organized the great talent hunt, and McNamara was by all odds Shriver's prize catch. No one is quite certain how it all started, although Adam Yarmolinsky, a Washington lawyer who worked with Shriver during and after the campaign, remembers "tossing around" McNamara's name before election day.

"Sometimes, when we got tired enough, we would sit around and discuss what would happen when it was all over, and who would be in the Cabinet," Yarmolinsky recalls. "I had met McNamara once when I was visiting the University of Michigan and he invited me to the house. I remember I was impressed with him, and the thought may have entered my head that this was the kind of business executive—young, brilliant, and public-spirited—who belonged on the New Frontier. But I was not really the efficacious source."

Further research established that the "efficacious source" in this case was probably a Wall Street investment banker named T. Herbert Shriver, Sargent's brother. Sargent Shriver had stopped in New York on the way back to Washington from his first scouting trip to Boston. In an effort to be helpful his banker brother mentioned that a fellow named McNamara out in Detroit was very highly regarded by Harold James Berry, executive vice president of Harriman, Ripley and Company. Sargent Shriver found it hard to believe that a man who had been elected president of the country's second biggest automobile company a few days earlier would consider walking out to take a public job which had tarnished more reputations than it enhanced. But he liked what Berry had to say about McNamara's intellectual power and managerial achievements. There was no harm, Shriver told Berry, in making a few discreet inquiries to determine whether or not the new Ford president might be available. After checking with associates in Wall Street and Detroit's Griswold Street, Berry reported back somewhat encouraged but still uncertain.

Shriver duly entered McNamara's name on the card file of prospects although no one had him in mind at the time for the Defense job. Kennedy was still hoping that Robert A. Lovett could be persuaded to accept the Secretaryship of the Treasury. McNamara was being considered as a possible Under Secretary and heir-apparent to Lovett.

At this point—it was mid-November—Shriver talked on the telephone with Neil M. Staebler, a wealthy Ann Arbor businessman who had rebuilt the Michigan Democratic party by applying his brain and his energies to the problems of precinct politics. Staebler was not only a close friend and neighbor of McNamara, he was to dine at the Ford president's home that evening. Shriver sounded out Staebler. "Why, Bob McNamara is the sort of fellow who has actually read *The Affluent Society!*" the Michigan party chairman reported with rising enthusiasm. "I think he might be ready to do some things for the new administration. He might be willing to serve, for example, on advisory committees or boards." Even Staebler could not bring himself to believe that McNamara would consider leaving Ford.

When Lovett, on the advice of his physician, turned down Kennedy's Cabinet offer, the search turned elsewhere. Without tipping his hand, Shriver kept asking people he met, "By the way, what do you know about Bob McNamara?" He got warm endorsements from Lovett himself and from Charles Bates Thornton, who had been McNamara's wartime boss in the Army Air Force and his senior colleague at Ford before moving on to California where he became president and board chairman of Litton Industries.

The inquiries spread around the country, but they remained seemingly casual and wholly confidential. Some approaches were so roundabout that the men questioned had no idea whether it was McNamara's credit rating or perhaps his personal habits that were being checked. Shriver, for example, asked Jack Sturgis, vice-president of a Chicago bank, to draw on his banking connections in Detroit for a report on McNamara. It was positive.

Other bits of unrelated data were filtering into the talent-scout headquarters at the Democratic National Committee: Staebler reported that McNamara might have voted for Kennedy (he did); that he had refused to support the Democratic candidate for governor, John Swainson; Kenneth O'Donnell, a presidential assistant, brought back word that Jack Conway, personal assistant to Walter Reuther of the United Automobile Workers, thought McNamara was highly intelligent, fair-minded, and a man who had astonished the few labor people he met by his breadth of interest.

To get a quick reading on how McNamara was rated by his faculty neighbors at the University of Michigan, Shriver called on Tom King, Jr., an employee of the Kennedy-owned Merchandise Mart in Chicago. King telephoned his father, a former director of athletics and now dean of students at Michigan State University in East Lansing. Dean King, in turn, consulted a friend of his on the Ann Arbor faculty who lived a few doors from the McNamaras. Again the report was positive.

Shriver was balked only once. He wanted to poll the caddies who might have carried McNamara's golf bags on the theory that next to a man's valet his caddy can be the shrewdest judge of his character. Unfortunately, McNamara was no golfer. He tried the game once, played badly, and quickly decided that climbing mountains was more of a challenge.

On the night of December 6 Shriver saw Kennedy and reported his findings: McNamara seemed to pass all the tests, but no man could say whether he would be interested in coming to Washington. The Treasury and Defense jobs were still open. The President, always a believer in direct action, said to Shriver: "If he's that good, who don't you fly out and see him?"

Shriver remembers his instructions: "If he lived up to the advance billing, I had the authority to sound out his interest in the Defense job. If I sensed any stiffening, I was prepared to move in the other direction—to see how he felt about the Treasury."

The next morning Shriver raced to Washington's National Airport. He missed the first plane to Detroit. While waiting for the second, he asked Robert Kennedy to telephone ahead and alert McNamara. When Shriver's plane reached Detroit, a Lincoln was waiting at the airport. He was whisked to Ford headquarters and into the president's office.

Shriver at once mentioned both defense and the treasury as possibilities. McNamara was soon delivering a well-organized discourse on the problems that would confront both new secretaries. He talked about the balance-of-payments problems and the nuclear-weapons race. "I was convinced we wanted this guy in the Administration," Shriver said afterward. "He seemed to know an amazing amount about weapons but he also showed a clear grasp of the Treasury situation."

McNamara said he supposed he would have to sell his Ford stock if he went to Washington. Shriver agreed. That would be no problem, McNamara observed, because he already had more money than anyone in his family had dreamed of. But he was not convinced that he could handle the Defense job. True, he had once served in the Air Force. But that was long ago, and besides he didn't stay long enough to become any kind of military expert.

Another obstacle, he told Shriver, was his sense of obligation to Henry Ford II and the company. He would have to consult Ford, as well as his wife, before saying yes or no. Ford happened to be in New York so the answer would have to wait a day or two. Shriver left without a commitment one way or the other but with a "seat of the pants feeling" that his time and effort had not been wasted. He stipulated that if McNamara was inclined to refuse he should talk with Kennedy before reaching his final decision.

The very next morning McNamara telephoned Shriver from New York. He had talked with Ford, with Lovett, and with Sidney Weinberg of Goldman, Sachs and Company, a director of the Ford company. "Mr. Ford didn't say a word to deter me, but he didn't make it easy, either," McNamara recalls. Weinberg and Lovett were more encouraging. When McNamara mentioned his obligation to Ford, Weinberg said the only things a young man should worry about were loyalty to his country and his family. "I suppose it sounds trite," McNamara says, "but Weinberg's words counted with me."

McNamara asked to see the President-elect, and Shriver fixed an appointment for six o'clock that evening, December 8. Rather than "hang around" New York, McNamara said he would catch the next plane to Washington, go straight to the Ford suite at the Shoreham Hotel, and wait all afternoon for Shriver to pick him up.

They slipped into the Kennedy home on N Street through the back door after dark to avoid the reporters and photographers bivouacked out in front. McNamara was sure in his own mind by this time that he would prefer the Defense assignment if he came to Washington at all. He talked about his own inadequacy. It might take a year or eighteen months before he was on top of the job. Could the country afford to wait that long?

Kennedy, who had been to the White House two days earlier for his first talk with President Eisenhower on the transfer of executive responsibility to the new administration, told McNamara that if the outgoing administration was right the United States would be far ahead of the Russians in nuclear striking power for many months to come. "If they are right," he said, "you will have the time to learn. If they are wrong, I want to find that out as quickly as possible and you're the man to do it."

McNamara had other reservations. The Symington report had just been published. It recommended a drastic overhaul of the Defense Department, including abolition of the separate Army, Navy, and Air Force departments. The young tycoon explained that he didn't know enough about the problem to endorse or disclaim the Symington recommendations. Kennedy said he had not made up his own mind. He suggested it would be wise to wait a year or more before undertaking any reorganization of the Pentagon, until both the incoming President and the new Defense Secretary knew more about their jobs. McNamara kept coming back to his own lack of qualifications. Kennedy at one point replied that he was not aware of any school for Cabinet officers, or Presidents either, for that matter.

Before leaving, McNamara promised a definite answer by Saturday, December 10. He wanted to ask Thomas S. Gates, the outgoing Defense Secretary, the biggest question on his mind—could any man, no matter how gifted and hard-working, ever make a success of running the Pentagon? As they walked away through the back alley, McNamara said not a word to Shriver for three or four blocks. Suddenly he found the words he was searching for:

"That's a very impressive brother-in-law you have."

"Well, you're very impressive yourself, Mr. McNamara," Shriver replied.

The following morning McNamara drove to the Pentagon and spent two hours with Gates. No one recognized the tall, professorial visitor, not even the alert Pentagon reporters. He flew back to Ann Arbor for the weekend "considerably reassured" that the Defense job could be handled, at least by a man of Gates's long experience, but obsessed by lingering doubts about his own qualifications. Saturday came with McNamara still undecided. He telephoned Washington to ask for more time. By Monday his mind was made up.

"I had been approached about an assistant secretary's job in the Defense Department under both the Truman and Eisenhower administrations," McNamara explained. "At the time I felt I wasn't ready, financially or otherwise. I had once told Henry Ford that I was interested in public service. At some particular point I felt I would have to do it if I was asked. You just can't go on saying no all your life."

On Tuesday, December 13, McNamara flew to Washington again and this time entered the house on N Street through the front door. The President-elect sat his guest before the open fire in the drawing room and, with a yellow legal pad on his knee, wrote out the statement he would read a few minutes later on the wind-swept stoop of the old federal house. McNamara was all the more impressed; in the automobile industry statements by very important persons are the product of vast public-relations departments headed by a vice-president.

Washington's way of transacting business was not Detroit's. The new Secretary of Defense made this unsettling discovery even before he took office. There were job seekers to contend with, some recommended by the President, others by powerful congressional leaders, and some backed by organized labor or the veterans' organizations.

The President, for example, once suggested that Franklin D. Roosevelt, Jr., might be considered for Secretary of the Navy. McNamara turned him down. Kennedy pointed out that he owed a political debt to young Roosevelt for his effective campaigning in the West Virginia primary. The Defense Secretary agreed to see Roosevelt and re-examine his qualifications. But he still felt Roosevelt was not the man he wanted and the President, in the end, gave way.

George Meany, president of the A.F.L.-C.I.O., had a candidate of his own for the job of Assistant Secretary for Manpower. The chosen one was Joseph D. Keenan, a devoted Kennedy man throughout the campaign and a stalwart of the building-trade unions. McNamara simply did not feel Keenan had the qualifications he wanted and told the President so.

Meany sulked in a cloud of cigar smoke at A.F.L.-C.I.O. headquarters, across Lafayette Park from the White House. A friendly emissary suggested that McNamara would do well to pick up the telephone and invite Meany to the Pentagon so they could talk over their misunderstanding. The go-between felt that a face-to-face meeting would be a useful part of McNamara's general orientation on the Washington scene, whether Keenan got the manpower job or not. "I'll go over and see him myself," the Defense Secretary decided.

The French would describe the disaster that followed as a "dialogue of the deaf." Straightforward to a fault, McNamara opened the conversation by announcing that he had come over to reassure Meany that he was not anti-labor. The A.F.L.-C.I.O. chief could not have been more flabbergasted if McNamara, whom he was meeting for the first time, had proclaimed that he was not a wife beater.

Launching into a fifteen-minute lecture on the virtues of his good friend Joe Keenan, Meany succeeded in blocking McNamara's belated efforts to steer the conversation into less controversial channels. The meeting broke up with McNamara only half-realizing the extent of his failure to communicate with Meany. As for the A.F.L.-C.I.O. president, he felt the man from Ann Arbor had cold-shouldered him. Their misunderstanding, in fact, was now complete.

McNamara is no admirer of the old-school labor leaders. His disdain applies with particular force to the building trades, which he has long regarded as dead set against technological progress and, therefore, reactionary. He does not put Walter Reuther in this category.

His first choice for the Pentagon man-power job was in fact Reuther's man, Conway. The Keenan incident ruled that out. McNamara was given to understand that Conway's appointment would have driven a wedge between Reuther and Meany, something neither wing of the labor federation wanted. Finally, the job went to Carlisle P. Runge, of the University of Wisconsin. Through all the pulling and hauling, Kennedy backed his Defense Secretary, although at times he may have wished that McNamara had grown the political antennae to match his administrative and analytical capabilities.

There were other unsettling incidents, which helped to correct the early impression that McNamara was a man without weaknesses. His most conspicuous failing, Washington soon discovered, was a total absence of political subtlety. "You ask him a question and he gives you the answer—bang, bang," said one associate. "He has yet to learn that certain things are better left unsaid, even if they happen to be true."

A good example was his celebrated "background conference" with the Pentagon reporters a few days after taking office. Somewhat foggy about the rules of this old Washington parlor game, McNamara talked freely and frankly about various delicate matters on which the new administration was still in the process of making policy decisions. He was horrified to hear on the radio three hours later and to read in some newspapers the next morning that the Kennedy administration had reached the tentative conclusion that there was no "missile gap." He was sure that he had said no such thing—and several of the experienced military writers who attended the conference upheld McNamara after carefully checking their notes. Some equally experienced members of the craft insisted he had left that unmistakable impression. It was one group's word against the other's; no stenographic record was taken.

Unhappily, the Defense Secretary was only dimly aware of the political dynamite attached to this issue. (In the 1960 campaign Kennedy had accused the Eisenhower administration of negligence and complacency in allowing the United States to fall behind Russia. Dwight Eisenhower's last word on the subject, in his valedictory message to Congress on the state of the union, was to dismiss the missile gap as fiction.) In a matter of hours after the publication of McNamara's reported remarks by the *Washington Post* and the *New York Times,* Republican spokesmen were demanding that Kennedy should apologize to Eisenhower for having raised a phony election issue.

There was a crumb of comfort for the Secretary in letters he received afterward from four of the correspondents, conceding that some of the things he said might have been torn out of context and thereby distorted. But he was shaken by the experience, deeply regretted the embarrassment he had caused the new Administration, and took care not to tempt the furies again by exposing himself to the press unnecessarily. The President, conditioned by fourteen years in Washington as a member of the House and Senate, took a calmer view of the incident. In public and private he defended Mc-Namara.

A more rugged test of the new Secretary's staying power came with his discovery that the Pentagon had no over-all strategic plan that he considered worthy of the name. There were short-term war plans, designed to meet a variety of contingencies. But the Army, Navy, and Air Force had failed to agree on a single national design for survival and victory in the event of war five or ten years from now. The Eisenhower administration, torn between the Air Force doctrine of "counterforce" and the Navy's "finite deterrent" theory, never made a clear choice. Unwilling to put all its eggs in one basket, the Administration went along with a mixture of plans and weapons, satisfying neither school.

The last formal restatement of United States strategy had been the John Foster Dulles doctrine of instantaneous and massive retaliation "by means and at places of our own choosing," enunciated in 1954. It implied a willingness to answer communist aggression anywhere in the world by dropping thermonuclear bombs on Moscow. Apart from alarming some allies and most neutral nations, the Dulles doctrine threatened to destroy the country's capacity for "brush-fire" or limited wars. As crisis followed crisis—Indo-China, Formosa, Hungary, Suez, and Lebanon—it became apparent that the United States hesitated to use its nuclear advantage. The day was long past when the West enjoyed a nuclear monopoly. As soon as the Russians developed their own atomic arsenal, the massive retaliation strategy became too hazardous to contemplate.

Moving into the vacuum, Navy strategists developed their own concept of the finite or invulnerable deterrent. They argued that fixed installations of Atlas and Titan missiles would hardly survive the first enemy strike. What the country needed, the Navy thinkers contended, was a mobile deterrent in the form of missile launchers which could be shunted around the country and fired from railway cars, Polaris submarines, more foot soldiers, and the ships and planes to transport them anywhere in the world. Any potential aggressor would find war unacceptable so long as he knew for certain that, even after the first blow was struck, America would be left with sufficient missile strength to retaliate effectively against his own cities.

"Counterforce," the Air Force answer devised by Rand Corporation scientists, stipulated that the United States must have enough manned bombers and missiles, operating from hardened and dispersed bases, to wipe out the whole of Russia's war-making potential, not merely her big cities. Survival also would demand a greatly expanded early-warning network, effective spy-in-the-sky satellites, and steady reconnaissance flights over Russian territory to detect any major shift in deployment. The theory was that rather than await the first blow more or less passively, the United States should strike as soon as the enemy deployment suggested imminent war.

McNamara feels the country must have a national plan without necessarily committing itself to either of these alternatives. There can be no final judgment about the uncertain future, in his view of the world. While the country girds itself for contingencies that may never arise, there is bound to be waste in military spending. But we must go on buying time and options, he believes, so that the country can choose the proper response when war threatens.

Testifying before the Senate Committee on Armed Services some ten weeks after he took office, McNamara outlined the Kennedy Administration's new approach: "In re-evaluating our general war position, our major concern was to reduce our dependence on deterrent forces, which are highly vulnerable to ballistic missile attack, or which rely for their survival on a hair-trigger response to the first indication of such an attack. Conversely, we sought to place greater emphasis on the second approach—the kind of forces which could ride out a massive nuclear attack and which could be applied with deliberation and always under the complete control of the constituted authority."

The decisions meant a buildup of conventional forces trained in guerrilla warfare, a speedup in production of the relatively invulnerable solid-fuel Polaris and Minuteman missiles, and an accelerated shift away from such "first generation" missiles as the highly vulnerable liquid-fuel Atlas and Titan. In full awareness of the outcry that would be raised by pressure groups, defense contractors, and congressmen whose home districts were affected, McNamara cut back development of the B-70 bomber, wiped out the long, costly, and so far fruitless effort to build a nuclear-powered airplane, and ordered the closing of seventy-three military installations and bases that no longer served a useful purpose.

Whether the country needed a new grand design for strategy or a more efficient organizational structure in the Pentagon, the new Secretary of Defense was willing to wait years for the armed services to submit an agreed blueprint. He provided the leadership himself. Under McNamara's direction, for example, four task forces carried out a sweeping review of America's defense policies during the first thirty days of the Kennedy administration's term. It was McNamara, not the Joint Chiefs of Staff, who picked the members and assigned their tasks. When the recommendations were complete —and only then—McNamara submitted the reports to the Joint Chiefs of Staff for ratification and comment. "I see my position as being that of a leader, not a judge," he told the Chiefs. "I'm here to originate, to stimulate new ideas and programs, and not just to adjudicate arguments."

To a former Harvard Business School professor, who had successfully applied his knowledge of management and statistical techniques to long-haul planning in the automobile industry, the Defense Department seemed an incredibly untidy and haphazard operation. He promptly set up a new Office of Management Planning under the wing of General Counsel Cyrus Vance, with the assignment of framing new proposals for a more rational organization.

At meetings in the Department the Secretary keeps the discussion moving briskly. He invites a clash of opinion around the table so he can be certain that all the relevant facts, pro and con, have been taken into account. Once a departmental decision is reached, however, he expects and insists upon the loyal support of all three services. At Ford it was, of course, inconceivable that the Lincoln-Comet-Mercury division would challenge a corporate decision and lobby against it in the newspapers. In the Pentagon—as Charles E. Wilson of General Motors and Neil McElroy of Procter and Gamble discovered in their time—such behavior is par for the course. In fact, a career officer's advancement often depends on loyalty to his own service even when that calls for a show of apparent disloyalty to the Defense Department or the White House. Consider the example of Admiral Arleigh Burke, the outgoing chief of naval operations. The fact that Burke was a key figure in the so-called Admirals' Revolt against the Truman administration, at the time of the B-36 controversy, made him a popular choice for the top job in his own service.

McNamara is still baffled when he hears that a two-star Air Force general, or a Navy vice-admiral, has slipped secret documents to a friendly reporter for use against the Army. His belief that this situation can be corrected by writing new directives for the armed services seems to most Pentagon old-timers a touching piece of naïveté. But he is learning fast that there will be leaks so long as the services must compete for appropriations on Capitol Hill.

If Congress can ever be persuaded to vote a lump-sum appropriation for the Secretary of Defense, who in turn would apportion it among the services according to his own best judgment, then McNamara's dream of a single defense plan for the country will come true. But until that day he can expect more bafflement and frustration at budget time.

McNamara, a lean, athletic six-footer who wears himself out on vacations by climbing mountains or skiing with ferocious dedication, brings to the Pentagon a first-class brain and a highly developed Presbyterian conscience. In the expense-account society he formerly inhabited, he was admired by some for his stern integrity and dismissed by many others as an oddball. On family trips, for example, he stubbornly refused all executive-suite perquisites such as the use of company cars. He tried to rent Fords at his own expense whenever possible. But he spent one happy European vacation cruising around in an Opel, built by General Motors. When he returned to Dearborn, McNamara reported that the Opel was a pretty good car and remembered to blister his good friend Tom Lilley of Ford International because he had found it impossible to rent a Ford product. When he traveled on business, Mrs. McNamara stayed home.

It is part of his creed that wealth can be a good thing, if properly used, but too much wealth is likely to corrupt most men, including his own children. When he quit Ford to become secretary of defense at $25,000 a year, McNamara gave up a salary of $175,000 plus bonus arrangements that would have pushed his personal earnings to almost $500,000 a year. His 1959 bonus as a Ford vice president amounted to $285,000.

According to McNamara's own rough estimate, he will forego profits of some $3 million over the next three or four years in anticipated earnings from the 24,250 Ford shares he was forced to sell and options he forfeited on 30,000 additional shares. But it was not the monetary loss that bothered him.

"I had not lived up to my income, or even a third of it, in Detroit," he says. "I didn't think it was healthy. As a boy my home was in Oakland but I went to school in Piedmont, where the rich kids lived. Those children didn't have anything I wanted my children to have."

Bob McNamara was born in San Francisco on June 9, 1916. He was a frail, spindly boy who loved to read and was quick with figures. His father, the sales manager of a wholesale shoe company, was twenty-five years older than his mother. Both parents doted on their firstborn and only son. A daughter, Margaret, was born three years later. The family lost most of its savings in the great crash of 1929, when Bob was thirteen. After that, though the McNamaras were never poor, they lived in modest circumstances.

He entered the University of California at Berkeley in 1933. It was the age of Franklin D. Roosevelt, of mass unemployment, soup kitchens, and bitter warfare between labor and management. At the end of his freshman year young McNamara haunted the San Francisco water front looking for a summer job. But the port was paralyzed by a maritime strike. One day he rushed home, bursting with pride. He had signed on a ship and couldn't wait to pack his gear. So single-minded was his search that the boy scarcely realized he had been hired as a strikebreaker. His father soon put a stop to that adventure. Although he was really "quite conservative," Robert James McNamara ruled that no son of his would ship out as a strikebreaker. It just wasn't the decent thing to do.

The following summer, with the long strike settled, young Bob fulfilled his seagoing ambition. Now a junior, who was doing his best to live down a newly-acquired Phi Beta Kappa key, he frequented the rough, tough hiring halls along the Embarcadero until he wangled a berth. He shipped out that summer as a probationary member of Harry Lundberg's Seafarers International Union of the Pacific. Twenty-five years later he was to cherish a copy of the union paper announcing that Brother McNamara, late of San Francisco, had made good in the East as a member of President Kennedy's Cabinet.

At Berkeley, in the class of 1937, Bob McNamara met Margaret Craig, a fellow student. They enjoyed being together and kept in touch by letter after Bob moved on to Boston, where he spent two years at the Harvard Graduate School of Business Administration. Although he won a $500 scholarship at the end of his first year, he continued working summers, once with an accounting firm and another time as a boys' camp counselor.

Returning to California in 1939, with a Master of Business Administration degree, he went to work for the accounting firm of Price, Waterhouse and Company. Within a year the Harvard Business School offered him an instructor's job. But there was one item of personal business to be settled first. Margaret Craig was in the East, traveling with her mother, at the time. Bob tracked her down in the Baltimore Y.W.C.A., proposed marriage by telephone, and was promptly accepted. They left California together the day of their marriage in August 1940. For the next three years McNamara taught at Harvard.

"He was a tough teacher," one former student recalls. "They use the case method at the Business School and Bob's mind was always one step ahead of anyone else's. He threw questions at you faster than you could hope to answer. He demanded performance and he got it."

It was at Harvard that McNamara first met a brilliant, handpicked group of Army Air Force officers whose guiding spirit was Colonel Thornton. "Tex" Thornton, all of twenty-nine years old, had persuaded Robert A. Lovett, then Assistant Secretary of War, that the Army Air Force needed a better management system to schedule the flow of men and equipment into the training pipeline and out to the war theaters. With a group of officers skilled in the techniques of statistical control, then a highly esoteric discipline, it would be possible to estimate a year in advance, for example, just how many tail gunners should be pushed into the training pipeline, after making due allowance for a certain percentage of washouts and casualties, so that the Air Force would have enough trained men for each combat command.

Harvard took on the assignment of organizing such a course and McNamara was one of the faculty members assigned to initiate the Air Force officers into the mysteries of "stat control." The War Department soon sent him to England as a civilian consultant to establish a new system in the European Theater. On his return, McNamara was commissioned an Army Air Force captain. He went to work on the B-29 program, winding up in the China-Burma-India Theater.

At the end of the war Colonel Thornton conceived the idea of keeping his first team together by offering its combined skill and experience in a single package to companies needing managerial talent. McNamara, the man he wanted as his own deputy, was recovering from a mild case of polio at Wright-Patterson Field in Ohio. A handsome prospectus was worked up and sent around to some twenty companies; about ten replied. George E. Moore, one of the original "stat control" officers and now a Washington businessman, happened to visit Detroit on home leave and heard something about "Young Henry" Ford's problems in taking command of the ailing company from his grandfather.

He and Thornton framed a telegram to young Ford, outlining the concept they had in mind. Lovett was their prime character reference. To their amazement, Ford replied in a matter of hours, showing definite interest in the unorthodox proposal. "I remember getting a long telegram," Henry Ford recalls. "I turned it over to a fellow named George Colton, who was then our office manager. We knew we had to rebuild and we were in the market for talent all right. But I wasn't sure exactly what these fellows had to offer, so we asked them to come in and talk about it. Colton saw them first and after a few minutes he rushed into my office. 'These guys are too hot for me to handle,' he said. So I saw them myself."

The Ford Motor Company, long the pace setter of the industry, was in worse trouble than any outsider realized. Its management was wholly discredited. Old Henry Ford had no use for engineering or styling departments, least of all for slide-rule planners. From his office in the garage of the Ford Administration Building at Dearborn Harry Bennett functioned as the old man's executive arm. It was not many years since Bennett's hired sluggers had taken care of labor-relations problems by a show of brute force. Because the company was family-owned its steady losses from 1928 to 1940 had been kept secret. Even during the war, when Ford built bombers at Willow Run on a cost-plus basis, it barely showed a profit.

After outlining his plan to "young Henry," Colonel Thornton inquired how many Air Force men the company could use and how much it would pay. Ford replied, "That's up to you."

Thornton first satisfied himself that McNamara, then a twenty-nine-year-old lieutenant colonel, wanted to be part of the package. Their final decision was to offer Ford ten men at salaries ranging from $9,000 to $14,000 a year. As the senior officer, Thornton got the top salary. McNamara, the second in command, was put down for $12,000. Moore, only twenty-five at the time, fell into the $9,000 category.

It was the wildest bargain Ford ever made. When McNamara resigned to join the Administration, he left behind in key positions five of the original group. James O. Wright was group vice president; Ben D. Mills, vice president and general manager of the Mercury-Comet-Lincoln division; Arjay R. Miller, vice president, finance; J. Edward Lundy, treasurer; and Charles E. Bosworth, director of purchasing. Thornton and Moore had moved on earlier, along with W. R. Anderson, who operates a van and storage business on the West Coast, and F. C. (Jack) Reith, president of the Avco Manufacturing Corporation's Crosley division at the time of his death.

For about three months the recruits moved from Ford department to department, asking questions about the whys and wherefores of the business. They were received without much warmth by the old-school executives. The "Quiz Kids" was what the old-timers called them. It was not meant to be a compliment.

Ford had brought in Ernest R. Breech, a former General Motors and Bendix executive, to take charge of the rebuilding operation. Breech in 1949 persuaded Theodore O. Yntema, a University of Chicago professor, to join the company as vice president, finance. The Quiz Kids dispersed into various divisions of the Ford industrial empire, to be heard from later. They saw in the Yntema appointment clear proof that the new management team was not afraid of brains.

McNamara, assigned to the newly-created planning and financial-analysis office, was among the first to make his presence felt. By 1949 he was named controller of the Ford company. Six years later he moved into the top echelon as vice-president and general manager of the division that builds Ford cars and trucks.

He did not pretend to know all the answers but he seemed to have more of them at his fingertips than anyone else. Henry Ford remarked one day: "The things that most men have to turn to books and reports for Bob is carrying around right in his head."

In 1957 McNamara moved up to the board of directors as group vice-president in charge of all the car and truck divisions. His Ford division colleagues presented him not with the conventional silver tray or cigarette box but a four-volume set of Toynbee's *An Outline of History*. This was a tribute to his stubborn eggheadedness, a quality no longer in short supply among Ford executives thanks to the rise of men such as Yntema and McNamara.

In Detroit, McNamara developed a reputation for shyness, perhaps because he did not socialize with other industry leaders. He is no backslapper, no party-hopper, not at all the country-club type. But any man who has spent an evening kicking ideas around with Bob McNamara must challenge the widespread notion that he is icicle-cold, self-righteous or aloof. He is certainly a man of deep inner reserve who felt he did not belong in Bloomfield Hills or Grosse Pointe, the handsome Detroit suburbs where most top-drawer automobile industry people make their homes. Besides, in the words of an admiring Ford colleague, "it didn't satisfy his appetite to meet the same people at night that he worked with all day."

McNamara preferred Ann Arbor, where he bought a five-bed-room English Tudor house not far from the University of Michigan campus, and spent ninety minutes a day driving thirty-eight miles each way to Ford headquarters at Dearborn. The move to Ann Arbor was quite deliberate. He wanted to live away from the closed world of the automobile industry, to shield his children from the pressures of the status race. Above all, McNamara was at home in the college-town atmosphere. He befriended members of the Michigan faculty, attended concerts, read strenuously, and seized every opportunity to inform himself about problems most auto-mobile people have no time for—the quality of teaching in the public schools, what makes one painting a great work of art while another is merely a competent representation, the meaning of existentialism, or the rights and wrongs of recognizing Communist China.

A close friend submits this thumbnail description of McNamara at home in Ann Arbor:

"Even off the job, Bob is not quite the average slob. His idea of getting away from the job is just about as intensive as the job itself. He consistently reads heavy stuff, probing in new directions. I've never seen him pick up a detective story just for relaxation. He is not a hermit, by any means. In Ann Arbor he enjoyed going out to dinner with congenial people. But his mind kept working and there was no particular limit to the range of his interests. For ex-ample, he developed quite a strong interest in interracial housing a few years back, and then in fine arts. If he ran into a real expert at a party, he would drag the guy off into a corner and ply him with questions. On a business trip to London not long ago he flew by way of Rome, if you please, to look at some paintings. It meant staying up all night to reach London in time with that long detour. But he thought that was just fine—and brought home some inter-esting modern paintings.

"You have the feeling Bob is still consciously broadening him-self, not to impress other people but because something inside keeps driving him to learn more about, well, almost any subject."

A good example of McNamara's rage for self-education was the now-famous study group he organized in Ann Arbor. For three or four years it met once a month to hear a report on a new book and discuss it. Passive listening was not encouraged. All of the members—husbands and wives—were required to read the book choice for that month and come prepared to argue its merits.

McNamara and Tom Lilley were the only automobile industry members. The regular membership included Staebler—and a neurologist, a historian, an expert on natural resources, and a fine-arts teacher from the university. They plowed through such books as John Kenneth Galbraith's *The Affluent Society;* Jacques Barzun's *The House of Intellect; Impatient Giant,* a report on Communist China by the Canadian correspondent, Gerald Clark; William Barrett's *Irrational Man,* a study of existentialism, and painter Ben Shahn's *The Shape of Content.*

McNamara enjoyed the Barzun book but was annoyed by what he took to be the author's pedantic, cocksure manner. The Barrett book, in his view, was a thoroughly rational treatment of the irrational, but he could not buy the strange merchandise of existential philosophy. As for *The American Voter,* a monumental study of American behavior at the polls also on the reading list, McNamara considered it an elucidation of the obvious.

He discovered politics a few years ago, persuaded himself it was important and, with characteristic intensity, plunged into a far-ranging study of public issues. Although in past elections he had voted Republican more often than not, McNamara actively supported Michigan Democrat Philip A. Hart for the Senate in 1958 because he felt Hart was better qualified than the Republican incumbent, Charles E. Potter.

Before leaving California twenty years ago he had registered as a Republican. But he voted for Franklin D. Roosevelt against Wendell Willkie in 1940.

A straw poll of the Harvard Business School faculty that year showed a 98 to 2 landslide for Willkie. McNamara wondered who the other maverick might be. After some weeks the fellow heretic identified himself as Eugene Zuckert, assistant dean of the Business School. Today Zuckert is Secretary of the Air Force under McNamara.

As a political animal McNamara defies classification. In 1960 he made four campaign contributions. Three of the candidates he supported were liberal Republicans—Senators Clifford Case of New Jersey and John Sherman Cooper of Kentucky, and Paul Bagwell, the unsuccessful Republican candidate for governor of Michigan. The fourth was a Democrat, John F. Kennedy.

Asked to state his position, McNamara says: "The Republicans think I'm a Democrat and the Democrats think I'm a Republican, and I don't get the benefits of either."

But he is seldom at a loss for solid reasons to explain his political behavior. A day or two after he was elected president of Ford he was invited to call on Michigan's new governor, John B. Swainson. McNamara wasted no time on the little courtesies appropriate to such occasions. He told Swainson that his own ballot had been marked for Bagwell. The reasons? Because Swainson had refused to declare himself on a new tax program, a position that McNamara regarded as "immoral," and because the Governor-elect did not endorse the ballot proposition to call a state constitutional convention until organized labor shifted its position on the issue.

Swainson grinned and said in his own defense: "Well, you have to credit me with the ability to be elected." McNamara thought that was "a damn poor answer" and said as much to the Governor.

His own immersion in public affairs started with the formation of Citizens for Michigan, a bipartisan organization headed by George Romney, president of American Motors. The state was on the edge of bankruptcy thanks to a perennial deadlock on tax legislation between the Republican State Senate and the Democratic governor, G. Mennen Williams. "I was troubled by the terrible polarization between big business and big labor," McNamara recalls. "There was a real need for new ideas. So I joined."

At Ford he had taken no part in collective bargaining with Reuther's Auto Workers' Union. In fact, he had little or no personal contact with labor people until he sat side by side with Jack Conway at meetings of the Citizens for Michigan. The two found themselves taking a similar analytical view of state problems. They served together on Romney's tax committee and developed a strong mutual respect, verging on admiration. Conway's recollection is that they never talked collective bargaining or politics outside of

Michigan. But they touched on every other topic in range. "This man has a way of boring in on a problem," Conway said. "He is able to talk sense on almost any subject. One night at dinner, for example, we spent a solid hour comparing European technology with our own. We talked of comparative hours of work, labor costs, taxes, and volume. The interesting thing was that there were few points of difference between his analysis and mine."

It is not easy to pinpoint McNamara's specific contribution to the postwar success of Ford. In any enterprise of Ford's size the decisions that count are group decisions. Henry Ford himself and lesser company executives agree that it was McNamara who developed the facts and pressed hard to bring out a four-seater Thunderbird against considerable opposition. The original two-seater model, an American classic, had been successful beyond Ford's fondest calculations. Some Dearborn purists wanted to leave well enough alone, fearful that any radical change would ruin the Thunderbird. McNamara argued that while two-seaters were just fine for bachelors and childless couples, his studies showed a four-seater model would do even better. Of course the sales figures proved him right.

He also is credited with a major contribution to the success of Ford's best-selling compact car, the Falcon. "He didn't originate the idea," Henry Ford says, "but he handled the project from the time it was just a sheet of paper. McNamara set the price level and the specifications. All the other divisions or departments reported to him. He also controlled the total investment in the Falcon project. It was a tough job because he had to work with people who were not under his jurisdiction. But he did it."

His final victory, before leaving Ford, was the new twelve-month or 12,000-mile warranty policy, which the rest of the industry adopted in a matter of hours. This was a project close to McNamara's heart. He worked up a set of figures to prove that the added cost to the company would be partially offset by strengthened customer loyalty. Some Ford executives were, and still are, dubious. The warranty idea appealed to McNamara's conscience; it made for higher quality and better value to the customer. "He is the kind of chap who needs to justify what he does in terms of responsibility to the public," one associate explained.

The qualities that set McNamara apart from other successful executives can be summed up in a clumsy way as all-around out-standingness. Five men who know him well were asked the same question: What's so special about Bob McNamara?

"The fellow can digest more relevant information more quickly and more thoroughly than anyone I know," said one long-time associate. "He always gets the point the first time. The other big difference is his integrity."

Henry Ford added: "You can't say it's any one quality. It's the combination: a keen, analytical mind that gets rid of all the fluff for one thing. He was always ahead of the others in analyzing facts and figures."

A trade-union official: "Hell, he's an intelligent man."

Staebler: "His mind is like a beautiful piece of machinery."

Arjay Miller: "The way he fastens on the heart of the matter and eliminates the irrelevant. When he evaluated a problem it was in terms of its total impact on the company and the community. Al-ways there was responsibility. I've also heard him admit that he was wrong on occasion."

McNamara has always been a great setter of deadlines, for him-self and others. Punctual to the point of fetishism, he boasted to friends that Mrs. McNamara, on her first visit to Washington, had managed to rent a furnished house and settle their younger chil-dren, Kathleen, sixteen, and Robert Craig, ten, at Sidwell Friends School in a single day. Their elder daughter Margaret, nineteen, is at Stanford University.

There is something misleading about the Defense Secretary's scrubbed features, rimless spectacles, and Tom Dewey haircut. They suggest small-town virtue and just a touch of righteousness. And, in truth, he is not a man to crack jokes at Cabinet meetings. The twelve-hour day he puts in at the Pentagon wears out two shifts of lady Marine receptionists. Mrs. McNamara, fearing for her husband's health, recently instructed his secretary to schedule no more evening appointments except in genuine emergency situa-tions. A close friend confessed: "I'm worried about Bob; the guy is so damned dedicated he never knows when to quit. He needs to be reminded that every man has his breaking point."

At the end of the day in his office, or at home on Kalorama Circle, however, the workaday stiffness vanishes. A Pentagon colleague, seeing the unbuttoned McNamara for the first time, reported with awe that the boss had engaged him in a half-hour talk about the novels of C. P. Snow, taking the time out to make a left-handed notation of one Snow title he had missed. Finally there is the testimony of a thirteen-year-old Ann Arbor schoolboy, who knew McNamara as a family friend and a good neighbor. In an impromptu theme on "the most unforgettable person" he had ever met, the youngster wrote:

"I shall call him Mack Robert. He is an admirable man, probably the most industrious man in the business world. . . . You would probably expect this man to be a stone-cold business executive with his only love that of sheer business competition. Well, that is exactly what Mack Robert is not.

"For a man with this position he is kind and loving to everybody he is intimately associated with. Although he works long hours and takes business very seriously, he considers his family above all else. Even when his day at the office has been very hard he always comes home to his house (sic) with a good spirit and no hard or harsh words for anybody."

8.

BROTHER ON THE SPOT

Robert Kennedy

By HUGH SIDEY

SNOW BANKED THE CURBS OF WASHINGTON'S STREETS IN MID-December of 1960 as Robert Francis Kennedy walked through the chill air toward the Justice Department on Pennsylvania Avenue. His head was down, as is his habit when he is thinking. He wore no hat. Around his eyes were lines of weariness etched by months of unceasing work.

On this morning he was contemplating a personal problem, perhaps as important as any he had ever faced. As the brother and closest confidant of the President-elect of the United States he was trying to decide if he should accept appointment as attorney general in the new Cabinet of John Kennedy's administration.

The day after the election Jack had come to Bobby and in one of those brief, mumbling conversations that only these two brothers can understand had suggested that perhaps Bobby should take over the Justice Department. Bobby had been emphatic in his rejection of the idea. He said he planned to get completely out of government.

In the following weeks, as he struggled to staff the New Frontier with the type of men Jack Kennedy wanted, Bobby changed his mind. He conceded that he would work for his brother—but not on the Cabinet level. Very little was said between the two men. There was no question that the President-elect wanted his brother as Attorney General. But he, too, knew the dangers of public criticism of the Kennedy family. "That's the most sensitive kind of criticism you can get," explained Jack. Then he added: "But he's the best man I can get for the job."

In his long deliberation Bobby Kennedy considered taking a sub-Cabinet post in the Defense or State Departments. "I've been chasing bad guys all my life," he confided to a friend. "I'd like a change." It wasn't that easy. John Kennedy was having difficulty finding the type of men he wanted. It also became starkly clear that the President-elect intended to rely on the judgment of his brother. Thus to have a subordinate officer in a key department closer to the President than the top man presented an intolerable situation for a new Cabinet officer. Bobby Kennedy realized this.

As Christmas approached, the pressures mounted for him to become Attorney General. The patriarch of the Kennedy clan, Joe Kennedy, fretted up in New York. "I don't know what's wrong with him. Jack needs all the good men he can get around him down there. There's none better than Bobby. You know for six years he hasn't told me what he wants to do."

Besides the problems of the New Frontier, Bobby Kennedy was wrestling with career problems of his own. If he wanted to carve out a political life for himself, he would have to start soon. Although still a young man, he was rather old to launch a search for elective office. Should he run for governor of Massachusetts in two years? His brother had confided that he thought Bobby could win easily. The soon-to-be-vacated Senate seat of Jack's was Bobby's if he wanted it. ("I won't take that," snapped Bobby. "The only way I'll go to the Senate is run for it.") He had toyed with the idea of buying a newspaper. Government service appealed to him more, however. Joe Kennedy, now seventy-two, soon would need someone to take over the huge business and financial machinery of the family. Bobby, always described as the son most like the father, was suggested for this duty. Yet Bobby didn't relish a task he regarded as merely the making of money.

Jack Kennedy needed Bobby's decision that week. The President-elect wanted to complete his cabinet and move on in building his administration. Bobby went unnoticed through the massive doorway of the Justice Department and walked quietly to the office of J. Edgar Hoover, director of the Federal Bureau of Investigation. From Hoover he wanted advice. Was there still a great deal of work to be done at the Justice Department in combating crime? Could he, Bobby Kennedy, do any good? Hoover was enthusiastic about the possibilities in a reinvigorated war on crime under the young man who sat in front of him. But Bobby still had not edged nearer a decision as he left the Justice Department and headed for Capitol Hill. In the quiet of the Supreme Court Building he lunched with an old friend, Justice William O. Douglas. From New Deal days Justice Douglas had been friends with the Kennedy family. He and Bobby had been early travelers in Russia when restrictions were lifted. For more than an hour Bobby plied the craggy Douglas with questions and listened to his advice.

All afternoon he brooded. He took half an hour out and went back to the Justice Department for a talk with retiring Attorney General Bill Rogers. Toward evening he began to lean toward his earlier conclusion that he should not accept the appointment. Newspapers were criticizing the suggestion. Republicans, recalling Milton Eisenhower's refusal to take a full-time job in Washington with his brother, were scornful of the idea. Bobby phoned Jack at his Georgetown home that night and said he did not think he would take the appointment. The President-elect, however, did not accept this answer.

"Let's talk it over at breakfast tomorrow," he suggested.

Bobby agreed. Next morning he made his way to 3307 N Street. Jack was more insistent now. He needed and wanted Bobby; he felt that the criticism, already voiced in many papers, had about run out. There would be a flurry of it at the announcement, but then it would die. ("I must say," said Bobby later, "Jack had the guts of a burglar.") This time Bobby decided for sure—he would take the appointment as Attorney General.

The decision seemed to ease things for him. That afternoon the old Kennedy sense of humor returned with all its flavor. As he finished a phone conversation with the President-elect, he added one last thought. "On my announcement," he said, "why

don't you paraphrase another prominent American, Dwight Eisenhower. You can say: 'I know he's my brother, but I need him.' "
The two Kennedy boys let loose dry chuckles of delight. Then Robert Kennedy began preparing for another new job.

Many were skeptical over the thirty-five-year-old Bobby's legal experience and ability. He had never been in private law practice and all his government career had been in investigative work, first on Senator Joe McCarthy's Investigations Subcommittee, later on Senator John McClellan's Rackets Committee. A man of imposing legal stature was needed, it was suggested, not someone appointed mainly because he was the President's brother.

The Justice Department is essentially the nation's lawyer. It pursues criminals, keeps them in prison, enforces civil rights, fights price fixing, handles suits arising over government property, helps regulate the flow of immigrants into the country, settles water disputes, and a thousand other things.

"There is nothing that you could do to fully prepare yourself for being Attorney General," Bobby argued back. The President agreed. The most important things needed in the job were sound judgment, integrity, willingness to work, and ability to learn. "Bobby's got all that," declared the new Chief Executive.

Technical legal talent abounded in the Justice Department, friends of Bobby pointed out. What it needed was leadership. Bobby felt that the Justice Department, like all government departments, had lost initiative, that it reacted to crisis instead of trying to prevent it. The President took some of the heat off the appointment with his wit. Making his first social outing after taking office with an appearance at Washington's Alfalfa Club, he cracked: "What's wrong with a fellow getting a little legal training before he goes into the practice of law?"

Whatever his preparations for the job, Bobby started fast, as he always does. He launched a study of juvenile delinquency and concluded that for the 5,000 juveniles in federal institutions special counseling and adjustment centers were needed to prepare them for return to normal life. He asked Congress for $618,000 to get this going. It was a pilot project, designed to show what could be done. One weekend he quietly left Washington and with his friend David Hackett flew to New York. There in shirt sleeves he walked through New York's Harlem seeing for himself the living conditions, talking with members of two youth gangs.

From his Rackets Committee days Bobby had learned that dishonest attorneys and businessmen can be as sinister as any hoodlum. Dishonest management breeds corrupt labor, he believes. He was thus appalled at the electrical companies' price-fixing scandal uncovered by his predecessors at the Justice Department. He promised war on price fixing in virtually every major community across the nation. Bobby also sent off to Congress a legislative package to fight organized crime that would extend the jurisdiction of the FBI when the states ask for help from the federal agency.

He fully expects civil rights to be his most inflammatory issue. There will be a shower of voting rights cases in time, Bobby says. And of course there will continue to be trouble over school integration with which he must grapple. He is not approaching civil rights gingerly or timidly. Already his hand has been felt in New Orleans.

On the telephone he told Louisiana's Attorney General Jack P. F. Gremillion that his department would use every weapon at hand to see that the courts were obeyed and New Orleans schools continued to be integrated. At the same time he offered to listen to Gremillion, who flew to Washington. When the Louisiana Legislature failed to advance needed money for New Orleans school salaries, Bobby didn't budge. He hinted that in addition to legal war against Governor Jimmy Davis and the legislature there would be political reprisals against the state. Suddenly Davis found money in a special fund to set aside for the teachers.

Yet these are just the opening skirmishes in a long war. The question remains, can Bobby Kennedy win the long and arduous battles where patience and intelligence as well as administrative skill and guts are needed?

Beyond his legal duties in the federal government lies perhaps an even more important role. That is confidant to the President who faces some of the most critical hours in history. Few will be closer than Bobby Kennedy.

The pattern already is forming. When Democrats sought to liberalize the House Rules Committee so that the Kennedy program would stand more of a chance in Congress, Bobby moved in and organized the assault on Capitol Hill. As the White House organization shakes down, Bobby will be doing fewer of these tasks personally. But his advice always will be sought. There are phone conversations almost daily between the brothers about the entire range of federal problems. Although not an expert in foreign affairs, Bobby is kept informed up to the minute by the President. The broad views of national purpose and direction are talked over thoroughly by the two when Bobby goes to dinner quietly at the White House. Both men have their eyes warily cocked on the 1964 election and no voice will outweigh Bobby's in these matters.

If there is one consistent theme in the life of Robert Kennedy, it is the fact that always he seems to have been working for someone else, that he has lived in a shadow. He has been distinguished in his own right, for certain, but others—particularly Jack—have gained as much from his inexhaustible energy. So it is now.

Bobby Kennedy, like all the Kennedy children except the youngest boy Edward (Teddy), was born in a bedroom in a homely, two-story house in Brookline, Massachusetts. It was November 20, 1925, a rather hectic but plentiful period in Joe Kennedy's life in terms of both money and children—Bobby was the seventh of nine.

Before Bobby really could remember much of anything the family moved to Riverdale, New York, while Joe went in quest of his millions and Joe, Jr., the eldest of the brood, set the house on fire with his chemistry set. The fire—not the millions—is one of Bobby's very early memories.

His schooling was so transitory that Bobby himself has trouble remembering the chronology of all the schools he attended. "I went to about twelve schools, at least," he exaggerates, painfully trying to sort them out. He began in Riverdale's public schools but before long he had shifted through a couple of private schools and the family had moved to Bronxville and he was in the third grade of the Bronxville public schools. In a few years he found himself in Gibbs School in London and before he got to Harvard he had toured the classrooms of St. Paul's (Concord, New Hampshire), Portsmouth (New Hampshire), Priory and Milton (Massachusetts) Academy.

Bobby's greatest talent from the early days was not studying. Even then his fierce combativeness was evident. He liked football, baseball, swimming, tennis, and sailing ("just about anything outdoors," he says). All his energy was not channeled into such healthy pastimes. Out in the Bronxville tool shed he pulled over an old radiator and it hit his foot, breaking his second toe. His fear of what his family would say about such a deed was more troublesome than the pain from the smashed toe. For almost half an hour he bore his anguish, refusing to remove his shoe. When he did, the blood was spotted and Bobby was rushed to the doctor.

His mischievous sister Eunice once rolled up the chocolate frosting from a cake and threw it at Bobby at the dinner table. He responded with spirit and chased Eunice through the Bronxville house until he felt he had her cornered. She was standing in front of a table. Bobby lowered his head and charged like a bull. Eunice gracefully stepped aside and Bobby hit the table, blood poured down over his face from a gaping wound, and once more he was whisked to the doctor.

Bobby became somewhat of a naturalist during these early years. He always seemed to have an animal around the house and he still does today. In order to supplement his ten-cent weekly allowance Bobby decided to raise white rabbits for sale ("just plain white rabbits, the kind that have a lot of babies"). He set up a hutch in the tool shed and dutifully tended his wards. They indeed did multiply as advertised, and before long Bobby was doing a good neighborhood business in white rabbits. His mother, the patient and encouraging Rose Kennedy, opened a savings account for him in Hyannis, Massachusetts, the location of their summer home. The account still is in force and now has a grand total of $42.00.

A little later Joe, Jr., presented Bobby with a pig he had won. The younger brother immediately named it "Porky" and set up housekeeping for it in the tool shed along with the rabbits. Porky became a good pet. Neighbors of the Bronxville era can remember the familiar sight of Bobby Kennedy aboard his bicycle pedaling proudly down the family drive with Porky trotting beside.

Bobby tried his hand at commerce while his father was conquering Wall Street. He became a salesman for the *Saturday Evening Post* and the *Ladies' Home Journal.* He is reluctant to tell all the details of the enterprise but those who remember it say it was a three-part drama. "When he started," recalls his wife Ethel, "there was Bobby delivering his magazines from his bicycle with Porky following behind. The next thing the neighbors saw was Bobby and his magazines in the back seat of the family Rolls-Royce and Dave, the chauffeur, driving him around to make sales. No more bike and no more Porky. And finally Dave was all by himself with the magazines and you could barely get into Bobby's room, there were so many unsold magazines stacked around."

When he was ten Bobby left for England with his family. His father had been appointed Ambassador to the Court of St. James by President Franklin Roosevelt. As best he could, Bobby continued the activities that interested him in this country. He joined the English Boy Scouts after they allowed him to change the oath so that he did not have to swear allegiance to the King. He played cricket and soccer at Gibbs and even joined the juvenile social whirl, attending kids' parties with Princesses Margaret Rose and Elizabeth. (He hasn't seen them since.)

Although he was extremely young, he was already being edged into the adult world, as was the habit of the stern father for his entire family. In those years the great war clouds were looming just across the English Channel. The Kennedys toured the Continent. Bobby saw all the European nations on the eve of conflict. He still has vivid recollections of the awesome scenes in Germany as the Nazis paraded and cried out their "Heil, Hitlers!"

There was constant yard fighting with British school companions. The tussles always seemed to be touched off over discussions of which country, the United States or England, was better and

which of the two really had won World War I. He won his share
of the scraps but lost some.

His pursuit of sports and the outdoor life continued. He was not
a reader, as was his older brother Jack. He did manage to get
fair marks in school but rarely lifted them above that. When war
came Joe Kennedy sent his family back to this country. And
Bobby went off to school. At Milton he began to emerge. He not
only made the football team as quarterback but also discovered
books. Slowly at first, but with increasing zest, he pursued history and biography, in much the same pattern as Jack, though
certainly with not the ease and speed of the elder brother. In
fact, just about everything Bobby did seemed to come harder than
it had for his two older brothers. "It was much tougher in school
for him than the others—socially, in football, with studies," says
a friend. "But he made up for it with hard work."

In many ways he was different from the other students. "He
didn't drink or smoke," recalls classmate David Hackett. "He did
other things for a good time." (At age twenty-one Bobby collected $2,000 from his father because he had neither smoked nor
drank. Jack sipped beer in college and lost out.) Bobby Kennedy
tried almost everything. "He sang in the glee club although he
couldn't sing," says Hackett. He played tennis, too. When he left
Milton in 1943 he was as popular as any student although still,
as one classmate says: "He was no good on small talk. He was no
good on social amenities. He was no great lover."

Like all the Kennedy clan the days of the family gatherings at
Hyannis Port meant more to Bobby than virtually anything else in
his life. There had always been the gentle but insistent guidance
from Rose Kennedy. From the early years she read to the children,
made sure they studied their catechism every Friday, insisted that
they constantly try to improve themselves. She would not allow
small talk at the table, even when her brood were tiny. She took
special care to make sure they were aware of their historical
heritage by taking them to national shrines. At Hyannis Port there
was the feel of Father Joe's hand. During much of Bobby's life
Joe had been busy with the stock market or off in Hollywood
making more millions in the movie industry. But his presence was

felt. He encouraged the fierce competitive spirit. Bobby can recall he and Jack racing their sailboat on Nantucket Sound and Joe Kennedy splashing along beside them in his motor cruiser watching every move they made so he could offer advice. He wasn't happy if the boys lost. Joe would stand out in the yard and throw the baseball with his sons, or watch them closely as they played touch football.

In Joe's long absences the spirit was carried on by Joe, Jr. Although Bobby was closer in age and companionship to his younger brother Teddy, Joe, Jr., was a great force. He watched over the younger ones. He taught Bobby to swim, sail, and play football with the same drive to win that the father had imparted in him.

The war was on when Bobby came out of Milton. He had been wooed by Joe, Jr., a naval aviator, and he signed up in the V-5 naval-aviation program. He was shipped to Bates College in Maine for eight months. As the tide of war began to turn he was transferred from V-5 to V-12, the program for regular naval officer training. He was sent to Harvard and put in the naval R.O.T.C. and then he could stand it no longer. He arranged to see an old family friend, Secretary of the Navy James Forrestal, and from him he got an assignment at sea. It was on the newly-commissioned destroyer *Joseph P. Kennedy, Jr.,* named after his older brother who had been killed on a daring volunteer bombing mission.

His sea duty was hardly what he sought, either. For four months Seaman Second Class Robert Kennedy scraped paint in the Caribbean and for two months he watched the blip go around in the ship's radar shack. He never saw an enemy. It was hardly a record to match his other two brothers', one who died as a hero, the other who won the Navy and Marine Corps medal for a fifteen-hour struggle in the water rescuing crew members after his PT-boat was sliced in two by a Japanese destroyer.

Out of the Navy in 1946, Bobby got his first taste of politics. Jack was running for Congress from Boston's 11th District. He pressed Bobby into service. It was the younger Kennedy's task to get votes in East Cambridge, an extremely poor section. There were no instructions, no plans, no titles. "I went from house to house ringing doorbells," he says. "I don't remember what I said to them. I guess I just asked them to vote for my brother." Enough of them followed his advice, and Jack won the Democratic primary, which was tantamount to winning the election.

After a two-month swing through Latin America with K. LeMoyne Billings, one of Jack's Choate roommates, Bobby was back and ready to get a Harvard education. His first love, however, was football. "He had no right to be on the varsity team," says Ken O'Donnell who became a teammate and close friend. "It was just after the war and all the men were back from the service. We had eight ends who were bigger, faster, and had been high-school stars."

Yet Bobby beat most of them and made a place on the team. "He wasn't fast, he wasn't shifty," continues O'Donnell. "He had another quality." That quality was determination. It was in all his five feet, ten inches and 165 pounds. At first Bobby couldn't catch passes very well. He asked O'Donnell to throw the ball for him so he could practice. He would come an hour ahead of the rest of the team and stay an hour longer than anyone. "He was a quick, tough guy who worked five times as hard as anybody," says O'Donnell. "He'd come in from his end like a wild Indian. If you were blocking Bobby, you'd knock him down, but he'd be up again going after the play. He never let up."

At one practice session Bobby was having trouble blocking his man. A tackle opposing him kept slipping through the line. Over and over the team ran the play as Coach Dick Harlow grew more irritated with Bobby. Suddenly, almost in tears with anger, Bobby collapsed. They took him off the field and found he had a broken leg.

His Harvard academic achievements were average. "I didn't go to class very much to tell you the truth," he admitted years later. "I used to talk and argue a lot, mostly about sports and politics." But the Kennedy fire that came out on the playing field also showed itself in other matters. While attending a Catholic seminar with a friend, he heard a cleric declare that all non-Catholics were going to go to hell. He was incensed, and even though he was a guest he disagreed openly with the man. Bobby's friend was horrified, suggested that the next day he go around and apologize. He refused, stoutly insisted that no Catholic had a right to teach this. (The cleric was later excommunicated for this teaching.)

The Kennedy social life had not improved much over his Milton days. He was not a recluse but he didn't care for the frantic round of parties and dates that a student of his wealth could have had for the asking. He was a member of Hasty Pudding, the Spee Club, and the Varsity Club, where he spent most of his time. Once he took the entire football team with him to the exclusive Spee Club, shocking the members so much that he was threatened with expulsion, whereupon he suggested where the club could go. He was not expelled.

On another occasion he called up a Boston girl friend and asked her if he could bring some teammates along with him to her coming-out party. She agreed, but the affair proved to be such a strain for all involved, "we never went again," he says. "It wasn't our cup of tea."

His attitude toward the social circuit remains the same today: "Nobody who goes to those things all the time makes any real contribution."

From 1944 throughout his college years he kept seeing progressively more of a lively, warmhearted girl named Ethel Skakel. He had met her, a friend of his younger sister Jean's, on a Canadian skiing trip. Sixth in a family of seven from Greenwich, Connecticut, she was much like Bobby. She enjoyed the out-of-doors and sports. They were married in 1950 but not until Bobby had toured the roiling Middle East as a correspondent for the *Boston Post,* then drifted up north to watch the Berlin Airlift.

Back in the United States he felt suddenly that he was unprepared and unequipped to do much of anything. He enrolled in the University of Virginia Law School and this time he went to work on his studies. His grades were high but his campus activity was even better. He helped revive the dormant Student Legal Forum and became its president. He brought in speakers such as Supreme Court Justice Bill Douglas, *New York Times*

pundit Arthur Krock, and Senator Joe McCarthy, just then be-
ginning to attract attention. He had to fight determinedly to get
Ralph Bunche admitted to the campus for a lecture. But he won
the battle and with it got his first real splash of national publicity.
Out of law school in 1951, Bobby was ready for his public career.
He began in the Justice Department.

From the start of his legal career Bobby got some good breaks.
When he joined Justice he was put in the Internal Security Di-
vision and one of his first cases was the Owen Lattimore loyalty
investigation. From that he plunged into the corruption of the
Truman administration. He was one of three lawyers on this duty,
and his biggest job was in Brooklyn when he presented to the
Grand Jury a major share of the case against Commissioner of
Internal Revenue Joe Nunan.

In May 1952 Jack Kennedy challenged the Senate seat of
Henry Cabot Lodge. Bobby left his Washington duties to manage
the campaign. He was twenty-six years old. But it was then that
he began to formulate some of the solid political premises which
eight years later would pay off in Jack Kennedy's presidential
drive. After a careful look around, Bobby decided that the major
ingredients lacking in existing political systems were hard work
and common sense. He vowed to add these features. "Those politicians," he grumped to a friend later, "just wanted to sit around
and talk about it and have their pictures taken at the rallies.
That's all they did."

Side by side with Larry O'Brien, the shrewd young organizer
from Springfield, Massachusetts, and his friend Kenny O'Donnell,
Bobby began to devise the Kennedy system. "The key to that victory," he says, "was that we got a large number of people to do
some work instead of trying to get a few people to do a lot of
work."

Committees on virtually everything and everybody were set up
for Jack Kennedy. There were Poles for Kennedy, Dentists for
Kennedy, Italians for Kennedy, and Teachers for Kennedy. Some
of the groups overlapped, but Bobby didn't care. Everyone was
getting a sense of participation.

Bobby and his staff members culled police lists of residents and

voter lists to find out if those in Democratic districts were not
registered. They discovered many a rich lode of untapped Democratic votes. A state-wide registration drive was launched and some
100,000 new names were added to the rolls. The Massachusetts
Democratic party always had reasoned that if a candidate won
Boston by a large enough margin he would win the state. Bobby
and Jack were not content with that. Bobby tried to organize every
town of more than six hundred voting population.

During the summer and fall, as they battled the powerful political stature of Henry Cabot Lodge, Bobby lost ten pounds from
the seven-day work weeks, the twenty-hour days. Even this early
he began to get his reputation for being tough. Paul Dever, running for governor, wanted Jack to link his campaign to the Dever
effort. The Kennedys wanted no part of the rest of the confused
Massachusetts setting. Bobby Kennedy was the man who went
to dinner in the Ritz with Dever and his henchmen and put it firmly
and coldly that the Kennedy campaign would be independent.
Dever was angered by the brush off from such an upstart. (The
two later became friends.)

When a group of Boston politicians walked casually into the
Kennedy headquarters one day to offer their help to the campaign
manager, their first shock was the confrontation with Bobby Kennedy, a mere boy by their standards. The second came when
he suggested that right then and there they could help lick envelopes that were being mailed out with campaign literature. The
politicians walked out the door and didn't come back.

Bobby Kennedy wasn't above licking envelopes, however. He
also rang doorbells, gave speeches, drove voters to the polls—and
helped win the election. The night of the vote Jack rolled up the
big city margin as expected. Then the out-state results began to
come in. The Kennedy margin began to dwindle. The political
hacks around the Kennedy headquarters who had been so gay
at the start of the evening faded away, the usual sign of political
death. One old-timer drifted in and announced: "You're dead.
You've lost." But Bobby's new brand of politics didn't rely on
the hunches of the old-timers.

He watched the tote board and noticed that even though they

were being beaten out state, their margin of defeat was some 5 per cent less than the traditional Democratic trouncing. Bobby had equipped himself with a slide rule that evening and learned to use it in the few minutes before the votes were chalked up. From the start he figured that the improved showing out state would save Jack. Paul Dever, who had ignored the small cities and towns, lost by 25,000 votes. Jack Kennedy won by 70,000.

Back in Washington, Bobby went to work for Senator Joe McCarthy's Government Operations Subcommittee on Investigations which was just then beginning to stir up dust. Today Bobby insists that Joe McCarthy was not the reason he joined the investigations. "I felt it was work that needed to be done then," he says. The controversial Roy Cohn, chief counsel for the Committee, had eight assistants. Francis (Flip) Flanagan, general counsel, had four, one of whom was Bobby. He worked hard as always and before long distinguished himself by uncovering the case of the two ships flying the British flag which had carried supplies up the China coast for the Red Chinese then fighting the United States in Korea.

Bobby, however, was not happy. He felt Cohn was mishandling the communist cases. At one point he went to McCarthy and said that if Cohn continued to be counsel the Committee was headed for disaster. Bobby wanted to resign. McCarthy asked him to stay on, promising to straighten out the Committee. But he never acted, and Bobby did resign. Next he joined the Hoover Commission then assembling its massive recommendations for administrative reform in government. However, a lull developed in this work and Bobby got restless again. Meantime, the three Democratic members of the McCarthy committee—John McClellan, Stuart Symington, and Henry Jackson—who had walked out in protest of McCarthy techniques had come back to the Committee again. They asked Bobby to become minority counsel, and he accepted immediately.

Clash with Roy Cohn was inevitable. The two battled on virtually every major case. When Senator Jackson in public hearing showed how ludicrous an investigator Cohn's friend and assistant David Schine had been, Cohn came menacingly around the committee table after the hearing. "You tell your friend Scoop Jackson we're going to get him on Monday," threatened Cohn.

"Get lost," snapped Bobby.

His relationship with McCarthy was under severe strain. He said publicly that McCarthy mismanaged the Committee. And McCarthy, fearing he would lose support of some powerful backers if he fired Cohn and Schine, refused to do anything about the operations of the two which Bobby found to be "inefficient, inaccurate, and untrustworthy."

As the power and influence of McCarthy began to wane, Bobby played a major role in writing the report on the hearings, a report approved by both parties—no small accomplishment in such supercharged atmosphere. Early in 1955 the Democrats took over Congress and Bobby moved up as counsel for the permanent Subcommittee on Investigations.

That year he took seven weeks out with Justice Douglas for an extensive tour of Russia and the surrounding area. They were among the first persons allowed into Siberia, and Bobby once again returned momentarily to journalism, writing and taking pictures for the *New York Times Sunday Magazine*.

Just a few weeks before the 1956 presidential convention in Chicago, Jack Kennedy and his intimates began to get the feeling that he might have a chance for the vice-presidential nomination. Bobby sounded out people on Jack's chances, asked rather casually here and there for support if it developed that the junior Senator from Massachusetts got into the running. Up until the night before the ballot the brothers had not decided for sure whether they should try. Then Adlai Stevenson threw open the convention and they decided to go after it. This was a desperate and unorganized lunge for the wire. Bobby took charge of the tiny band of workers he had. Most of them were family members. They hurried out into the Chicago night and haunted the hotel corridors until daylight. Eunice Shriver was sent to appeal to the Mississippi delegation. Bobby tackled Arkansas's John McClellan and other friends from Congress. Connecticut's Governor Abe Ribicoff and State Chairman John Bailey pursued New York delegates and brother-in-law R. Sargent Shriver worked on Maryland, his home state.

Bobby stood on the floor of the convention hall and watched victory slip away. For a few minutes he was bitterly disappointed to have been in a major battle and to have lost. Then the reality of the situation began to sink in. He walked over to his brother's hotel room. He still was dejected from the idea of losing a fight, but he blurted to Jack: "This is the luckiest thing that ever happened to you." A lot of others agreed.

The convention had been one more political lesson in Bobby Kennedy's expanding bank of experience. "It really struck me then," he said later, "that it wasn't the issues which mattered so much, it was the friendships. So many people had come up to me and said they would like to vote for Jack but they were going to vote for Estes Kefauver because he had sent them a card or visited in their home. I said right there that as well as paying attention to the issues we should send Christmas cards next time."

There was no question then that both Kennedys felt 1960 would be the year for Jack to try for the presidential nomination. They did not discuss it much. Once again there was an unspoken understanding between these two brothers, who had grown closer together as they had matured.

As an aide to Jim Finnegan, Adlai Stevenson's campaign manager, Bobby rode the Stevenson campaign train the fall of 1956. He had nothing to do and would have left the campaign except he was curious. There was a vague feeling that someday he might have to know how to run a campaign. He stayed for seven long weeks. He noted that Stevenson hated whistle stopping and often came to the rear platform and read his speeches, failing to arouse any feeling in his audiences. At one stop a Stevenson aide came out on the platform and told the impatient crowd that Adlai would not be along for a few minutes; he was having a cup of coffee. Bobby watched the Stevenson relationship with the press crumble because no one paid any attention to the reporters. He saw that Stevenson was drawing TV audiences of only a million and a half when he should have gotten twelve or fifteen million; yet nothing was done. All these facts he put away in his mental archives.

In Washington again he dived into his work with a new flurry, and for the next three years Bobby Kennedy gained more national attention than his elder brother. As the chief counsel of John McClellan's famous Rackets Committee Bobby pursued relentlessly the hoodlums of the big labor unions and to a lesser degree sought out abuses by management. His first quarry was roly-poly Dave Beck, president of the giant Teamsters Union. Beck and his henchmen had made millions by misusing the funds of the Union. Beck was forced out of his job, eventually convicted of larceny. But it was not that easy with his replacement James Riddle Hoffa.

Although Bobby claimed Hoffa had misused Teamsters' money far more extensively than Beck, he declared this was not the most sinister element in Hoffa's character. Bobby charged Hoffa with encouraging hoodlums and racketeers to move into his union to help him achieve total power. In virtually every major city, Kennedy said, the underworld had linked up with Hoffa and taken command of the Teamsters local, or was trying to do so.

Day after day, week after week, Bobby Kennedy sent his investigators out into the field to study union records and track down the frightened witnesses to some of Hoffa's gangland techniques which included beatings, bombings, and even suspected murder. Bobby's days were sixteen hours and longer. He prowled like a caged animal back and forth in his cluttered, windowless office of the Senate Office Building's first floor, preparing the complex cases. "It was like playing Notre Dame every day," he said. Then up in the marble caucus room in front of the harsh kleig lights of TV he shot questions at the cast of sinister characters, many of whom ducked behind the Fifth Amendment or just ducked.

Nobody was more evasive than Hoffa himself. Once Hoffa was arrested and charged with trying to bribe one of Bobby's investigators to get information. The F.B.I. had been in on the case, movies had been taken. The case seemed so tight against Hoffa that Bobby rashly said he would jump off the Capitol dome if Hoffa wasn't convicted. With the help of one of the nation's leading criminal attorneys, Edward Bennett Williams, Hoffa won acquittal before a jury. Williams offered to send Bobby a parachute.

Hoffa became Bobby's obsession. The more he worked, the more he felt Hoffa's hand was everywhere in the misuse of union money and power. Hoffa had more than a hundred attorneys working for him and his cronies. (In the Caucus Room the group became known as Hoffa's Bar Association.) Hundreds of thousands of dollars were poured into legal fees for the defense of the racketeers in the Teamsters.

The face and voice of Bobby Kennedy became household items as the nation looked, listened, and then gasped at some of the abuses uncovered. But as often as not there was another profile on those TV screens. It was that of brother Jack, a member of the Select Committee to Investigate Improper Activities in Labor-Management Relations. Sometimes the image blurred and the casual viewer did not really know which brother was which. The name Kennedy, however, was indelibly printed on the national brain.

The country's outcry was felt in Congress finally in 1959, and a labor reform bill far harsher than the big unions wanted passed both Senate and House and was signed into law. Convictions of some of the more notorious offenders uncovered by Bobby's thirty-five investigators began to trickle in from courts around the country. But the top men still remained free, and a court Board of Monitors appointed to watch over the Teamsters began to bog down in a morass of legal entanglements thrown up by Hoffa's lawyers. The passion in the public for reform had died and Bobby Kennedy and his band of investigators began to make plans to dissolve the committee. Besides, in the fall of 1959 Jack Kennedy's drive for the presidential nomination was taking on such momentum that it no longer could be handled by a small staff working out of the Senator's office on Capitol Hill. It needed a manager.

Before taking over direction of Jack's campaign Bobby began a book about his three years of investigations. His work hours were as long as ever. But the conditions were more pleasant. Most of the work was done on his beautiful McLean, Virginia, estate. Often he would write beside the swimming pool, soaking up the sun, taking an occasional minute out to romp with his children. His family had grown to seven and his five acres were aswarm with them, their friends, and their pets. By December of 1959 he had finished *The Enemy Within,* shipped it off to the publisher, and at last he could turn full time to presidential politics.

The Kennedy brothers summoned friends and family for the biggest project they'd ever undertaken. Down from Springfield, Massachusetts, came organizer Larry O'Brien. Kenny O'Donnell, who had been Bobby's chief of staff on the Rackets Committee, joined the campaign as did Pierre Salinger, a key investigator from Committee days. Brother-in-law Stephen Smith moved from New York to Washington to help. Sarg Shriver worked from Chicago.

Jack Kennedy had to beat the professional politicians who felt that his youth and his Catholicism were such huge disadvantages that he could never win a runoff with Richard Nixon, who had been maturing in the Vice President's chair for eight years. To win popular support and disprove the old political theorems, Jack planned to enter and win the presidential preference elections. The first vital one was April 5 in Wisconsin.

Bobby Kennedy was never officially named campaign manager in those early days, but everybody knew he ran the show. He dusted off all the lessons he had learned since he first rang doorbells in 1946. One thing was certain—in politics you can't be sure of hearsay, you've got to find out the facts for yourself. Scorning all advice, Bobby made an early foray himself into Wisconsin. For seven days he tramped through the snow talking to the local politicians, sometimes quizzing people on the street, sizing up the strength of the state's Democratic organization. The Kennedy opponent in Wisconsin would be Hubert Humphrey, a neighbor from Minnesota, a man skilled in the likes and dislikes of the farm folks. Bobby's tour convinced him that they could not rely on any Wisconsin Democratic organization. They would have to build a new one for Jack Kennedy. "That's the mistake that Hubert made," says Bobby. "He didn't find out until it was too late that you couldn't depend on the Wisconsin organization."

Bobby drove thousands of miles helping set up local organizations. O'Brien revised and reissued his famous manual of organization for conducting a campaign on the local level. Bobby showed up in the early dawn at many factory gates to shake hands and ask for votes. He gave speeches, some of them no more than, "I'm here to ask you to vote for my brother Jack."

The press had picked up the chant that if Kennedy didn't win all ten Wisconsin districts it would not be a clean-cut victory. In the final days of the campaign Hubert Humphrey lashed out hard and cut into the Kennedy tide. Jack Kennedy won six districts and carried the heavily-Catholic state by 107,000 votes, acquiring 20½ delegates out of the total of 31. He had taken 56 per cent of the vote but because of the attitude of the press it was not considered a hard win. "It wasn't as glorious an occasion as it might have been," said Bobby Kennedy, and the very next day he flew to West Virginia to begin work on what was to be the second crucial battle. Again the opponent was Hubert Humphrey. But West Virginia was entirely different from Wisconsin. Only an estimated 4 per cent of the population was Catholic. Vast depressed areas seemed to be ready to hear and believe Hubert Humphrey's flamboyant liberalism. At one point Bobby sent emissaries to try indirectly to persuade Humphrey to pull out. This failed, so he split the state into districts and brought in one of his men for each district. Bobby divided his time between stumping and organizing. The week before the vote on May 10 he felt that Jack would win. He had liked what he found in his tours of the mines. The miners were the tough, spirited individuals that Bobby found appealing. They seemed to like Jack. But the weekend before the election he talked to pessimistic newsmen and on his own he went out again, this time running into the strong religious prejudice. He was discouraged on May 10. Jack flew back to Washington expecting the worst, not wanting to be in West Virginia if he lost.

Ethel Kennedy hurried into Charleston to be with Bobby in his time of discouragement. It was raining on election eve. Ethel stood at the edge of the airport ramp shielding herself from the mist. Suddenly Hubert Humphrey appeared. His spirits were up; he plainly felt he would win this one. He rushed up to Ethel and gripped her hand. "When this is all over and our temperatures are down some, I hope we can get together with our families," said Hubert.

"That was rather sweet of him," said Ethel, staring after him, then remembering her own mission of comfort, she rushed off to find the glum Bobby.

"Half an hour after results began to come in we knew we'd won," says Bobby. While the exuberant Humphrey began to fade, the Kennedy morale began to rise. Toward midnight Bobby was on the phone with his brother. "Should I fly out?" asked Jack.

"Yes, you'd better come," answered Bobby.

While Jack flew toward Charleston, Bobby Kennedy quietly slipped out of the Kennedy headquarters and through the dark, wet streets to Humphrey's suite in the Ruffner Hotel. "I just came over to say hello," murmured Bobby as he shook Humphrey's hand, trying to ease defeat in some way.

John Kennedy's West Virginia upset reached huge proportions. He won 65 per cent of the vote. With that victory Bobby felt sure the Democratic nomination was theirs. He did not leave it to chance, however. As Jack wound up his primary victories with number seven in Oregon, Bobby was in Washington preparing for the July convention. He and others went to see every delegate elected. Convinced that one reason Jack's efforts in 1956 to get the vice presidential nomination had been so futile was because they had no communication system on the convention floor, Bobby flew to Los Angeles six weeks ahead to plan an elaborate system of telephones and walkie-talkies so the Kennedy scouts would know within seconds every floor development. Plans were laid for a daily Kennedy tabloid to be delivered in the hotels. A card on every delegate was prepared, a system set up to get hourly reports from each state delegation once the convention started. Long before the fateful night of July 13, when Jack Kennedy won the nomination on the first ballot, the outcome had been decided. Nobody knew it better than Bobby. From his headquarters just outside the Los Angeles Sports Arena he watched calmly as the count rose above the 761 needed. The final vote differed only 10 votes from his predicted total. In a few minutes Jack was in the room with him. The two brothers talked calmly in the corner, away from the growing horde of politicians pushing in to congratulate Jack. The only burst of emotion came from Bobby. He rammed his right fist into his left palm repeatedly and he wore a slight smile.

Perhaps the ultimate praise came when his father called him and said: "It's the best organization job I've ever seen in politics."

Up until this time the hardened Democratic professionals tended to treat Bobby Kennedy, the boy wonder, as something of a myth. They had not really believed what they saw. Suddenly Bobby was named national campaign manager. This slight figure, his eyes constantly showing deep fatigue, in shirt sleeves, tie loosened, began to plan for a Democratic victory, and the old-timers still wouldn't quite believe it. "He might have been good in Massachusetts or West Virginia," scoffed one, "but this is different. We'll see."

As Bobby moved his old regulars and a cadre of new young friends into the party, there was more muttering. "Complaints?" snorted one politician. "No, not many. Only about a million a day."

"People get mad," said Jack Kennedy, somewhat amused at his brother's unrelenting toughness. "But they get mad whatever you do. Whatever moves things upsets someone. You can't make an omelet without breaking the egg. I don't pay any attention to the beefs. Every politician in Massachusetts was mad at Bobby after 1952 but we had the best organization in history."

But could Bobby do it again? New York, the richest lode of electoral votes in the land, was being consumed by internecine Democratic war. The giant wounds in California were not healed. There were rumblings in the South against Lyndon Johnson's nomination for Vice-President. Then the rump session of Congress which Johnson had cooked up prior to the national convention in hopes of increasing his own potential as a presidential nominee caught both Kennedy and Johnson in August. For three weeks Congress frustrated any attempt to get through key Democratic legislation and finally adjourned leaving doubt about Kennedy's ability to deal with Congress.

"Just wait until Jack can get out to the people," reassured Bobby as he listened to the early clucking about how Nixon had gained the edge. All of Bobby's political theories hinged on the solid belief that his brother was the most attractive and talented candidate in the business. With enthusiasm growing over the Kennedy campaign, Bobby could go out and set things up his way. Few dared to defy him for fear of losing out with the best prospect the Democrats had had in years.

Bobby's reputation for being tough increased. He invaded fragmented New York State and for three days he huddled with the warring factions. To Herbert Lehman's reformers he rasped: "Gentlemen, I don't give a damn if the state and county organizations survive after November, and I don't give a damn if you survive. I want to elect John F. Kennedy." To the bosses Carmine DeSapio and Mike Prendergast he was equally blunt. "The only thing I'm interested in is electing Senator Kennedy for president."

It was obvious that he could not choose a person from either side to head the Kennedy drive in New York. Instead, he placed perennially unsuccessful congressional candidate Anthony Akers in charge of the local effort. But he also moved in a "Kennedy co-ordinator" who could watch, listen, and advise and report straight back to Bobby. He was a Georgetown artist friend of the Kennedys named William Walton. Into twenty-nine other key states went out-of-state co-ordinators whose jobs were to keep small hurts from becoming open wounds. "It's like the Gaza strip," said Bobby, remembering his stint as a reporter in the Middle East. "You have to watch it all the time and make sure the little fights don't become wars."

Bobby launched a drive to register ten million voters, figuring six or seven million would be Democrats. He put it under the direction of New Jersey's colorful Congressman Frank Thompson. Only hours after Thompson had been told he had the job, Bobby asked what he had done so far. Thompson, who knew the Kennedy ways, had anticipated such impatience. He had hired a secretary, set up an office, and summoned key Democrats to a meeting. Bobby was almost satisfied.

From Denver Bobby summoned Byron (Whizzer) White, the

former Colorado University All-American and Rhodes scholar, to head the Citizens for Kennedy and Johnson. White had performed impressively in the Rocky Mountain area before the convention. If Bobby Kennedy had worked hard on previous projects, he broke all records now. "I don't even have to think about organization," marveled Jack. "I just show up. Bobby's easily the best man I've ever seen. He's the hardest worker. He's the greatest organizer. He's taken no time off. He's fantastic. He's living on nerves." And even Father Joe had to wonder a bit. "Jack works harder than any mortal man can," he said. "Bobby goes a little further."

The cries from irked Democrats all across the land increased as the campaign began to roll. Some of them ran to Jack. "Bobby has the strong support of his staff and the people who really want to do some work and help us," Jack told a friend. "What friend who was really worth while has he lost? I don't know a one. There's nothing you can do about the people who complain. They don't like me either. They don't like our success."

Some politicians complained bitterly that Bobby was utterly ruthless. "I'm not running a popularity contest," said Bobby. "It doesn't matter if they like me or not. Jack can be nice to them. I don't try to antagonize people but somebody has to be able to say no. If people are not getting off their behinds and working enough, how do you say that nicely? Every time you make a decision in this business you make somebody mad."

Bobby had one immense advantage in his national political dealings. He could be tough because he was the candidate's brother, a peculiar position for politics, indeed. Nobody was jealous of his position since it was one of birth. He sought no special job nor was he under any outside influence. He was in the strongest possible position from which to say no. Before the end of the campaign he concluded that one of the great Republican weaknesses was that there was no man at G.O.P. headquarters who could act with the same decisiveness without fear of trouble.

The Democratic party began to come alive under the whip, and after watching Jack Kennedy stand up to Richard Nixon in the

first of the famous TV debates, the local headquarters were flooded
with people who wanted to work. Money came easier. As Bobby
watched the progress, he was elated. "It won't even be close," he
predicted.

But even as the news continued to be good there remained the
rumblings over Bobby Kennedy. There were constant stories about
disagreement between the brothers. In fact, for a year there had
persisted whispers how the two didn't agree on some crucial matters. To believe such reports was to show misunderstanding of
how the two brothers got along. There were differences of opinion.
Sometimes they were expressed. But inevitably they were talked
out in calm. Once the decision was made by Jack, there was no
more discussion. For a few days Jack had been glum over the
decision to enter the West Virginia primary, a decision based
largely on Bobby's advice. Jack does not look back long, however. Bobby was at first shocked by the liberal opposition to
Lyndon Johnson on the ticket and questioned whether Lyndon
was worth it or not. When Jack said he was, the matter was
dropped. On little things Jack sometimes smarted. When Bobby
publicly attacked Nixon supporter Jackie Robinson, Jack heard
about it on his airplane, grimaced, and moaned, "We are running
against Nixon not Jackie Robinson." But always their relationship came down to their feeling about each other.

"Jack has the best political judgment of anybody I know," said
Bobby.

"I'll take Bobby's word over anybody's," declared Jack.

There were no defections among the men who worked for
Bobby Kennedy. Every last man who labored closely with him
back in the Rackets Committee days swore by him. (When the
committee broke up, Bobby made sure each person had at least
one satisfactory job offer.) Those who got to know him during
the campaign came away with the same respect.

"He is more concerned with morality and personal integrity
than anybody I know," said one friend. "He doesn't like to compromise." A driving sense of integrity, however, can sometimes
be a prime irritant to those who don't relish such rigid living. "The

men around Bobby are men who believe in a cause," said one friend. "Those who don't, don't stay long."

Indeed, in the moments when Bobby had time to talk about anything but political organization he could be philosophical. "I'm not doing this just because of the family," he said, "just because Jack is my brother. I sincerely feel that this will make a hell of a difference to the country. I really believe that we've gone soft in America. We've got to wake up."

But as soon as someone said with admiration that a young man of his talent and wealth was making a tremendous sacrifice to do this work, he replied: "That's ridiculous. This is the greatest thing in the world. It's a rewarding way to live. I'd rather do it than anything else."

On the night of November 8, as Jack Kennedy was elected President of the United States, Bobby Kennedy watched and listened from the second story of his green-shuttered white cottage at Hyannis Port. He was surprised and disappointed at the closeness of the election. Victory, nevertheless, was sweet, and there was no time for brooding—a government had to be formed. Once again Bobby Kennedy took no rest.

Flying back to Washington only days after the Kennedy victory, Bobby organized a team of talent scouts to scour the country for the men who wanted to join the New Frontier. His relationship with his brother became even closer in these days. In the final hours of deliberation over key Cabinet members only Bobby knew what the President-elect was really thinking. And then it was Bobby's turn to decide if he wanted to come along to the New Frontier.

Young Kennedy's quick and energetic start as Attorney General has quieted the critics, at least for now. But the issue of nepotism still lurks under the surface. Republicans who, after threatening to challenge his confirmation, joined in singing his praises still mutter that if he slips they will make his position a public issue.

There are some friends who feel the tightrope Bobby will have to walk in the next years has changed him. There are fewer flaring temper bursts than in the days of the Rackets Committee. He doesn't relish throwing fully-clothed guests into his swimming pool quite so much as he used to. Yet there remains the zest for life that Joe Kennedy instilled in Bobby and the rest of his amazing family. It wasn't long after he became Attorney General that Bobby, brother Teddy, and a group of friends gathered on his lawn in Virginia in six inches of snow for a game of touch football.

9.

HONEST ABE—THE VOTE-GETTER

Abraham Ribicoff

By BEN H. BAGDIKIAN

WHILE HE WAS A REPRESENTATIVE FROM CONNECTICUT, ABRAHAM Ribicoff once asked financier Bernard Baruch for a contribution to his political campaign. The shrewd old investor turned him down. Instead, he offered some advice: "Get out and get around. Let them see your face and you won't have any trouble."

With his celebrated eye for profitable assets, Baruch had fastened on young Ribicoff's most valuable political possession. It was Ribicoff's face and his personality that had already brought him to the halls of Congress and would take him less than a decade later to the inner circle of men running the United States government.

It is his image and his genius for projecting it that have raised Ribicoff above the cross fire of normal partisan politics and enabled him to overcome some major paradoxes in his career. Consider: Ribicoff once voted against the creation of the Department of Health, Education, and Welfare, then asked for the job of running it. After a political career based largely on damning bureaucracy, he committed himself to promote the fastest-growing bureaucracy in American society. He never received an ordinary college degree, yet he is now the federal high chief of education.

The Ribicoff face is handsome, purposeful, and grave. Black hair touched with silver sweeps back, parted—without political significance he would insist—slightly left of center. Dark brows,

213

deep brown eyes, and a suggestion of heavy beard lead downward to mouth and chin set in a perpetual look of unrelenting virtue. The expression of the face is normally one of profound seriousness, of determination with a hint of tolerant wisdom able to dissolve into a slow smile. But it returns quickly to a look of gravity.

There is no reason to believe this a stage face. Its owner is a shrewd political strategist, a genius at public relations who possesses one of the most photographed smiles in Washington. But Abraham Ribicoff at heart is a solemn man.

Once, while governor of Connecticut, he had seemed so impelled by a sense of mission in delivering a series of public exhortations to civic virtue that the State House press corps planned to memorialize this messianic behavior by sending Ribicoff a birthday card on Christmas. But Ribicoff takes no relief in slapstick, irreverence, or spontaneous wit. The newspapermen decided against the birthday card because, even though they considered themselves personal friends of the Governor, they feared he would fail to see the humor.

In his native New England Ribicoff was the first Jewish governor. To many observers his character has seemed a merger of the Yankee ethic of self-reliance and hard work and the Hebrew sense of righteousness and devotion to higher service. He had the legendary poor boy's background, but today he insists it was the best possible life a young man could have. Ribicoff's parents came from Slonim, Poland, now a part of White Russia. They arrived in the United States in 1909 and moved to New Britain in central Connecticut, a small, pleasant city on a branch of the New York, New Haven & Hartford Railroad. They lived in a third-floor tenement on Star Street where on April 9, 1910, Abraham Alexander Ribicoff, second of three children, was born with the help of a midwife.

His father, Samuel Ribicoff, worked as a wood turner in a local hardware factory for his first ten years in this country, then built up a bakery route. They were Orthodox Jews who kept a kosher house, spoke Yiddish, Polish, synagogue Hebrew, and English with an accent. Theirs was a working-class neighborhood with other immigrants, mostly Poles, with some Irish and Italians. The stereotype of such neighborhoods is one of squalor, brutality, and religious persecution, but along the Connecticut Valley before the depression life had a sunny, small-town intimacy. Ribicoff today is rhapsodic about his youth.

"If I had to do it all over again, I'd still choose New Britain, Connecticut, to grow up in. We had railroad tracks in New Britain but they were a physical division, not a personal one. People on both sides of the track respected each other. In New Britain you weren't a Jew or an Irishman or a Pole—you were either a good guy or a stinker."

No anti-Semitism scratched his personality, he says. "I was never conscious of being Jewish, of being different. The fact that my parents were immigrants, that I was Jewish, that we were poor— these never left a scar. The Irish kids would visit our house at Purim and I'd walk to church with them when they went to confession."

He appears impatient with the "self-consciousness" of many minority groups. "They look for slights when there are none. If they are rejected, they believe it's because of their religion or their race. If I ever failed, it was because of me, not because of my being a Jew." This, he knows, was partly good luck. "I never felt the corrosive effect of prejudice. Later it made me realize what it means for a kid to be accepted for himself."

His parents urged upon their children the qualities of hard work, thrift, and education. Abe carried coal from the basement to their third-floor stove and then, in the pre-petroleum ritual of the American home, carried the ashes to the cellar and sifted them for unburned nuggets. "We always lived on a third floor because the rent was a little cheaper," he recalls.

And he worked after school. "I have worked ever since I was eight years old." He ran errands, delivered milk, peddled papers, sold vegetables, labored with pick and shovel in a construction gang. His parents, neither rich nor destitute, never took any money from him. His father told him to save it for a college education.

Saturdays he brought back books from the New Britain public library. "I was the greatest reader of anyone. I read anything— fiction, history, biography, anything. I guess that's why the University of Chicago let me into their law school even though I didn't have a college degree."

After high school he lacked money for immediate entry to college so he went to work keeping track of orders in the G. E. Prentice Mfg. Co. zipper factory in the next town, Kensington. A year later he enrolled at New York University. But after one year of college, when he was nineteen, he accepted the Prentice Company offer to run their Chicago sales office for $70.00 a week.

In Chicago from early morning to late afternoon he sold zippers and shoe buckles, wholesale, to the satisfaction of his home office. From late afternoon to late evening he studied law at the University of Chicago Law School, to the satisfaction of the faculty. He became editor of the school's *Law Review* in his final year, was elected to the honorary Order of the Coif, and was graduated *cum laude* in 1933. But because he lacked a college degree he received a Bachelor of Laws degree instead of a Doctor of Jurisprudence as most other graduates did. "I didn't really care," he says without much conviction.

While still a law student he had gone back to Connecticut to marry Ruth Siegel, a short, pretty girl from Hartford. They had met at a dance in New Britain when she was sixteen. They returned to Chicago, to an efficiency apartment with a Murphy bed and a blanket stretched across the room to shield the kitchenette. It was the beginning of a close marriage and a working partnership in every activity of Abraham Ribicoff. "Everyone warned me about marrying a boy who was still going to school," Mrs. Ribicoff once said. "But I never doubted for a moment that Abe would be successful."

In the *Law Review* of May 1933 Ribicoff had written a paper on the jurisdiction of the United States Supreme Court in hearing certain kinds of appeals from state courts. The article caught the eye of Herman Oliphant, lawyer and later general counsel for Franklin Roosevelt's Department of the Treasury. The United States had just gone off the gold standard and Oliphant called the twenty-three-year-old Ribicoff to Washington and offered him a job at $3,800 to worry about the economics of gold. Ribicoff recalled recently that this had no appeal for him and that he told Oliphant: "I don't want to work in Washington with gold. If I became an expert on gold, what would I do afterward? I'd have to work on Wall Street and I don't want to work on Wall Street. I want to live in a small town."

He also turned down $4,800 a year to work for the newly-created Tennessee Valley Authority with his classmate from Chicago, Gordon Clapp. Years later, when Clapp became head of T.V.A., he told Representative Ribicoff's colleagues on a congressional committee: "I'm glad Abe turned down the T.V.A. job in 1933 because if he had taken it, he'd be the head of T.V.A. now instead of me." Ribicoff said he was never tempted by the big offers. "I believe this small-town philosophy. Do you know how much $4,800 a year was in 1933? It was fabulous. But I meant it about small towns. The most important thing for a man is to find what kind of town he wants to live in. It doesn't make any difference where it is. If you've got something, you'll succeed no matter where you are."

His wife's family lawyer, Abraham S. Bordon, took young Ribicoff into his firm at the lowest level. At night Ribicoff opened his own office in Kensington, a town of 1,700 population, twelve miles from Hartford. The Bordon office was in a building at 750 Main Street, Hartford, a structure that was to house a number of symbolic scenes for Ribicoff. Here he and his wife acted out a daily scene of homely thrift and devotion, here he met John Bailey, whose curious alliance brought them both to power, and here it was that Bailey ripped apart Ribicoff's written withdrawal from politics and thrust Ribicoff onto the national scene.

Like so much of the Ribicoff story, the scene at 750 Main Street begins with a demonstration of simple virtue. The bright young lawyer, having left a $70.00-a-week job selling zippers in order to learn a profession, having rejected $73.00-a-week security as a bureaucrat in the nation's capital, returned to his native state, moved in with his in-laws, and went to work in a family firm, searching real-estate titles at $30.00 a week.

Mrs. Ribicoff played an important supporting role. Before her marriage she had worked for an uncle as a medical receptionist. While Abe was in Chicago, she did the same work there. Now, while Abe worked in the Bordon office on the seventh floor, she worked as a receptionist in a doctor's office on the eleventh floor.

Each morning Ruth would pack two lunches and take them to her office. At noon, when the doctor went out to lunch, Abe would come upstairs and they would eat their sandwiches together.

As they sat inside eating their sandwiches, back on the seventh floor, John Bailey, a lawyer far more affluent than Abe, five years older, tough and effective in Connecticut Democratic politics, took the elevator downward for the fashionable restaurants of downtown Hartford. Today the two legal alumni of the seventh floor of 750 Main Street are major figures in American politics, John Bailey the national Democratic chairman, and Abraham Ribicoff the Secretary of the Department of Health, Education, and Welfare and confidant of the President of the United States.

From the start Ribicoff wanted to get into politics. He has no specific explanation for it except: "There's nothing as interesting as politics." It is easy to believe this instinctual explanation. The Ribicoff manner is outwardly calm, restrained, measured. He tends to speak publicly in lofty terms of broad ideas. But when he begins talking of the political wars, of the rebellions and alliances, the maneuvers and feints, his eyes glisten, his head thrusts forward, he uses his arms expressively, he is a man surrounded by excitement.

It occurred to him that he would run for alderman of the city of Hartford. But he found that being one of the brightest law graduates of the Class of 1933 at the University of Chicago was no key to the hearts of the hard-boiled hierarchy of Hartford politics. He began by pushing doorbells in the precincts. By 1938 he had pushed a lot of doorbells. What is more important, he had developed a friendship with John Bailey. It was the start of a long relationship that had its ups and downs, but the downs were seldom as deep as they seemed in public. Together—Ribicoff, the thoughtful Jewish independent, and Bailey, the Irish party-line boss—they spanned a great deal of Hartford County political sentiment.

It so happened that in 1938 Bailey, the organization man, had a falling out with the city Democratic boss, Thomas J. Spellacy. This placed him in the unnatural position of being anti-organization. So was Ribicoff. They worked together and beat the organization. In the process Abraham Ribicoff became elected to the state House of Representatives. "That's when the Bailey-Ribicoff combination started," Ribicoff explains.

During his first term in the Connecticut legislature newspapermen voted Ribicoff the legislature's "most promising freshman." Unlike many winners of "most promising" polls, he did not forthwith march into oblivion. The next term they voted him "the most able representative."

Abraham Ribicoff had begun a political career based on the image of integrity and high purpose, qualities that his political opposition has never been able to contradict. They were qualities propagated through his peculiar genius for winning newspapermen and influencing voters.

At the same time Ribicoff was never sentimental about the realities of party politics. As a member of the House Judiciary Committee, he had his friend and mentor, John Bailey, made police court judge for Hartford. Later, when he was governor, he made his old party enemy, Spellacy, state insurance commissioner. When his national reputation was based on his inflexible administration of state traffic laws, he fired his deputy registrar of motor vehicles with indignation because the man was accused of fixing a traffic charge. But the next day the discharged official went on the pay roll of the state Democratic committee at exactly his former pay. Ribicoff did not arrange this, but he did not stop it. "In politics, this is very important," says Ribicoff, raising a pedagogical finger: "You should always be a gracious winner."

Yet what happened next was important in the Ribicoff career: He learned to be a more-or-less gracious loser. At the end of his second term in the state legislature Ribicoff in the House and Joseph Cooney in the Senate took part in a Young Turk's rebellion within the Democratic party. Bailey and Spellacy joined forces again to beat down the revolt and Ribicoff was purged. "They thought I was too independent."

But Ribicoff's opponents had learned the Ribicoff Rule of Gracious Success: Abe was named Hartford police court judge. He thinks now that those six years out of politics was a period that made the difference between his being a successful politician in Hartford and being a successful politician in the United States.

During this time he heard minor infractions of law and decided traffic cases. He built up his law practice, in partnership with his older brother, Irving. He paid attention to the public mood, quietly began joining high-level nonpartisan reform groups. He became chairman of the Connecticut Assembly of Municipal Court Judges, chairman of a state committee to study alcoholism and crime, and hearing examiner under the state Fair Employment Practices Act. He joined the Hartford Charter Revision Commission whose purpose was to drive party politics out of the city.

As a police court judge Ribicoff attracted considerable attention. He had a temperament and knowledge not always found in the lowest court. A Hartford newspaperman recalled the impact of the judge: "I had covered the court before the war and was impressed with the dignity and purpose Ribicoff brought to a bench that was not always dignified before. He was obviously a big leaguer on a farm team."

Ribicoff never kept his eye off politics. He watched the politicians in the snake pit of the Hartford legislature, a body that during this period was not an inspiring demonstration for civic classes. Lobbyists operated with the usual vigor but with more than usual candor. The law firm of John Bailey, then Democratic state chairman, was lobbyist for liquor interests, considered one of the best accounts at the capital. A well-known Republican leader was also thought to share in the liquor interests; his brother officially represented liquor interests. It was not a unique pattern. A friendly bipartisan spirit governed handling of state insurance premiums. With a traditionally Republican House and a Democratic Senate, opposing party functionaries found many mutual interests in state politics.

"Party politics" increasingly became a tainted phrase. Some of the public began to grumble. So did a few politicians. Most acutely uncomfortable of the politicians, perhaps, was the respected Democratic senator, Brien McMahon. From Washington McMahon could see that Democrats in Connecticut were headed for trouble. He kept nagging Bailey to find a fresh face. Once he said passionately, "John, will you find some bright young guy who's good? We've *got* to find someone like that!"

Such scenes were a long way, in time, in geography, in political history, from another scene twelve years later in which a man in a country-club telephone booth in Hollywood, Florida, heard another man in a comfortable summer estate fifty miles away in Palm Beach greet him with an innocuous, "Abe, how are you?" It was the President-elect of the United States inviting the Governor of Connecticut to lunch, to play golf, and to take his pick of practically any appointive job in the United States government.

It was a long way from Hartford to Palm Beach, but a clue to Ribicoff's future success was already at hand in 1948. Abraham Ribicoff was never known to take a cheap short cut; as a child he had always wanted to be "a good guy" not "a stinker," and by 1948 when phrases like "some bright young guy who's good" were used in Connecticut, a picture of Abe Ribicoff came to mind.

Bailey and Ribicoff had been public political enemies, but they never let party fights interfere with their personal relations. Ribicoff, who is not modest or blind to reality, says: "At the end of those six years I was above party politics, untouched by turmoil. The fact that I had been out of politics was a great asset."

Ribicoff's critics, including some of his former colleagues in the anti-political Charter Revision Commission, thought that when Ribicoff began dealing with Bailey once more he was trading with the enemy. No matter what anyone thought, it happened. One day in 1948 John Bailey dropped in at Judge Ribicoff's office, put his feet up on the desk, and said, "Abe, how about running for Congress?"

Recalling that day, Ribicoff salutes Bailey, "This was the genius of John Bailey. He harbors no grudges and he knows that a political leader has one requirement—to win. And there is only one thing you can win with—a good candidate. Bailey had to come to me."

That day Ribicoff stared past the Bailey feet and into the impassive Bailey face. "Don't make me laugh. I'm out of politics. I have a good practice. I've got a wife and two kids. I'm happy. Besides, you're going to lose."

Bailey took his feet off the desk, said, "Think it over," and walked out.

Both men knew things looked dark for the Democrats. President

Truman was considered beaten even before the national convention, and a lot of local Democrats would go down with him. Connecticut, considered a Republican state, was tired of politics. Bailey had Chester Bowles to run for governor but it was no secret that his chances were shaky.

Ribicoff finally wrote out a formal letter turning down the offer. He put it in letter form so that Bailey could prove he had tried to get a do-gooder. The letter sang with the classical cadences of such documents, "I wish to thank you for the honor . . . nevertheless, for personal reasons . . . but be assured I will give my wholehearted support . . ."

Bailey read the letter, tore it up, dropped the pieces into a wastebasket, and said, "The hell with that." He made daily visits to the Ribicoff office, repeating assurances Ribicoff could be nominated and win. A week later Ribicoff said yes. In Connecticut, a mutual yes between party boss and candidate is usually enough for nomination.

Ribicoff ran against the Republican incumbent Representative William J. Miller, from the First District, Hartford County. It was a largely industrial, retail, commercial area that Ribicoff knew well. He won by a plurality of 25,000 votes, and his success in drawing out the large Hartford vote was credited with giving Chester Bowles his slim margin of victory as governor. In 1950 Ribicoff ran for reelection and won by a plurality of 38,000.

When Ribicoff entered Congress he wanted what all freshman congressmen want: a prestigious committee assignment. Among the choicest of these is membership in the House Foreign Affairs Committee. Older men in the House were waiting in line for such an assignment. But Ribicoff got on his first year. He had taken the pains to have John Bailey go to Boston with him to see Representative John W. McCormack, House majority leader, and arrange the appointment.

From the start the Ribicoff record in Congress spanned a broad spectrum from which there emerged an image of sometimes conflicting qualities: party loyalty and personal independence; liberalism and conservatism; internationalism but protection of American business.

He supported the Democrats on most party issues, but he voted for the communist control bill over President Truman's veto and opposed Truman's proposal to create a Department of Health, Education, and Welfare. When some of his personal friends asked him to introduce a bill extending subsidies to Connecticut shade tobacco growers, he did—and then voted against the bill. Like most congressmen he denounced "pork-barrel" spending of the taxpayer's money for federal projects strewn over the map. But, unlike most other congressmen, when a $32,000,000 project came up for his own district, he voted against it. He helped push through a second appropriation for the Marshall Plan but he insisted on earmarking $300,000,000 to guarantee the foreign investments of private American businessmen. He co-sponsored a joint resolution with Senator McMahon calling for more friendship with the people of Russia, and he sponsored a resolution calling for an anti-communist alliance in the Pacific.

This independent course brought printed praise nationally, such as the Stewart Alsop column in the Republican *New York Herald Tribune* in 1950: "It is a rare experience these days—and, therefore, a rather moving one—to come upon honesty, intelligence, and real courage anywhere in Washington. . . . Yet all three of these qualities are to be found in the person of a certain freshman representative, Abraham A. Ribicoff."

Back in Hartford the insurance executives, bankers, manufacturers, and, in the outlying countryside, the Yankee farmers, were heard to speak with respect of "Abe" Ribicoff. Within the Democratic party there was some private grumbling. Ribicoff was playing the conservative game. A party leader at a private dinner called him "The Jewish Lausche." When this was reported to Frank Lausche, the Ohio Democrat whose anti-spending conservatism was famous, he burst out laughing and predicted that at the rate Abe's reputation was growing they'd be calling Lausche "The Slovenian Ribicoff."

Ribicoff himself is serious about his political course. "I consider myself as having followed an independent course in politics. I am not doctrinaire. I am not extreme. This is why liberals are often after me. Basically, I have always been positive in my campaigns and in office. I never indulge in personalities. If you do that people respect you."

Senator McMahon died in July 1952. Ribicoff ran against Prescott Bush for the remaining four years of McMahon's term in a campaign that was quick and hectic. It was Eisenhower's landslide year and although Ribicoff ran far ahead of his party, he lost by 30,000 votes out of a total exceeding one million.

He returned to Hartford to practice law with his brother. He made some speeches, made some money, and waited. In June of 1954 he was nominated to run for governor against the Republican incumbent, John Davis Lodge, brother of Henry Cabot Lodge.

For Ribicoff the 1954 campaign was important and difficult. Some of the freshness in his reputation had faded with the 1952 defeat. The Eisenhower *mystique* was powerful. He was a Democratic Jew running against a Republican Yankee, not in his own urban Hartford but in all Connecticut, including the upper-class preserves in the west and the small conservative communities tucked into the hills and valleys throughout the state. And 1954, like 1952 and 1950, was a dirty year in American politics. The charge of "communism" volleyed in a thousand campaigns. Personal defamation had risen from the marshes of whispering campaigns to become part of the atmosphere in broad daylight. Ribicoff began his campaign by announcing, "If we cannot win decently, I do not want to win at all." His opponent, Lodge, took the pledge for a clean campaign. Both men stuck to it. Ribicoff promised to abolish the archaic county governments, to build better highways, and to expand schools and institutions for mental patients.

To observers of the Ribicoff career, what distinguished his campaign throughout the state, and later his success in office, was the effect he had on the press. The proprietors of the Connecticut press were overwhelmingly conservative, which was not unusual, but some were also respected and listened to. He had their conservative editorials to contend with and their corps of reporters to deal with. His basic asset was his own personality and history. No corruption or sleaziness had been associated with his name. He was, somewhat like Eisenhower, above politics.

He had his face, which was photogenic and reinforced the image

of his career. Underneath it all he had a shrewd politician's judgment of how to please the right people at the right time and an
instinct about what makes news. His first explanation for his success with the press is, "I happen to like newspapermen. I never
kidded them along."

But all politicians love all newspapermen, or practically all, during a campaign. Why did he score so heavily and so consistently?
"You've got to have a feel for it. It's a visceral feeling, right inside
you, an automatic response. You don't think about it, you just
know. From the day I hit Washington I was in the news." One of
the most common questions to his staff during a campaign for office
or for legislation is, "What impression will this make on the public?" Every politician worries about this, but few worry as produc-
tively as Ribicoff.

He followed the editorials of the conservative *Hartford Courant*
meticulously. Each morning during the campaign Mrs. Ribicoff
would bring in the *Courant* and read the editorials to her husband
before he got dressed. They would discuss the arguments and
plan the responses. (According to those close to the couple, Mrs.
Ribicoff showed perception and wisdom in her recommendations.
More than once she made the decisions on tactics.) His staff has
little doubt that Ribicoff gave major attention to making an impact
on the proprietors of Connecticut papers.

Ribicoff, with his campaign to win independent and conservative
votes, was not always found on the same side of the street as Bailey.
The candidate once said, "I will run the government and Bailey
will run the party." Bailey tended to the messy details of political
machinery and didn't seem surprised if Ribicoff took public swipes
at him for doing so. At a luncheon attended by newspapermen,
politicians, and businessmen, Ribicoff denounced "the delegate
brokers" of his party and made it clear that he was referring to
Bailey and another party leader. The other party leader stopped
talking to Ribicoff. Bailey was understanding.

Another time Ribicoff said, "There are some who are retailers
for votes and others who are wholesalers. The retailers . . . get
votes, one by one, individually, by favors given or patronage dis-
tributed. I am a wholesaler. I go after whole blocs of votes—by the

thousands—by following principles I believe in and know other people not in politics believe in also."

Wavering Republicans of Connecticut listened carefully to Ribicoff. Dissident Democrats who refused to work with Bailey came to work with Ribicoff. But if Ribicoff concentrated on wholesale lots and Bailey concentrated on retail lots, they met almost every night of the campaign to add up the day's results.

Ribicoff not only paid respectful attention to the powerful publishers. He paid special attention to the newspapermen whose work ended on Page One. In his understanding of the uses of news, Ribicoff approached genius. His personal relations with reporters were close. He asked their advice. He is a good listener when he wants to be and he listened to reporters' ideas. He could be infinitely engaging, not with buttering smiles or routine flattery, but with flashes of candor unexpected from politicians. "I like to think of candor," he once wrote, "as a straight ball that is thrown just when everyone, including the batter, is sure it's going to be a curve." In office or out, he was, until he joined the Cabinet, the most available man in Connecticut public life.

In the end, the conservative thunderers of Hartford could not find him truly offensive in their editorials. And his photogenic face and his lively news stories kept landing on Page One. His major themes were for positive programs, moderation, and without putting it in so many words, the honesty, integrity, and intelligence of Abraham Ribicoff. He won by 3,115 votes.

He was the only Democrat on the state ticket to win, and even before he took office he began his permanent residence on the front pages of Connecticut newspapers. Connecticut law requires the incoming governor to hold budget hearings, a monotonous ritual always performed obscurely in the State House. Ribicoff announced he would hold each budget hearing at the institution whose appropriation was being considered. "I held those hearings in the prisons, in the schools for retarded children, in the mental hospitals. Where the Governor goes, the press goes. This was the first time most of the press had ever been in those places. They had never seen anything like it. It's one thing to talk about appropriations for the retarded but when you see a forty-five-year-old woman sitting in a basket, you're not dealing with statistics any more. The impact on the press was tremendous."

He followed a Ribicoff dictum of never fighting with anyone in public if you can help it. And he dealt with everyone all over the political spectrum. He telephoned powerful Republican financiers for advice, he appointed important businessmen to state commissions. His inaugural address was an ode to bipartisan co-operation, "what I should like to call the integrity of compromise."

But he wasn't proposing a moratorium on politics. His use of the press brought Republican legislative leaders close to apoplexy. The Governor instituted not one, but two press conferences a day. The first was at 10 A.M., which meant that he pre-empted the front pages of the afternoon papers, frequently getting his side of an issue out first. The legislature usually convened at noon and picked up the challenge with a rejoinder to the Governor. But at 4 P.M. the Governor held his second press conference, replying to the as-yet-unpublished Republican statement. The lead political stories, morning and afternoon, always seemed to be quoting the Governor, and he always seemed to have the last word.

When he wanted to say something to the public, he spoke it in his own voice. "Stay away from handouts," he tells his subordinates. "Nothing gives warmth and personality to something as much as each reporter writing his own story."

Like the Old Testament Prophet Ezekiel, Ribicoff's ordinary prose can be dull and pedagogic, his frequent sermons on virtue leaden with lugubrious goodness. He repeated one exemplary story from his youth so often that it became known to reporters in the State House as "The Parable of the Doughnuts." It seems that young Abe used to walk to school with another boy in New Britain. Every day they passed a bakery from whence came the fragrance of fresh-baked pastries. One day the other boy had some money. He went inside and bought a large bag full of freshly baked doughnuts. As he and Abe walked side by side to school the other boy ate his doughnuts and never once offered one to Abe. This was indicative of a serious flaw in the boy's nature, Ribicoff would tell his audience, because the other fellow some years later went to prison and Abe Ribicoff went on to become governor.

But like the Prophet Ezekiel, Ribicoff knows how to dramatize a lesson, and his public acts can be spectacular and bring awe to the people. In 1955 disastrous floods filled valleys in parts of Connecticut. Governor Ribicoff at once took to a helicopter, set down in isolated places, talked with the stranded and the destitute. He issued orders on the fly. Most of the orders could have been issued more readily from the State House. But on the scene, his presence gave heart to the stricken, urgency to the bureaucracy, and made spectacular stories for the newspapers.

In 1958 two important events occurred in Ribicoff's life. He was re-elected governor by the biggest plurality in Connecticut history. And he announced that he would work to nominate John F. Kennedy for President of the United States. President Kennedy has been quoted as saying: "Abe Ribicoff was the first man who thought I could be President of the United States."

The two had met in the House of Representatives in 1949, Kennedy in his second term, Ribicoff in his first. The Jewish freshman from Connecticut sat down beside the Irish sophomore from Massachusetts, introduced himself, and began to chat. "Our philosophies were pretty much the same," Ribicoff says. "I recognized right away that Jack Kennedy had a certain quality about him. I wrote to a Hartford newspaperwoman back then, in 1949, that Jack Kennedy would be the first Roman Catholic President of the United States."

Six years later, at the Democratic state convention in Worcester, Massachusetts, Governor Ribicoff, of Connecticut, said in his keynote speech that the Democrats ought to nominate John Kennedy for Vice-President of the United States at the national convention. This earliest recorded plug for Kennedy made no impact. But afterward in the back of the hall Ribicoff said, "Jack, I really mean it."

Kennedy, from some reports, was unsure of the wisdom of an attempt for the national ticket in 1956. His father was even less sure, afraid a premature attempt would be fatal. But Ribicoff was insistent, and plainly no one told him to stop. His promotion of the Kennedy candidacy finally made front-page news that June at the annual Governors' Conference, another annual forum from which Ribicoff had always drawn extra dividends of news coverage.

"Bailey and I organized New England behind Kennedy," Ribicoff says. "But Jack was uncertain all the time, and just before the convention he wanted to back out. I had the floor for a nomination at one o'clock at the convention but as the time came I had no word how Jack had decided. At five minutes of one Bobby Kennedy finally came down and said, 'Go ahead, Abe. Nominate him.' "

Kennedy came close in 1956, but lost to Estes Kefauver. Ribicoff immediately set his sights, along with other Kennedy intimates, for the presidential nomination in 1960. He worked at the governor's level from 1956 to 1958, and after his re-election in 1958 operated on a popular level. Ribicoff was the only important public figure speaking consistently for the Kennedy candidacy during the four years after 1956. He had important company only in January of 1960 when Ohio Governor Michael DiSalle joined him. It was Ribicoff, however, with Bailey *sotto voce,* whose voice set off the chorus.

There seems little doubt that, offered his choice of jobs by a grateful President, Ribicoff wants to be a Justice of the United States Supreme Court. Asked about it today, he turns aside the question with: "He who does not seek is often found. The one thing you should never seek is the Supreme Court."

Court appointments must wait for vacancies, and the President-elect had no vacancies awaiting him on the bench. One of the major political waiting rooms for the Supreme Court is the Attorney Generalship, which a new President can fill. It was generally assumed, widely published, and privately acknowledged that Ribicoff was about to enter the waiting room.

By tradition, the political and regional composition of the Supreme Court has been preserved, with a "New England chair" a fixture in the history of the Court. This means that Ribicoff, if tradition were followed, would take the place of Justice Felix Frankfurter of Massachusetts, who is also Jewish. But Justice Frankfurter, a spry seventy-eight, has given no sign of resigning in the near future.

Whatever the reason, the plans for Ribicoff changed. He was no longer mentioned as the new Attorney General. He has said he changed his mind about Attorney General because that job is negative, telling people what they can't do, while Health, Education, and Welfare is positive. In addition, he said he told the President, "I don't think a Catholic President should have a Jewish Attorney General forcing the integration of Negroes upon white Protestants." Others point out that in pressing racial integration Ribicoff might have alienated powerful southern senators, with rights of confirmation over Supreme Court appointments.

Ribicoff had scarcely been sworn in as Secretary of Health, Education, and Welfare before he began to make news in the dramatic Ribicoff manner. (He has said, significantly, "Except for the State Department, this department makes more news than any other activity in government.") The President asked him to do something about Cuban refugees pouring into the Miami area. As he did with the Connecticut floods, he made his presence felt and recorded on the scene.

"I went down there. I talked to people, smelled them, saw them. There were decisions to be made that no one had made all this time. I made decisions on the spot. Some of our people said, 'Where will the money come from? What will we tell the Comptroller General?' You know what I told them? 'The hell with the Comptroller General. If the damn money isn't going into our pockets and is going to help human beings in need, then spend it. Once it's spent nobody can do anything about it. Let me worry about the Comptroller General.' " When the new Secretary left Florida the Miami *News* ran a front-page editorial entitled, "Thank you, Mr. Ribicoff."

Thus, in his first public act Ribicoff had overcome the impersonal routine of a great executive department whose employees are controlled by the civil service and whose money is supervised by the Congress and the Bureau of the Budget. Whether he can continue to shine through the enveloping mass remains to be seen.

Secretary Ribicoff's agency is a social mechanism so vast it is difficult to comprehend the span of its bureaucracy and the variety of life to which it administers. It is a massive agglomeration of federal functions. Practically every federal ministration applied to the training and health of Americans is handled by H.E.W.

The Department examines, treats, and hospitalizes the country's Indians and Eskimos, some 380,000 in over 200 tribes, in 52 hospitals, 23 health centers, and hundreds of field stations. But it ministers to a larger tribe yet, the Average American, which looks more and more to government to fight disease, keep poisons out of the environment, foster its education, and keep the children of the poor from slipping down the social drain.

The Public Health Service measures microbes in water and analyzes motor exhausts and radioactive fallout in the air. It shields continental United States from plagues and pests abroad by inspecting 70,000 airplanes and 33,000 ships a year. It watches epidemics from poliomyelitis to gonorrhea, sets standards of freshness for milk and lobsters, and keeps life-and-death statistics on the population. It makes some rare vaccines, like that for Rocky Mountain spotted fever, and regulates others injected into the bodies of millions of Americans. Probably the world's greatest single assault on disease is made at the Department's huge National Institutes of Health, just outside of Washington. Its National Library of Medicine with 1,049,000 works is the greatest collection of medical literature in history.

The Department's Food and Drug Administration tries to keep dirt and poisons out of whatever Americans swallow and nags at producers to label their foods truthfully. H.E.W.'s Office of Education is the focal point of a renaissance in American intellect, with functions added almost weekly. Even in a quiet year it makes more than one hundred thousand loans to college students, administers 6,500,000 tests, teaches 3,700,000 adults, and distributes 2,500,000 pamphlets. Social Security, run by H.E.W., is the largest insurance company in the country, with a $22 billion fund to cover 81,000,000 insured workers for pensions in their old age and payments to their survivors or benefits when they are disabled. Already the system pays monthly checks to 13,000,000 Americans. H.E.W. is the country's biggest welfare agency, doling out $2 billion of federal money to help support 5,800,000 destitute adults and dependent children, the blind, and the disabled.

This vast total of activity cost $3.7 billion this year and will run to at least $4 billion next year. And it seems destined to grow. When President Eisenhower was elected in 1952 he opposed "the welfare state" and more federal spending. He welded the collection of special agencies and independent activities then known as the Federal Security Agency into a single Cabinet-level Department of Health, Education, and Welfare. President Eisenhower appointed Oveta Culp Hobby the first Secretary. Thus he controlled its activities directly, was able to organize it along his own lines, and write its budget. But under the Eisenhower administration the Department of Health, Education, and Welfare doubled its employees, from 35,000 to 70,000, and more than doubled its first budget of $1.5 billion.

The man who now presides over this great mechanism is the first Democrat in the job. His headquarters are in the departmental building on Independence Avenue, one of that class of faceless architecture that blurs the capital. One enters an onyx lobby, past proletarian murals of the 1930's, rises to the fifth floor where signs of executive rank begin to show—wall-to-wall carpeting, wooden desks instead of steel ones, oil paintings instead of photographs, the governmental brand on the furniture placed discreetly out of sight. Here hang portraits of the earlier Secretaries: Mrs. Hobby, Marion Folsom, Arthur Flemming.

Ribicoff sits in a huge office, his desk at one end, a conference table at the other. Asked why he voted against creation of the organization when it was first proposed by President Truman, he said: "I don't like expanded government. I was against another department, another bureau, more bureaucracy. It's ironical but true."

Then why does he sit there at its head, when he had almost any job available to him? "Everything about H.E.W. is affirmative. Everything about it is directed toward the betterment of individuals and the betterment of society."

In his public propagation of the virtue of the affirmative approach Abraham Ribicoff can sound positively like the Reverend Norman Vincent Peale. "I hate to knock anyone. Be positive. Tell people what you are doing, not what someone else isn't doing. I don't like to take the negative approach ever."

Yet, privately, his approach may not always be one of affirmation. Behind closed doors he demands performance from his staff. When he is under stress he can get tense, have trouble sleeping, explode with language in the tradition of men who have worked at every sociological level of a colorful society. People who have worked with him say his mind does not absorb details readily but is capable of penetrating to the essence of problems. He seems impatient with minutiae and statistics, but once having understood the crux of a matter shows common sense and an ability to reduce issues to ordinary language.

Early in his administration of the Department he met the nine regional H.E.W. directors who had been called in for the occasion. As the Secretary entered, they rose from their seats around the eight-sided conference table, a company of veteran career officers, secure in civil-service tenure, hardened by the bureaucratic wars, most of them with the Social-Security system from its inception in 1935. They were cagy observers of Secretaries who have come and gone and who had called them into introductory sessions before. Much personal charm, urgent appeal, and brave new policy had been proclaimed before them but year after year they have had to run their distant duchies without the glamor and ambition of national office.

Ribicoff had met only two of the nine before, knew only one, Lawrence J. Bresnahan, of Boston, on a first-name basis. After the handshakes they all sat down, Ribicoff at the center. He began a sermon on positive action. The faces wore a steady noncommittal stare and it was easy to imagine the rhetoric washing down well-worn sluices through their minds. But as he talked, the Secretary drifted gradually from his public concern with positive thinking and began to exhibit some of his inner toughness and directness. He delivered a homily on small towns. "When I took this job, I deliberately stayed away from the Washington types. Washington is a company town. Everyone or almost everyone works for the Government. They aren't like other Americans who work on farms or have stores or jobs in factories. I deliberately took my top people from all over the country. Like Wally Turner, here, from Portland, Oregon. He's not my publicity man. I don't have one. He's an information man. But I told him, 'Wally, when you put out information, don't talk to the people of Washington, talk to the people of Portland, Oregon.' "

He instructed the directors on the power of positive publicity. "I know what it's like. A program is announced here and makes Page One in the Washington papers and perhaps in your towns it gets on Page 33." A few hard-boiled heads nodded. "Nothing that comes from here will make an impact on people in your area so well as something you do or say yourself. Make speeches. Be positive. Don't fight your critics. Tell what you're doing for people. If you do something for the aged or for children, send a feature story to the local papers. Almost everything you do is news if you can put it in human terms."

He warned them that they all had more work coming their way. "I'm not an empire builder. I don't look for more work. If anyone wants to steal functions from this department—and I've told them this—if anyone wants to take away jobs from the Department of Health, Education, and Welfare, let them. Fine! I'll be happy. We'll grow no matter what anyone does. Most of the new things the President of the United States wants to do are going to end up right in this department."

One of the regional directors said that a number of them had been waiting for a decision on a technical policy. Ribicoff, apparently reaching behind the question to a state of mind, said at once: "Yes, I know your problem. The trouble with bureaucracy is that decisions take too long. By the time you've written a letter and got a request for a memorandum and had a committee appointed, the problem has been chewed over a dozen times, all the life has gone out of it, all the freshness. In a bureaucracy it's always safer not to do something. By the time you get a decision, it's too late and nobody gives a damn any more."

By now the balding heads were nodding, the eye-blink rate was faster, backs were stiffer and closer to the edge of chairs. Beneath the tough hides a nerve had been touched. "I want you to know," the Secretary said, "that I'm a direct-action guy. I'm easy to see. When you've got a policy problem, send it to me. I'll give you an answer: Yes or no. That's my job: to make decisions. If decisions aren't made, everything piles up behind them and the life goes out of work. Come to me and you'll get decisions. You won't always like the decisions, but you'll get them."

A director, now smiling, brought up a specific, involved problem. Ribicoff listened a moment and then broke in: "I don't know what you're talking about. I can't give you a decision because I don't know what you mean. But before you leave, tell it to the Under Secretary here and we'll give you a decision when I understand the problem."

Thus Ribicoff rules a great organization, an enormous organism with a mass and a momentum of its own capable of swallowing an unwary leader without a trace. In his office Ribicoff meditated on how a single man can influence so vast an activity. He dug his fingers into a bowl on his desk and contemptuously held up a snarl of paper clips. "You don't count paper clips!" He slammed his palm on the desk. "You don't count blotters! There are people to do things like that.

"You make decisions. You keep producing ideas. You have to keep your mind fresh, open to assimilate new things. You've got to let people know you're aware of their work and that you think their work is important. Everyone wants his work to be respected. The nature of man is such that basically he wants to be constructive. I've got to keep that feeling alive in this department."

Yet it was widely known that he would like to be a Justice on the United States Supreme Court. And associates of Ribicoff speculate that the man who had been influential in making John Kennedy the first Roman Catholic President might envision himself the first Jewish President or Vice-President—speculation Ribicoff conventionally laughs at.

The monument he wishes to leave along the New Frontier is modest enough: "I would like history to say that I helped President Kennedy put his program across."

It is a modest ambition for a man who has striven for primacy, but it is a complex task. It is composed of the daily demands for commanding a bureaucracy, of an endless round of testimony and cajolery to push legislation through Congress, of Cabinet meetings. In this Ribicoff sees John Kennedy and speaks to him more often than he did during the pre-election years. The President appears to be as receptive as ever to the man who early waved the Kennedy banner. But still there are other men of first magnitude in the executive collection of national and world figures. It is not easy to be the brightest star in such a constellation. If Ribicoff failed to maintain his personal impact upon his department and upon his times, he might merely be remembered as the fourth Secretary of Health, Education, and Welfare.

At the end of a day Ribicoff's face shows signs of weariness. He is no inexhaustible dynamo. But the mouth still carries the hard set of determination and the face a lonely sense of driving duty. He had once said that he admired the Yankee ability of not being overly emotional about anything. He had also said, "In politics, the top man has got to be independent, strong enough in himself so that he isn't the slave of any single group. You've got to keep everyone at arm's length."

Behind his desk he sits in the high blue leather chair that had once been his as governor of Connecticut, and lays his head against the embossed gold seal of the state of Connecticut with the Latin letters still visible: *Qui Transtulit Sustinet*—He who transplanted, sustains.

In his lonely drive for political success he was now near the top, an achievement with all the hazards of high altitude. In the rarefied air of national leadership a new order of personal strength is needed; in the midst of power politics, a superior sense of balance. But the paper boy from Star Street has been transplanted before and has been sustained before. The men around Abraham Ribicoff insist there is no reason to expect him to stop.

10.

BUSINESSMEN IN POLITICS

Luther Hodges
J. Edward Day

By DON OBERDORFER
and WALTER PINCUS

BACK IN THE SPRING OF 1952 THE CASHIER IN A BEANERY NEAR
Goldsboro in the tobacco country of North Carolina was startled
when a well-dressed gentleman thrust a campaign card at her
and blurted a political message.

"I'm Luther Hodges and I'm running for lieutenant governor
and I've never been in office and I wish you'd vote for me," he
said in a sweat as he rushed out the door.

"I'm for you because you ain't in Raleigh or Washington
now," the cashier called after him.

"I started from there," recalls Luther Hodges. At age fifty-four,
with a successful career in business behind him, he entered the
world of politics. Nine years later he was a national figure and
John F. Kennedy's first and only choice for Secretary of Commerce.

In the summer of 1950 Adlai E. Stevenson, then governor of
Illinois, traveled one day to his sister's home in Bloomington for
some relaxation. At the time he faced the problem of finding a new
state insurance commissioner. During the day Stevenson asked
another of the guests, the president of a large insurance concern,
for some suggestions. "Get a hard-hitting young lawyer not tied
to any faction of the insurance business," Stevenson was advised.

The Governor drove back to Springfield that night with J. Edward Day, his thirty-five-year-old staff aide, and Day's wife, Mary Louise. While Stevenson curled up in the back seat of their car for the sixty-mile drive, the Days discussed the insurance official's advice.

"That sounds like you, Ed," Mrs. Day finally said. A few weeks later J. Edward Day was Illinois's insurance commissioner. The post led, three years later, to a career as an insurance company executive, which in turn was the steppingstone eight years after to appointment as John Kennedy's Postmaster General.

Hodges and Day are the two "political businessmen" in the Kennedy Cabinet. As secretary of commerce, Hodges speaks for the business community and is charged with bringing it along to the New Frontier. Day runs the Post Office, which with half a million permanent employees is itself the largest retail and service establishment in the country.

Neither man is a professional politician in the usual sense. Neither has any discernible political organization behind him. But both have considerable experience in using their own capabilities in both business and government to get ahead rapidly. This much they have in common, but the two men as individuals are very different.

LUTHER H. HODGES IS UNIQUE IN MANY WAYS IN THE KENNEDY coterie. He is the only man in the Cabinet born in the nineteenth century. He lacks the lean sophistication or political savvy of his colleagues. Hodges is cut from different cloth. He is a promoter and a salesman at heart, rather than a deep or original thinker. He would be any city's most successful Chamber of Commerce man, although the policies he hawks are progressive by business standards.

Luther Hodges came up the hard way. The story of his career reads like a Horatio Alger tale, compounded of hard work, determination, shrewd decisions—plus a heavy dose of luck. His birth on March 9, 1898, was a politician's dream. It took place in a cabin on his father's tenant farm in Pittsylvania County, Virginia. The cabin was stark enough to impress anybody with his humble beginnings; happily, it was also sturdy enough to stand even today as a local landmark.

Hodges was the eighth of nine children and the only boy in the family to attend college. He earned the money to enter the University of North Carolina selling newspapers on the Norfolk & Western Railroad. His chief recollection today of the start of World War I, in fact, is that he sold more papers that day.

At the university Hodges waited on tables, fired furnaces, was elected president of the student body, and was picked the best all-around member of his class. After graduation he went home to Leaksville, North Carolina, and worked in the local textile mill as secretary to the general manager. This was in 1919. Hodges soon organized the first personnel department in the mill, owned by the Marshall Field family of Chicago. He rose rapidly in the organization: 1927—manager of the blanket mill; 1934—production manager of all mills in the Leaksville area; 1938—general manager of all twenty-nine Field mills in the United States and abroad; 1943—vice president in charge of manufacturing for Marshall Field enterprises and living in New York City.

In 1950, despite a salary of more than $75,000 a year, Hodges decided he had enough. He quit Marshall Field and told his friends he would spend the rest of his life in public service. Hodges made good on that promise. He went from Marshall Field to Marshall Plan, becoming chief of the Industry Division of the reconstruction effort in West Germany.

A business friend in North Carolina suggested he run for lieutenant governor in 1952. The political novice was expected to run a poor third in a field of three, but he won big. Two years later Governor William Umstead died of a heart attack, and Hodges moved into the statehouse. In 1956 he was elected to a four-year term of his own. At the conclusion of his term in 1960 he was a natural to join the Kennedy administration.

This, in brief, is the career of Luther H. Hodges up until the time he entered the Cabinet. But what kind of man is he? How did he manage to pull his way up so fast?

"It sounds strange," an associate says, "but one secret of his success is that physically he is healthy as hell. He has a burst of health." Hodges retires almost every night at ten, and has been known to walk out on an evening guest. ("I just tell them, excuse me, I'm going to bed.")

Hodges wakes up at six thirty, lands running, and goes hard all day. He doesn't smoke and drinks little. His favorite foods are white beans, turnip salad, and corn bread. His refusal to take coffee breaks or allow them for less Spartan state employees caused a ruckus in the North Carolina state government. When Hodges is finished for the day, he stops dead. Friends say he rarely looks back, almost never worries about decisions he has made. "I don't carry problems to bed with me," he says.

Hodges' relentless drive and ambition can be traced to his early family life in the mill town of Leaksville. Most of his brothers and sisters, in keeping with the practice of those days, went to work in the mill as soon as they reached their early teens. Young Luther had only two and one-half years of high school before his time came. He recalls that his father discouraged the idea of college. But Luther was determined, and made it to the University at Chapel Hill mostly on his own steam. Hodges has continued to work hard all his life. North Carolina Senator B. Everett Jordan, a long-standing business associate and friend (Hodges appointed him to the United States Senate when an incumbent died), analyzes Hodges' success this way: "He's just good country native stock with a lot of brains. He scrambled for a living and worked like hell."

All through his life Hodges has had a knack for success in business. "Making money," he has said, "is the easiest thing I know. The way I do it is to keep my eyes open and pick out something that has good, money-making possibilities. This is rather a cold-blooded thing. Best thing you can do is pick out something that people destroy, something they eat or smoke or drink. Borrow a lot of money, as much as you can afford, and let the other fellow's money pay for all your growth."

For almost thirty-five years Hodges has applied this formula to one or another side-line venture. It has been these spare-time ventures, rather than his full-time executive jobs in business and government, which produced his present nest egg of more than $500,000.

It all started, however, with one bad investment. While managing the blanket mill in the 1920's Hodges put $1,000 (borrowed at 6 per cent from the Leaksville bank) into a local furniture factory. His father was convinced to put up an additional $1,500. Eventually they lost every penny. Another investment opportunity was soon offered to the popular young mill manager. This one fit the Hodges pattern, being a share of something people burn up— fuel oil and gasoline. Hodges and two partners put up $1,000 each to become local distributors for Shell Oil Company, which was moving East in the late twenties. Five years later Hodges and a Danville, Virginia, chiropractor bought out the other partner for $34,000. Trading as "Clark Oil Company," the two remaining entrepreneurs built up a system of 100 service stations in Rockingham and Caswell counties, North Carolina, and Henry and Pittsylvania counties, Virginia. They each took $6,000 out of the business almost every year, and sold the concern for more than a half million dollars several years after Hodges became governor. Hodges was grateful to have the chiropractor, an inveterate penny watcher, for a partner. This is because Hodges considers himself "a plunger" who is "a little fast with money" once he gets into a business.

Neither partner made the oil-distributing business his regular work. Hodges says he always followed a rule of refusing to discuss his oil company or other outside investments while working on his regular job. As governor he instructed aides to refuse any calls for him about such matters. "You'll have to get me at home or on weekends," he said.

The only time Hodges worked full time on one of his side-line ventures was in the early 1950's when he "discovered" Howard Johnson restaurants. He traveled to the company's operation and management meetings in several states. Once Howard Johnson himself got sore when Hodges presented a lengthy list of suggested improvements. Everett Jordan, now co-owner with Hodges of several

Howard Johnson franchises, said that his partner got to know "everything there is to know" about the restaurant business by diligent study and unabated curiosity. Hodges figured out the operating margins for food and labor. He knew everything but how much meat to put in the hamburgers, Jordan says.

Although the Commerce Secretary has sold all his transportation and other industrial stocks to avoid any "conflict of interest," he still maintains ownership in Howard Johnson restaurants in Durham, Fayetteville, Raleigh, Greensboro, and Charlotte, North Carolina, as well as in several motels. He periodically inspects the kitchens of his restaurants. A man who is finicky about his food ("I want it cooked right and with good service"), Hodges sees economic as well as sanitary values in kitchen cleanliness. "You can keep the place clean as cheaply as you can keep it dirty," he tells his cooks.

His restaurant ventures illustrate an important Hodges characteristic. Given a new idea, he will study all the angles extensively. Once committed, he sets to work in a personal campaign to sell others on his venture. He is an intensely practical man, little concerned with profound theory. This is the pattern of a good salesman or promotion man, which is what Hodges has been all his life—in business or in government. Selling textiles, promoting German recovery, inviting industry to North Carolina, asking American business to step up production—in all these tasks Hodges has been a man with a sample case, a salesman well prepared.

The drive and good business sense which led to his financial success were also, not surprisingly, the foundations for his enterprise in the field of politics. Significantly, his career in elective office began with a typical Hodges look before the leap. The first people he consulted about the race for lieutenant governor of North Carolina in 1952 were fellow businessmen.

"I discovered the thing we all know now," Hodges recalls about the lieutenant governor's post. "It was a strategic job. The lieutenant governor named certain committees which control legislation and there were certain interests, lobbyists, who usually had something to do with this. It just came to me somehow that this is a very important job and yet, having talked to one or two lieutenant governors, I found they had not worked to get the job. They had been selected."

His campaign shattered tradition. "Poor Hodges, he'll finish last," the professional politicians snickered. But they failed to reckon with two things: Hodges was a joiner and a relentless worker. He covered all 100 counties in the state, beginning with the surprised cashier in that Goldsboro eatery. He bought $1.00 worth of gas at a time, handing out campaign cards at each filling station. He paid all his own campaign expenses, about $6,000. He visited every courthouse in the state. In each area he had friends in the Rotary Club, which had long been his favorite means of socializing. (Even as a vice president of Marshall Field he was president of the New York City Rotary Club.)

Hodges won. Elected without the help of the usual political forces in the state, Hodges felt little allegiance to workaday politicians. As presiding officer of the state senate, Lieutenant Governor Hodges abruptly reorganized the antique committee structure. "There must have been about thirty-five to thirty-seven committees. I cut out ten or twelve. The unfortunate part is that I cut out a few secretaries at the same time without realizing it and made some eternal enemies. If I had known what I was up against I don't know if I would have had the courage because they could have cut my throat."

On Sunday morning, November 7, 1954, Lieutenant Governor Hodges and his wife, Martha, a former schoolteacher, were preparing to go to Sunday school at Leaksville Methodist Church. The telephone rang. Hodges says he'll never forget it. "The call came from Ed Rankin, Governor Umstead's secretary. He said, 'Governor Hodges'—Yes, he said, 'Governor Hodges, Mr. Umstead passed away a few minutes ago.' "

The businessman-governor lost no time in impressing statehouse employees that he was a different political breed. In his first hour in the governor's office he played the role of an innocent in Babylon and prepared the state workers for an era of governmental changes.

"There was a series of buttons on the desk," he recalls. "Partly for devilment and partly to find what would happen, I began punching them. People started coming in from back offices and everywhere. They came in and I was brand new and didn't even know them. I said, 'What do you do, and why do you do it?' That was the basic approach, and it created, er-ah, tremendous interest."

Even in the governor's chair Hodges paid little heed to organization politics. He looked around the state for a smart lawyer with good government background but no political ties to help him run the statehouse. Professor Paul Johnston of the Institute of Government at the University of North Carolina became his man. Johnston was dubious at first, later found him fascinating: "He wanted to do a good job and he didn't give a turkey damn about politics."

In the early days Johnston and Ed Rankin, a holdover from the Umstead staff, devised a special "selection form" to help Hodges make state appointments. The paper listed the job, the pay, the incumbent, and the name of his Democratic county chairman, along with the names and backgrounds of leading candidates—and the identity of their Democratic county chairmen.

The new governor was surprised and irritated to find Democratic county politicians listed on the form. He did not want to be bound by their recommendations in filling state jobs. So the political data were quickly dropped from the poop sheets. The jobs were patronage no longer. This set the pattern for all Hodges' appointments. During his governorship he named more than thirty state judges. "A man could run a state for twenty-five years on that much good will," says Johnston. But Hodges paid little attention to party politics in choosing his judges. Instead, he consulted the leading nonpolitical legal figures in the state, and even solicited suggestions from members of the State Supreme Court.

One of the most unusual aspects of Hodges' tenure in office is that his close relatives did not seem to benefit. Brothers or brothers-in-law of southern governors have often enjoyed spectacular commercial successes in the wake of family political prominence. Today one of Hodges' brothers is a Shell service station operator in Leaksville. Another is a supervisor at a state prison camp. Three widowed sisters are retired millworkers. Another sister is a schoolteacher. The other surviving sister lives with her retired husband.

During his term as governor Hodges reorganized many facets of state government. The upshot of his reforms was always the same: elimination of waste and insulation of state government from traditional politics. He appointed Paul Johnston as head of a new Department of Administration with substantial powers to cut the payroll and red tape. His most controversial move was to abolish the old system of regional highway commissioners whose power over roadbuilding had made them local political barons. Instead, Hodges set up a state-wide roads commission, supposedly "nonpolitical" in outlook. The pros at the statehouse laughed at the idea of a "nonpolitical" public road system, but the old power was undercut.

Some ascribe Hodges' distaste for politics to lack of imagination or naïveté, others to a rough-hewn honesty. The trait is often displayed in men who came to their politics late in life and feel uncomfortable in an alien world. Whatever the motive, Hodges has always been an administrator who took his ideas more from the executive suite than from the courthouse. He sees politics as something that gets in the way of efficiency.

As a result of all this Luther Hodges created a political machine the likes of which had never been seen in North Carolina. In fact, nobody could find it at all. Luckily for him, rival politicians were so awed by his obvious public popularity that the only opponents in his 1956 race for a full four-year term were a couple of unfortunate unknowns. Hodges went through the motions of a campaign, just as if a powerful foe were threatening him with political extinction. He won in a landslide.

In 1960, as he prepared to retire from the governor's chair, Hodges set out to pick his successor. He encouraged Attorney General Malcolm Seawell to enter the Democratic primary, helped raise funds for him, and passed the word to his friends to swing behind Seawell. But Hodges couldn't transfer his personal popularity. The Attorney General finished a poor third in a field of four candidates. The top two candidates were Terry Sanford, a young attorney and favorite of the liberal forces in the state, and former North Carolina Assistant Attorney General I. Beverly Lake, who promised to take the state back to a rigid pattern of racial segregation. In the runoff primary Hodges supported Sanford, who won.

During his six years as North Carolina's governor Hodges be came nationally known for two major reasons: he led North Carolina to a moderate position on the overpowering social problem of school desegregation; and building on this accomplishment, he spearheaded a strong drive to bring new industry to the state.

Only six months before Hodges became governor the United States Supreme Court shattered the southern calm with its epochal decision against school segregation. Hodges describes the resulting crisis as the toughest problem he had faced. *Time* magazine, going further, said of his situation: "Suddenly the tenant farmer's son stood amid the biggest crisis since Appomatox."

To the north and the south of his state Hodges saw the utterly unyielding racial policies of Virginia and South Carolina. But the Tar Heel state between, long before denied the slave trade because of the great reefs off its seacoast, had been settled by yeoman farmers with few slaves. It had never been as much a part of plantation society of the Old South as its haughtier neighbors. "A valley of humility between two mountains of conceit," a home-grown philosopher once called North Carolina.

Hodges picked Robert Giles, a smart young lawyer from the university, to study the court's ruling and North Carolina's options. Working with worried leaders of the state's business community, Hodges settled on a plan and led the fight for its ratification by the legislature and the people. Instead of barring all change, the North Carolina approach permitted local school boards to accept Negro pupils in previously all-white schools on an individual application basis. But it allowed a "safety valve" for segregationists by providing that local schools could be closed by a majority of votes of citizens affected.

Although publicly keeping state hands off local school-board decisions, Hodges' aides actually met secretly with schoolmen from the state's urban areas. After some quiet collaboration, school boards in Charlotte, Winston-Salem, and Greensboro all announced on the same day in 1957 their decisions to admit the first Negro pupils, a token number, to white public schools. The North Carolina plan of selective integration has withstood all court tests to date and managed to neutralize the racial issue to an extent unknown in most southern states. Although getting national credit for its voluntary compliance with the high court, North Carolina today has less than one hundred Negro students in integrated public schools. In neighboring Virginia, which received a national black eye for its ill-fated defiance, more than two hundred Negro students attend integrated schools after court decrees.

With the integration crisis abated, North Carolina was in a good position to attract outside industry. It had a clear advantage over other southern states still facing potential racial blowups. Hodges was quick to capitalize on his opportunity. Well-publicized industry-hunting expeditions to the North bore fruit. North Carolina's development program during Hodges' administration brought the state 2,324 new or expanded plants, 318,233 new jobs, $431 million in new pay roll annually, and a capital investment of more than $1.1 billion.

The most serious setback to North Carolina during the Hodges era arose from the long and bitter textile-mill strike at Henderson in 1959. Hodges tried to stay aloof from it but was forced to try to mediate when tempers became aroused. The union and the millowner reached an agreement after Hodges stepped in, but management backtracked on the understanding before it could be implemented. Hodges said he was "misled" by the company. Nevertheless, amid all sorts of recriminations, Hodges called out the National Guard to maintain order as nonunion workers were brought into the area each day. The arrest and conviction on conspiracy charges of eight union members, including the Carolina director of the Textile Workers Union, broke the back of the strike but left bitter feelings against Hodges.

Labor leaders in the state charge that Hodges is "antiunion." They hold him responsible for much of the Henderson turmoil. Officials of the Textile Workers Union cited Hodges' own record as employer. The union won a plant election at the Marshall Field's Leaksville mill in 1938. But it was unable to work out a bargaining arrangement with Hodges. The union finally had to haul the mill management before the National Labor Relations Board on unfair-labor-practice charges before the company agreed to bargain satisfactorily. This agreement settled the labor board case.

Although he has had his troubles with unions, Hodges helped convince the legislature to pass the first state minimum-wage law in the South in 1959. Thousands of workers were brought up to the state wage floor of seventy-five cents an hour. Even the union leaders were enthusiastic about this law.

One of the keys to Hodges' political success has been his unusual knack for publicity. Although he seems today a born public-relations man, Hodges was woefully naïve about publicity when he first entered public life. During his first year as lieutenant governor a *Business Week* magazine editor called long distance and asked if he could send a crew to Raleigh to get an eight-hour interview and one hundred pictures on the life of a businessman in politics. "My answer," says Hodges, "was that I never talked to anybody longer than an hour in my life and I couldn't say anything intelligent after an hour. I told the man I had a mat and a picture of myself and I'd mail them." *Business Week* finally convinced him that a "political businessman" had a story to tell. The result was his first big national display.

Since then Hodges has needed little convincing. He became the first governor to pose for *Life* magazine in his underwear (to show he wore North Carolina products from the skin out). He took a shower in his suit for another publicity shot, and once allowed himself to be heaved into the ocean to publicize a state fishing contest. The magazines were full of pictures of the white-haired Governor, looking like a Santa Claus with a shave. "That Hodges is a wonderful guy," says a nationally-known news cameraman. "He'll do anything you ask."

Any good promotion man knows it helps to have a personal trademark. Hodges picked up a white carnation for his buttonhole the day he became governor and was hardly ever without one during his tenure. While on a 1959 trip to Russia with several other governors, Hodges wore a plastic carnation that looked so real that

Soviet security men were suspicious about his source of daily supply.

His traveling companions on the Russian foray, finding humor in Hodges' widespread distribution of North Carolina cigarettes among the startled Soviets, tried to find a camel to pose with Hodges for a home-consumption publicity photo. To the Carolinian's relief the Russian state was unable to produce the beast. Hodges was worried about the reaction of the competitors of Camel's cigarettes.

Hodges also used public relations to further his state's reputation for progressivism, even at considerable political risk to himself. In 1959 he agreed to State Department requests that he play host to a visit to North Carolina by President Sekou Touré of the new African state of Guinea. Both the visiting Africans and prominent North Carolina Negroes were entertained at an interracial banquet given by Hodges. He also opened the publicly-owned Carolina Inn at Chapel Hill, heretofore "for whites only," to Negro newsmen as well as the Africans. The visit drew plaudits from Washington, from Touré himself, and from such national publications as the *New York Times* and *Time* magazine.

Not all of Hodges' promotional efforts, however, went off so smoothly. He was scheduled to appear on *Time*'s May 1959 cover as the symbol of "North Carolina: The South's New Leader." The cover was canceled when the Henderson strike situation exploded in violence. Later *Time* presented Hodges with the portrait its artist had prepared to grace the cover. Reminiscing about it now Hodges says, "If you didn't have a sense of humor, it would make you sick."

Under North Carolina law an elected governor cannot succeed himself in an elected term. As he approached the end of his tenure Hodges began surveying the possibilities for his future. He was determined to remain in public service. His background and his recent activities made him eminently eligible for prominent posts in several different areas. His business career, industry-hunting success, and trip to Europe made him a natural candidate for an important government or foundation job in commerce. His experience in West Germany, his well-publicized trips to Russia and Europe, along with his hospitality to Sekou Touré, made him an acceptable candidate for a diplomatic post. His reputation as a moderate on racial matters gave him additional appeal on the national scene.

So at the beginning of 1960 Luther Hodges realized that his own future in public service hinged on the coming national election. As the leader of an important Democratic state, he was sought out by representatives of leading Democratic presidential hopefuls. Robert Kennedy found him not antagonistic but definitely leaning to Lyndon Johnson. Says Hodges, "I thought it would be a Democratic year, and that any decent candidate would win." Hodges even told the younger Kennedy that his brother's religion would hurt him. But if John Kennedy were nominated, Hodges added, he would cover as much territory as possible and emphasize the need for religious tolerance.

Kennedy forces worked on Hodges' successor Terry Sanford, who became the first prominent southern politician to desert the Johnson camp. The night before the dramatic Sanford announcement Bob Kennedy met Hodges in a corridor outside Sanford's hotel room. Hodges knew what was going to happen but raised no objection.

Several weeks after the nomination John Kennedy telephoned Hodges and asked him to become honorary national chairman of the Businessmen-for-Kennedy drive. Hodges accepted. In that post he traveled widely throughout the country, and true to his word, he constantly discussed the religious issue. Hodges also labored to make Kennedy more acceptable to conservatives by organizing groups of businessmen in each state to support publicly the Democratic ticket. The Kennedy hierarchy now feels that this effort was extremely effective in helping to neutralize potentially damaging attacks on the Democrats as labor-dominated.

From the very beginning John Kennedy had only Hodges in mind for his Secretary of Commerce. He had all the attributes for the office: Kennedy needed a prominent southerner in the cabinet; Hodges was well respected by the business community and had a reputation for progressivism that would fit in with the New Frontier. In the Kennedy inner circle it had been simply taken for granted that Hodges would get the job. But nobody said so to the

North Carolina governor until Kennedy called him to Palm Beach to "discuss the Commerce Department." By then Hodges had long since been "announced" as the official choice for Commerce by many newspapers. Actually, he was not offered the job until fifteen minutes before Kennedy led him onto a patio at Palm Beach, December 3, 1960, to announce the selection.

From that moment Hodges went to work in his typically intense way to discover all he could about his new job. He quickly found that the job would be what he made of it. The Secretary of Commerce presides over an assortment of unrelated bureaus and responsibilities. This hodgepodge of activities includes the Census Bureau, the Coast and Geodetic Survey, the Business and Defense Services Administration, the Office of Business Economics, the Patent Office, the Bureau of Public Roads, the Inland Waterway Corporation, the National Bureau of Standards, the Maritime Administration, and the Weather Bureau. Most of these outfits could run along reasonably well if there were no Commerce Secretary. Some of them were in business even before the Department of Commerce was created in 1903. The Commerce post has rarely been one of great influence within a President's cabinet, a reflection of the men chosen as much as of their functions.

Herbert Hoover, Commerce Secretary from 1921 to 1928, was the only holder of the office who was able to use it to enhance his own political fortunes. But Hoover already had unusual prestige before he came to the office. President-elect Harding begged him to take the commerce job, and Hoover insisted on his right to participate in the making of all important economic decisions involving business, agriculture, labor, finance, or foreign affairs. Harding agreed to inform the other Cabinet members of Hoover's special status.

As Commerce Secretary, Hoover was a big power. The Secretary of State consulted him about disarmament. When the Mississippi River flooded, Hoover and a staff stayed at the scene three months directing a rescue and reconstruction effort. He battled the British on the price of rubber, and gave his views on Dutch activities in rubber-producing areas.

But Hoover was the exception. Later Commerce Secretaries either lacked his stature with the President or were in disfavor with the business community. Particularly under the Democrats, the "business seat" at the Cabinet table has often been uncomfortable. Franklin D. Roosevelt frequently admonished his first Commerce Secretary, "Uncle Dan" Roper, to "sit tight and be quiet." F.D.R. replaced Roper with Harry L. Hopkins in an attempt to build up Hopkins' political appeal. In one and a half years as Commerce Secretary the ailing Hopkins spent less than thirty days, off and on, in his office.

Jesse H. Jones agreed to take over Hopkins' job only on the condition that he retain direction of the Reconstruction Finance Corporation. An aide apparently ran the Commerce Department for Jones, who spent most of his time battling with Roosevelt and handing out R.F.C. loans. F.D.R. privately called him "Jesus H. Jones." After Roosevelt dismissed Jones, the angry Texan asked Congress to remove the R.F.C. from the Commerce Department and the hands of his successor, Henry A. Wallace. Congress overwhelmingly agreed.

Hodges is going to try, at least, to follow the Hoover pattern. A few weeks before taking office Hodges had several talks about the scope of his responsibilities with President-elect Kennedy. He came away with the understanding that he would be given a major role in such matters as transportation and area redevelopment.

Hodges conceives of his task basically as a salesman's job, with heavy emphasis on advance promotion. As his Under Secretary, Hodges picked Edward Gudeman, Jr., of Sears Roebuck ("he's probably the top merchandise man in the country"). Other marketing and selling experts were moved into key spots, along with Paul Johnston, the government administration expert from North Carolina, and Robert Giles, the young lawyer who studied the North Carolina racial problem for Hodges.

The Business Advisory Council of the Commerce Department was one of Hodges' early problems. This select group of top business executives had become industry's ultimate status symbol. To the public, however, it appeared to be big business's inside track to government. Congress resented its semiautonomous status. This situation was further complicated when Hodges took office; Ralph J. Cordiner, president of General Electric, was the council's chairman, and Cordiner's company had just been convicted for its part in a criminal price-fixing conspiracy.

The new Commerce Secretary set out to change the Business Advisory Council into a more acceptable institution. While Hodges worked to democratize the council, he was careful not to destroy its special meaning to businessmen. A series of delicate discussions with leaders of the council took place over many weeks. The result: Cordiner resigned, Hodges ended up with control over the council as its new presiding officer, and the B.A.C.'s meetings with government officials were opened to the public. In previous years, the businessmen had picked up the check for transportation and lodging of high government officials who attended the closed meetings of the council. Hodges ordered a stop to that relationship. The United States Treasury now foots the bills for federal officials.

Hodges stuck close to his old pattern in his first days in Cabinet office. He pushed the buttons on his desk to see who would respond. He called in all the chiefs of bureaus and sub-bureaus, spending twelve hours in one day listening to the most complete briefing ever demanded by a Commerce Secretary. He began to draw visits from top-ranking leaders of industry, such as Henry Ford and Frederic Donner, president of General Motors, and high-ranking government officials, including Chairman William McC. Martin of the Federal Reserve Board.

Hodges dropped his white carnation trademark the day he left state office, but he maintains his avid devotion to public relations. One of his first ideas was to require the Weather Bureau to identify each forecast as a Department of Commerce product. Hodges set out to hire a high-priced public-relations man, at regular government pay, to jazz up the image of the Department. They said it couldn't be done, but Hodges lured William Ruder, partner in a large New York P.R. firm. Ruder was making about $100,000, but he came to Washington at a salary of $16,500 a year.

Together Hodges and Ruder are brewing programs to make the public aware of Commerce. Before they were in office a month plans were well advanced for a TV film series based on the exploits of the Patent Office ("one of the greatest who-dunits in the whole world," said Ruder). They plan to focus intense publicity on the thirty-three Commerce Department field offices around the country and thus increase their use by businessmen. The offices are now receiving 900,000 inquiries from business a year, but the Hodges-Ruder target is two million a year.

Hodges' relationship with President Kennedy is difficult to assess. On the surface the two men would seem to have little in common. One is an Irish millionaire's son out of Harvard and the London School of Economics and an accomplished politician. The other is a tenant farmer's son who climbed up the hard way in the cotton mills, invested in gasoline, and became a governor noted for his distaste for organization politics. The two men don't really know each other well, and Hodges is not one of Kennedy's close advisers.

But John Kennedy admires competence, and he likes a job well done. The Kennedy-Hodges relationship is based on mutual respect. Kennedy needs an articulate and news-making spokesman for business in his entourage, and Hodges needs a place to expend, now at age sixty-three, his energies for public service. Old enough to be John Kennedy's father, Hodges is a generation apart from the most prominent New Frontiersman. But the man whose surging ambition has brought success as an administrator, salesman, and publicist has far too much vitality left to be the Polonius of the Kennedy court. "I may be the oldest man in the Cabinet," Luther Hodges is fond of saying, "but I drive a Thunderbird car."

THE JOB OF POSTMASTER GENERAL IS UNIVERSALLY CONSIDERED the least important in the Cabinet. And J. Edward Day, the man who fills it, was probably the least known of all the Cabinet choices. But Postmaster Day has impressed official Washington since he moved into office. His succinct and sensible comments on the state of the economy surprised his colleagues at Kennedy cabinet meetings. His quick and sure grasp of postal problems drew praise from the prickly House Appropriations Committee. His approach to his job impressed his own aides, mostly strangers to him before. "When

I look around to see which men will likely get into trouble and which ones will move ahead, Day impresses me as a real comer," a very high Kennedy aide remarked.

Once a protégé of Adlai Stevenson, Day retains many of his mentor's traits. He is witty, has a wide-ranging mind, and is a craftsman of the spoken and written word. Yet Day is also a quick, sure, decision maker and relishes minute details. Some have referred to him as "a practical Stevenson."

Day has a dry but active sense of humor. Standing on the White House steps with other Cabinet members after a formal reception, Day was asked by the doorman which Cadillac limousine was his. "I'm the Postmaster General," he replied, "mine is the one painted red, white, and blue." (His predecessor painted the nation's mailboxes and trucks but left his black Cadillac alone.)

Day has an extraordinary memory and a rare ability to express himself. He thinks nothing more enjoyable than to sit down for an hour or so to read from one of the three encyclopedias in his home. Another Day idea of fun was compiling and publishing a lengthy, detailed genealogy of his family, *Descendants of Christopher Day of Bucks County, Pennsylvania.*

At his first press conference reporters were astonished when Day, noting that the Post Office handles 65 billion pieces of mail a year, remarked, "that is as many seconds as have ticked by since the time of Julius Caesar." In testimony before the House Appropriations Committee after only a month in office Day answered questions on postal matters for several hours without referring to a single note. The congressmen were amazed.

James Edward Day was born October 11, 1914, in Jacksonville, Illinois. His father, like Day's grandfather and numerous other ancestors, was a doctor. Brought up in comfortable surroundings in Springfield, the heart of the Lincoln country, Day entered the University of Chicago in the depression year of 1932. This was the second year of the "Chicago plan," the daring educational innovation that brought fame to the school and to its president, Robert M. Hutchins. The plan permitted students to study as they pleased, without regular class attendance or examinations. A massive final examination was the only one that counted; when a student could pass it he received his degree, whether he had been at school four months, four years, or even longer. Day saw law school years ahead of him, and decided to finish his Chicago undergraduate work in three years. He did.

A classmate described him at the university as extremely popular: "He liked the gals and the gals liked him. But he made a basic decision that it was more important to pursue his career than be popular. He was not a grind but he was more conserving of his time and energy than most of us. He was the kind of guy who would have gone to the lectures, done his reading, and read the notes, a soft touch for anybody who was behind in his work and needed help, and yet he was a top scholar himself."

Along with his work Day found time to participate in limited extracurricular activities. Once he joined a raid on a girls' dormitory, forerunner of today's "panty raid." When the marauders got rough, Day's conscience got the better of him and he offered to help a housemother restore order. "What is your name?" she asked her volunteer aide. "Edward Day, ma'am," he replied. Later, when officials decided to punish the students for the raid, Day was the only name the housemother could recall. He drew a term on probation and complained to a friend that "just as soon as you get too tenderhearted, you get caught."

At Harvard Law School Day was a scholastic success. He did well enough to make the *Harvard Law Review,* reserved for the top scholars in the class. Adrian Fisher, now deputy to Disarmament Adviser John J. McCloy, was Day's note editor on the *Law Review.* "Ed was bright and very efficient," he recalls.

The summer after his first year at law school Day worked as a clerk in Abraham Lincoln's old law firm in Springfield. The following summer he clerked in Elihu Root's law office in New York. In 1938 he graduated *cum laude* from Harvard, and shortly after was hired as a clerk in the prominent Chicago law firm of Sidley, Austin, Burgess, and Harper. In 1941, with war hanging over the country, he married Mary Louise Burgess, the boss's daughter. At work he handled wills and estates, occasionally doing research for a partner in the firm whose name was Adlai E. Stevenson.

According to friends, Day spoke often and vehemently of the dangers of fascism's rise in Europe. Tired of just talking, he enlisted in the Navy's V-7 program in September 1940. But after a shakedown cruise Navy doctors found the future Postmaster General to be "hopelessly color blind." Adlai Stevenson moved to the Navy Department and from there helped Day get a desk job in the Naval Bureau of Aeronautics in Washington. (His division chief was then Captain Arthur W. Radford.) Day wanted sea duty and finally convinced Navy doctors there was really nothing wrong with his eyes. As he recalls, a four-stripe doctor gave him an old-fashioned color-blindness test instead of the new fancier kind. "I passed with flying colors," says Day.

On a destroyer escort in the Atlantic, Day whiled away the spare time writing a romantic novel he called *Bartholf Street*. This now-celebrated work was written as escape from the Navy routine. It portrayed the life and loves of a cynical young doctor who tells the story in the first person. After a wild fling at the "National Institute of Sanitary Surgery" in Vienna, the protagonist marries the attractive but equally cynical daughter of a Midwestern shoe magnate. The young doctor prospers in pediatrics with the help of his high-flying in-laws. Bored with his wife, he tries to woo her beautiful and idealistic sister. She spurns him for an Arizona religious retreat operated by the mother of two illegitimate children. Other characters in this improbable story include a period-piece radical who favors a universal state and an intellectual café dancer who is a cross between Mother Bloor and Gypsy Rose Lee.

After *Bartholf Street* was rejected by *Cosmopolitan* and several other magazines, Day took it in 1947 to Dorrance and Company of Philadelphia, which often publishes "cooperative" books, those in which the author shares expenses. Day paid about seven hundred dollars to get the volume printed. It featured a demure landscape for the apple-green jacket. He wrote a book-jacket blurb which warned that his story contained "expressions of some ideas which will be recognized by some readers as woefully unsound." Day explains that he didn't want anyone to think his literary diversion was autobiographical. The book sold less than a thousand copies. The royalties were so lean that Day received his last payment for sales, only forty cents, in postage stamps.

Although many who have read it consider *Bartholf Street* somewhat amateurish, Day retains a pride of authorship. At one time he even considered writing a second novel. But recent newspaper stories about *Bartholf Street* drew righteous indignation from Representative William Miller of New York, chairman of the Republican Congressional Committee. Miller, who had not read the book, called it "racy" and said the author, as Postmaster General, might be unable to clamp down on obscene literature in the mail because of his own handiwork. *Bartholf Street* contains several bedside scenes but nothing a reader of modern comic strips would find salacious.

After the war Day went back to work at his old Chicago law firm. In 1948 Adlai Stevenson was elected governor of Illinois. Day joined Stevenson as a personal assistant on legislative and legal matters, becoming a member of the informal "kitchen cabinet" of Stevenson intimates. After Stevenson and his wife separated, Ed and Mary Louise Day spent many an evening in the executive mansion with their friend to help him over his time of trouble. Day's office was in the mansion itself, and he lunched with Adlai frequently. Stevenson later described his younger associate as "a fellow with great wit, humor, and geniality, with a sharp, incisive mind and infinite capacity for work."

Day became Illinois insurance commissioner in 1950. The move from legal assistant to insurance commissioner at age thirty-five was a turning point in Day's life. Now he was an administrator, a job in which he excelled. And the new task was his introduction to the insurance industry which soon became his livelihood.

During his days in Springfield Day built a reputation as a writer of political verse. One of his most famous rhymes was written when State Senator Roland V. Libonati, now a congressman from Illinois, pushed a bill through the Illinois Senate requiring a cuspidor in every room of every state building. Day wrote:

A bill has passed the Senate about which some are skeptical,
Which would give a legal mandate to a rather crude receptacle.
For those among the public who may not approve of this,
We point out that good government should not be hit or miss.
We recommend approval for Libonati's legislation,
We trust that it will live up to our best expectoration.

When Adlai Stevenson ran for President in 1952 Day played a limited role in the campaign. He says he felt that an incumbent insurance commissioner should not take a leading role in politics. His main contribution was a long memorandum detailing Stevenson's years as governor, which served as background material for a number of magazine articles about the presidential candidate.

After the Stevenson administration in Illinois ended in 1953, Day was hired as associate general solicitor for the huge Prudential Insurance Company. Carrol Shanks, then president of Prudential, picked Day as a bright prospect and placed him in the company's main office at Newark, New Jersey. Shanks encouraged Day to learn all he could about the business, and Day began a round of travels to the "Pru's" operations all over the country. He became the company's leading expert on variable annuities, a type of investment insurance which was rapidly becoming important. In 1956 he was made associate general counsel of the Prudential. In 1957 he capped his rapid rise by being appointed a vice president of the company and director of its operations in thirteen western states. The new job took him to the West Coast, where he was responsible for 7,500 employees and $1.5 billion in investments. Shanks retired unexpectedly in December of 1960 after a conflict of interest furor and was replaced by Louis R. Menagh, a sixty-eight-year-old vice president. The new president's age encouraged rumors that Day may yet become the president of the second largest insurance company in the world.

As Prudential's man on the coast Day became active in civic and political affairs. He belonged to some thirty organizations, from the board of the Red Cross to the board of Claremont College. Things were so hectic, an assistant says, that one week Day went to five nightly banquets in a row.

Day lined up behind Edmund G. (Pat) Brown in California Democratic politics. When Brown was elected governor, he appointed Day to several state advisory committees. In 1958, just a year after coming to the Coast, Day helped organize "Democratic Associates," a committee of Los Angeles business leaders interested in finding good candidates for the party. The group was more conservative in character and outlook than the "Democratic Club" movement then sweeping California. Day's "Associates" included such figures as Dan Kimball, president of Aerojet General, and Edwin W. Pauley, the wealthy oil magnate. Day was picked as chairman of the "Associates" and became active in several other state Democratic party groups.

In the spring of 1959 John F. Kennedy visited Los Angeles, fishing for support for the presidential nomination. Day introduced Kennedy to a political meeting and was so impressed that he accompanied the Senator to five other similar meetings that day.

In February of 1960 Day and his wife traveled to Lake Forest, Illinois, for Adlai Stevenson's birthday celebration. During this gathering of close Stevenson friends, Day says, he became convinced that Adlai did not plan to become an active candidate for the presidential nomination. When he returned to California, he was one of the group that urged Governor Brown to support Kennedy. His stand became important early in 1960 when leading California politicians gathered together to draw up an official roster of delegates to the forthcoming Democratic national convention. The delegation was selected so that each of the major contenders was firmly represented, a circumstance which led to California's inability to function as a bloc at the convention. Day was picked as a Kennedy delegate. After the convention Day served as one of twenty-nine advisers to the ten-man Democratic campaign committee in California. But most of his time was consumed in a successful drive to win public approval of the issuance of bonds to finance the transmission of northern California water to southern California.

Following the Kennedy victory Day was consulted by R. Sargent Shriver and other top Kennedyites about prospective appointees to high office. They asked Day if he himself would be willing to come

East to the New Frontier, but at the time replied it was "not feasible." Meanwhile, back in Washington, Kennedy aides were shifting their attention to California for someone to fill a Cabinet post. Fred Dutton, former executive assistant to Governor Brown and a member of the Kennedy national campaign staff, circulated a memorandum emphasizing the political beachhead in the second largest state would be advantageous to the administration in 1964, particularly if Governor Nelson Rockefeller of New York were the G.O.P. presidential candidate. (The memo was so effective that in early 1961 another political paper made the rounds in top administration circles, this one warning that California was receiving more than a just share of the appointments.)

Although it is now officially denied, word went out during the Cabinet-picking days that the postmaster generalship would go to a southern Californian. First to be considered was State Senator Hugo Fisher of San Diego, but objections to him were raised within California Democratic circles. Then Day dawned on the "talent scouts" back in Washington.

One curious aspect of the search for a postmaster general was the announced "offer" of the job to Representative William L. Dawson, the Chicago Negro leader. Of the Dawson episode this much is known: His name was leaked early to reporters as a likely candidate for the postal job by Vice-President-elect Lyndon B. Johnson, an old political friend. The idea of naming the first Negro member to a presidential cabinet drew much interest. Actually, political scandals in Dawson's Chicago organization made him an unlikely choice from the start. In early December a fresh wave of stories from Washington erroneously naming Dawson as a likely Kennedy appointee added fuel to the fire. The President-elect was irritated at this turn of events. He found it particularly vexing because he was making a real effort to find qualified Negroes for high posts in his administration, but Dawson, the aged leader of an old-time Negro political machine, was not the type of man he sought. Even today the Kennedy high command is tight-lipped about the offer to Dawson, which was announced by the President-elect, along with the news that Dawson had declined to serve. The regular Kennedy "talent-scouts" organization, which was involved in most Cabinet choices, knew nothing of the Dawson offer until Kennedy announced it to the public.

On December 15 Day was attending an insurance industry cocktail party at the Biltmore Hotel in Los Angeles. About 4 P.M. (7 P.M. in Washington) he was called to the telephone. His secretary informed him that President-elect Kennedy was trying to get him. Day recalls he was told to ask for "Operator 60" in Washington. Sitting in a hotel phone booth, Day reached Mrs. Evelyn Lincoln, Kennedy's private secretary, at the President-elect's Georgetown home. Mrs. Lincoln said that Kennedy was busy on the front steps announcing the appointment of his secretary of agriculture and asked Day to wait. After twenty minutes in the phone booth Day got the call from Kennedy, who asked him to be postmaster general. Day says he never had a second thought about his on-the-spot decision to accept. Kennedy asked him to get aboard a jet flight to Washington that evening. Day called his wife with the news, warning her to keep it a secret. He then called Carroll Shanks, president of the Prudential, who was "delighted." Practicing careful secrecy about the forthcoming appointment, Day was surprised to be telephoned by a Los Angeles newspaper reporter while packing for the trip. The newsman already had the whole story.

When Day arrived the next morning at Friendship Airport in Baltimore, a reporter-photographer team from a press association was waiting for him. Day refused to comment on the rumored appointment but recalls he "gave them a number of views on postal matters." He flew with Kennedy from Washington to the vacation headquarters at Palm Beach and had the first chance for a long talk with his new boss on the trip. Kennedy announced Day's appointment December 17 on the patio where many other New Frontiersmen had been introduced to reporters. The selection of the small, somewhat prim-looking Day completed the Kennedy cabinet.

Day returned home to California to wind up his affairs. The postman who regularly delivered the mail to the Day family, a Negro letter carrier named Marvin Johnson, was so elated that he took the Postmaster General-designate down to the local substation for all the other carriers to meet. Johnson's personal interest in the Postmaster General did not die with that proud moment. A few weeks after Day had assumed his high office his fourteen-year-old daughter, Molly, still attending school in Los Angeles, sent her father a note through the mail. On the outside of the envelope she wrote, "Postman, postman, do your duty. Take this letter to my cutie." To which the dutiful postman appended, "O.K., it's on its way. Marvin." The Postmaster General keeps the envelope as a memento in his desk at the Post Office headquarters in Washington.

When he moved into office Day was in much the same position as when he became state insurance commissioner. He knew little or nothing about the details of his assignment. But soon he began to learn from two very different sources.

The first was H. W. (Bill) Brawley, long-time chief of staff of the Senate Post Office and Civil Service Committee. Brawley had worked in Kennedy headquarters during the campaign as a liaison man with Lyndon Johnson and helped Kennedy look around after the election for a likely prospect for Postmaster General. Kennedy announced Brawley's appointment as Deputy Postmaster General at the same time he announced Day's appointment for the top postal job. As top Democratic congressional staff aide on postal matters, Brawley had written many of the laws governing the Post Office. During the transition period Day and his deputy worked together from Brawley's Senate office.

The other source of Day's postal education was incumbent Postmaster General Arthur E. Summerfield. A series of eye-opening encounters with him revealed to Day a great deal about Summerfield and some surprising things about the state of the postal service. Summerfield telephoned Day in Los Angeles after the Palm Beach announcement. After brief congratulations Summerfield asked Day to retain his confidential secretary in her job. She had been Summerfield's secretary when he was Republican national chairman. Day considered this a very unusual request but he promised that the secretary would be "taken care of." Several other times during the transition period Summerfield pressed Day to keep the secretary in her job. After taking office Day learned that the confidential secretary had been placed under civil service and thus could not be easily fired. He says he also learned that the woman's husband, sister, and brother were on the Post Office pay roll. The confidential secretary was moved to a job in another office and the relatives retained as required by civil-service rules.

There was little real cooperation between the outgoing and incoming bosses of the Post Office Department during the preinaugural "transition period." Each time Day, Brawley, or other top officials-to-be went to see Summerfield, he greeted them heartily and then showed selected short movies on his program for commemorative stamps or other such matters. One of Day's first official moves was to slash Summerfield's rather large expenditures for promotion movies, in which Summerfield played a leading on-camera role, and generating other publicity about the Post Office Department and its leader.

Another surprise to the former Navy lieutenant was the seriousness with which postal employees took his new title. Nearly everybody addressed him as "General" and postal guards even snapped to a salute for Day on an inspection trip to the New York City Post Office. Day made an abortive attempt to reduce the formality at a meeting with postal subordinates, where he suggested the more democratic salutations of "Ed" or at most "Mr. Day." The postal workers looked shocked, and Day dropped the campaign. He discovered that the title of General had been taken seriously by the postal service for more than one hundred years.

Day's new rank made him a welcome guest at Washington social gatherings catering to high government officials. A few days before inauguration Day received a dinner invitation from a Washington hostess whose name he had never heard. Aides couldn't place the woman either. Finally a Senate employee was asked to check up on the sender of the mysterious invitation. He came back with a detailed credit report on her husband but no information on whether Day should attend the party. He discovered just in time the dinner given by Mrs. Jane Wheeler on inauguration night was the "official" affair for President Kennedy and his cabinet, sanctioned by the new President himself.

The Postmaster General has encountered continuing problems because he came to Washington as a relative unknown. House Speaker Sam Rayburn mistook Day for a bouncer at an early social gathering and ordered him to help clear the way for "the official party." When Day wrote an article on his first weeks in the nation's capital for the *New York Times* magazine section, errant editors captioned his picture as "NEW MAN IN TOWN—J. Clarence Day, the 'least known' Cabinet member." Day was miffed that he was so little known the *Times* editors didn't even remember their guest writer's name.

Other than relatively small difficulties, Day found the Post Office to be "generally getting along pretty well." He discovered many things to change but no major crisis. His largest continuing problem appeared to be the postal operating deficit of $800 million to $900 million a year. From colonial times to the present day the Post Office has often spent more money than it received in revenue. Day hopes to make the Post Office more nearly self-supporting, and postal rate increases are the only way to do this, he says.

Postmasters General have usually been important dispensers of political spoils for the entire administration. The hallway just outside the Postmaster General's immense office is lined even today with empty benches and chairs where once an army of favor seekers waited. Kennedy decided early in the game that political patronage would be handled primarily through the Democratic National Committee and a few key White House aides, not by the Postmaster General. Day says that he is "pleased that I am not expected to function on patronage matters for other departments."

Nevertheless, there is ample room in the Post Office itself for some political maneuvering. Despite the Republican attempt to "lock in" present postal employees under civil-service rules, many vacancies occur in the huge department. It is estimated that thirty thousand jobs open up each year. About twenty-five hundred are postmasterships, and an equal number are rural route carriers. These are traditional political sinecures for local party organizations. In addition, the Department keeps millions of dollars of public money in selected local banks and awards another $200 million yearly in builders' contracts.

In his first remarks to a gathering of Post Office Department workers Day laid out a standard for his regime. "For all our people, both the new management and the career personnel," he said, "we hope to set a tone of alertness, brightness, enthusiasm, and energy. It will do us good to sparkle a bit—even, at times, to show that we have a sense of humor." Nothing written sums up better the Postmaster General himself.

11.

KNIGHT OF THE BARGAINING TABLE

Arthur Goldberg

By ALAN E. ADAMS

ARTHUR JOSEPH GOLDBERG AT FIFTY-TWO IS, NEXT TO LUTHER Hodges, the oldest man in the Kennedy Cabinet, a fact he recites with relish as he races along the New Frontier. To Goldberg "everything in the Kennedy administration starts the day before yesterday," whether it is rushing into deadlocked tugboat negotiations in New York City, dashing to the airport for a hurried trip to Midwest centers of unemployment, driving on a moment's notice to Capitol Hill to sway legislative leaders, flying South to meet with union chiefs he once served, or going to the steel cities of Pennsylvania to see businessmen he once faced across the bargaining table.

It is a frenetic pace the ambitious Goldberg sets as the ninth Secretary of Labor, not because the specifics of the job demand it, but because it is his way of life. The White House, a bare three blocks from his office in the Labor Department, is a command post where he reports with astonishing frequency to the man he calls "my chief."

Even the Labor Secretary's private office is feeling the effects of Goldberg's eagerness to be in the thick of things. Before he came to the Department, the office had become practically insulated against the everyday hum of government activity. The Secretary's broad mahogany desk and high-backed leather turret

chair were located in a massive pine-paneled room which could
be reached only after overcoming a formidable array of receptionists in an outer waiting room, then an imposing set of secretaries in a second office, and finally an administrative assistant
whose own office door led to a conference room that could easily
seat all the policy makers in the Labor Department. Beyond the
far door of this room was the Secretary's office.

This was uncomfortable isolation for Goldberg. "I like to work
closely with people and have them close at hand," he said. "I
found the office a long distance away from where I thought I
ought to be."

Goldberg's discomfort behind this wall of departmental personnel was only a small thorn in a job that is beset by complex
problems and challenges. It is a job on which he thrives, however.
He brings to the task an initiative, aggressiveness, and bold imagination that have already won him a place as one of President
Kennedy's closest advisers on matters economic.

He approaches people directly, and most people in turn take
to his modest, informal manner. One day Robert Kennedy telephoned Goldberg, on his way to his brother's house in Georgetown,
where he was to be announced as the new attorney general. "Arthur," he said, "I need moral support. How about coming along
with me?" They rode together to the house on N Street. The
President-elect, watching the pair walk up the front steps, was
surprised to see his new Labor Secretary. "Don't tell me you're here
to resign already," he cracked.

The quip was a pertinent one. Kennedy has been challenged
by businessmen and others for picking a man from the ranks of
organized labor to head the Labor Department. Critics pointed
to the unsuccessful experiment with Martin Durkin, onetime president of the Plumbers' Union. Durkin had an unhappy reign as
President Eisenhower's first labor secretary, resigning before com-
pleting a year in office. But Goldberg, for all his ties to labor, never
was a union leader, emotionally blinded by one point of view. Thus
the position of the two men is not quite comparable.

When Arthur Goldberg left the labor movement for a place
in the Kennedy Cabinet he had become known as the man who

had set labor's pace at the bargaining table, who had fused the divisions in its ranks, who had cleansed it of elements of both communism and corruption, and who had led it through the intricate channels of legislation in Congress. Throughout the crises that beset labor it was Goldberg who managed to bridge the wide differences between the union leaders he served. When Walter Reuther of the C.I.O. and George Meany of the A.F.L. were searching for a way to end a twenty-year split in labor's ranks, Goldberg put together a formula in the new A.F.L.-C.I.O. constitution that satisfied both sides. When the federation had to face up to racketeering in the family, Goldberg was on hand to write the ethical practice codes that laid the ground rules for behavior of its officials. And then he set out to bring the offenders before labor's own court and before the McClellan committee.

Despite his achievements in the labor movement, Goldberg was not regarded as a union man by labor. The only union card he ever carried was issued by the Hod Carriers Union when he worked on construction projects to pay his way through law school. To George Meany, with whom he worked intimately for ten years, Goldberg was a "good man" but he did not fit Meany's prescription for the post of Labor Secretary. When it came time for Kennedy to fill the Cabinet office, Meany scribbled down the names of five men who would be acceptable to him: union presidents Joseph Beirne of the Communications Workers; George Harrison of the Railway Clerks; James Suffridge of the Retail Clerks; Al J. Hayes of the Machinists, and Secretary-Treasurer Joseph Keenan of the Electrical Workers. To leaders of the powerful building trades bloc Keenan alone was acceptable.

When Kennedy indicated his choice was Goldberg, a storm of protest blew up at A.F.L.-C.I.O. headquarters. Goldberg himself resisted the offer at first. He had served twenty-three years with the union movement as an attorney. The law, not labor, was his career, and he wanted to continue it in the Kennedy administration, hopefully as Attorney General or, barring that, as Solicitor General of the Department of Justice. "I am by education, by training, by experience of thirty-one years now a lawyer. I expect to remain one for the rest of my life," he has said. But as union resistance to him mounted, Goldberg's fighting instincts were aroused. He told the President-elect he would take the labor assignment "if George Meany approves." Meany gave his grudging okay. Early in the morning of December 15 Meany went before an angry assembly of building-trades chiefs, told them his decision, and persuaded them not to raise a protest. Later that same morning he and Goldberg stood smiling together on the steps in Georgetown as Kennedy announced his new Labor Secretary.

Fortune has effectively recorded Goldberg's long career in Washington as counsel to organized labor. In 1950 it bestowed the title "Labor's Man of the Year" on Goldberg for his efforts both as negotiator and legal counsel in the United Steelworkers' victorious fight to win company-financed pension plans. By 1960 his reputation had grown. "Goldberg is more than a resourceful bargainer for the Steelworkers," *Fortune* said. "He is also a roving minister without portfolio for the American labor movement at large, a theoretician, a policy maker, a diplomat, and an enormously useful contact-man-about-Washington." In the years between Goldberg sat in the high councils of labor, became a friend and confidant of Supreme Court Justices before whom he adroitly argued the union case, counseled officials of foreign governments as well as his own, dealt intimately with leaders in Congress, and steered labor's political support in the directions he felt it should go. During the 1960 presidential campaign he was in constant telephone contact with the Kennedys on the campaign trail and helped to win union backing for the Democratic aspirant.

Except that his thatch of wavy hair has turned almost totally gray, Goldberg appears the same serious, mild-mannered man who arrived on the Washington scene in 1948. His soft, throaty voice still bears traces of his native Chicago. His figure is trim and he keeps a conscientious eye on the scales to make sure they don't climb over one hundred and seventy pounds for his five feet, nine inches. He dresses in expensively cut suits, now leans toward dark, conservative colors in deference to his Cabinet ranking. When Goldberg talks, his hands are constantly in motion and he jabs the air for emphasis. When Goldberg listens, he rubs his hands together in a way that suggests thought rather than concern

His very seriousness, enhanced by horn-rimmed glasses, some-times makes him appear as youthful as the intellectual law student he was twenty-five years ago.

Goldberg has an ease on the public platform gained from long experience at union conventions, dinners, rallies, and the like. He is not a polished speaker but has improved over the years. At one time he disdained telling "opening" jokes, but now uses this traditional form. Sophisticated jokes can leave Goldberg unsmiling. ("They seem to go over his head," says a friend.) He is not known for a sense of humor, and the points of his jokes sometimes escape his friends. Goldberg gets his biggest laughs from gags about human relationships, where people get mixed up in ludicrous situations through misunderstandings.

Goldberg's first move after nomination as Labor Secretary was to sever his ties with the labor movement, effective December 31, 1960. (Until his confirmation by the Senate Labor Committee on January 21, 1961, he was unemployed for the first time since the age of twelve, when he started working after school.) "This is a complete and final severance," he said. Later, in office, he remarked, "It has always been part of the lawyer's tradition to devote time to public service. Many great lawyers have done this and returned to their careers where they left off. I don't intend to return to the labor practice. I think I made that clear because I did not feel that it was appropriate to do it in light of taking this post. Now I expect, when I have finished what I am doing, to return to private practice outside the field of labor."

Goldberg dropped all his clients and unloaded all financial holdings in his control, mainly real estate, including a share in the Condado Beach Hotel in San Juan, Puerto Rico. He resigned from his Washington law firm, Goldberg, Feller, and Bredhoff, where he was senior partner, and from the Chicago firm, Goldberg, Devoe, Shadur & Mikva. Goldberg's income at the time he took over the $25,000 Cabinet job was a reputed $100,000 a year. He also withdrew from a pension program of the United Steel-workers from which he would have received a substantial income at age sixty. He retains some real-estate holdings but has placed them in a trust where he has no power of decision over purchase, sale, lease, or power of direction.

When he was named Labor Secretary, Goldberg simultaneously held the following jobs: Special counsel of the A.F.L.-C.I.O.; general counsel of the United Steelworkers of America; general counsel of the Industrial Union Department of the A.F.L.-C.I.O.; special counsel for the C.I.O. Textile Workers Union; Washington counsel for the International Ladies' Garment Workers Union, and Washington counsel for the United Hat, Cap, and Millinery Workers Union. He also represented, on occasion, the Transport Workers Union, the American Newspaper Guild, the Hotel and Restaurant Workers Union, the United Federation of Teachers, and the Railway Clerks. He was a one-man ethical practices committee for the State, County, and Municipal Workers. And he was on the board of directors of the Fund for the Republic and the Carnegie Endowment for International Peace.

The man with this impressive array of tasks was born August 8, 1908, in Chicago, the youngest of eight children. His parents, Joseph and Rebecca Goldberg, were Russian immigrants. He was raised in the dreary sections of Chicago's West Side where his father earned a meager living hauling produce in a horse-drawn wagon. Life was a constant struggle for the family, particularly after his father's death, when Arthur was eight. On cold nights the family slept in the kitchen huddled by a wood-burning stove to keep warm. Arthur was twelve when he got his first job, at $3.80 a week, delivering shoes from factories to stores. He was fired from his second job as a wrapper in a clothing store when he refused the owner's demand that he work one night a week for only an extra fifty cents dinner pay. He quickly found another job.

Young Arthur was an excellent student, serious and intent. He taught himself to read when he was four years old, skipped kindergarten, and was thereafter among the youngest in his classes. He graduated from Chicago's Harrison High School at sixteen and entered Crane Junior College, a public institution where most of the students held outside jobs. There Goldberg became acquainted with a tiny, energetic teacher, Lillian Herstein, whose freshman English classes started at 9 A.M. Miss Herstein recalls that as she looked down the row of seats "I would see Arthur's head bobbing up and down and he would soon be asleep." When she approached her student, he assured her he wasn't ill, but admitted he didn't get to bed until 2 A.M. after working eight hours in the post office.

It was at Crane, through Lillian Herstein, that Goldberg got his first taste of the labor movement. She was deeply interested in the movement and taught classes in labor education for the American Federation of Labor. At the time she was the only woman member of the executive board of the Chicago Federation of Labor and on several occasions was a candidate for political office on the Farmer-Labor ticket. Miss Herstein's interests and enthusiasm spilled over to her students, and Arthur took an active part in the labor debates of the time. "Many of Arthur's fellow students were from lower and middle-class families, working part time or full time to pay for their books and clothes and even contribute to the family budget," she recalls. "They came to grips with social and economic problems early." But while other students became emotionally partisan in the debates, Miss Herstein remembers, "Arthur always listened to the other side."

Goldberg graduated in 1926 after three years at Crane, and entered Northwestern University Law School, after convincing the entrance board that working his way through wouldn't handicap his studies. "I can remember him sitting asleep in a chair with a lawbook in his lap and alarm clock in the crook of his arm," a sister has said. "He'd set the alarm for two hours, and then he'd wake up and study some more. He was a real scholar." Goldberg in his three years at Northwestern scored the school's highest scholastic average, with 89 credit hours of A grades and three of B, a record unsurpassed during the period letter grades were used at Northwestern. (In 1937 the Law School shifted to numerical grades.)

While attending Northwestern Goldberg worked part time in the law offices of Kamfner, Horwitz, Halligan, and Daniels. He passed his bar examinations at the end of three years of law school and petitioned the faculty for a waiver to permit him to work full time with the firm. At that time students who entered law school with only three years of undergraduate work as Goldberg had done were required to remain in residence for four years. The faculty granted Goldberg's request, provided he do some special work at the school and obtain a few additional credits. He received his law degree in 1930, graduating *summa cum laude* and winning the Charles B. Elder prize as the top student in his class. In his final year at the university Goldberg was also editor of the *Illinois Law Review*.

During law school Goldberg used to study in the Northwestern library with Dorothy Kurgans, an attractive dark-haired girl who had a special flair for painting and was taking art courses at night at the university. They were married in 1931 before Dorothy had a chance to complete her college course. Two years later Goldberg was already earning a good income as a lawyer and insisted his wife resume her education. She received her degree in art education from the University of Chicago.

After receiving his law degree Goldberg stayed on with Kamfner, Horwitz, Halligan, and Daniels. Although the depression was pervading the country, the firm had a lucrative real-estate practice. A fellow lawyer recalls that Goldberg's talent for mediation served him well in this practice. "Arthur could take a bankrupt property and convince the creditors that it should be saved. He reorganized the investments, located new funds, and in the reorganization secured some property rights himself." However, Goldberg decided abruptly to quit. Mrs. Goldberg recalls, "It was during the depression and it was a wonderful job. Arthur was doing so well and we had a very nice apartment on the South Side. He was supporting me and my mother. But Arthur decided he didn't want to spend his time foreclosing mortgages." The period that followed this decision was the only period, except during his youth, that Goldberg has been in financial trouble.

Mrs. Goldberg remembers "it wasn't too easy" when Arthur Goldberg began his own private practice in 1933. He became counsel to labor unions in Chicago, but much of the work was advisory and without fees. The nation was just beginning to recover from the depression and Goldberg took on labor clients more as a civic duty than as legal counsel. He worked on pioneer cases in social insurance and death benefits for the United Packing House Workers and other unions. One of his first law partners, says Goldberg, "was the kind of lawyer who would take on a case because he felt lawyers had a duty to the community, the way doctors do. In those days representing unions in their earliest attempts at organizing was not an easy thing to carry on. The atmosphere was fairly hostile, sometimes we forget, and it took great conviction not to feel the disapproval from the community." Goldberg persisted, and his list of clients began to grow. One of his big early assignments was defending the American Newspaper Guild against a damage suit by the Hearst Corporation.

By 1942 Goldberg had gained a reputation as a top labor attorney. He was called to Washington by William "Wild Bill" Donovan, who was then setting up the Office of Strategic Services, to organize a labor desk. The idea was to develop intelligence links with union resistance forces abroad. Goldberg developed a network of counterespionage agents in France, Germany, and North Africa, coordinating the resistance work of seamen, river-barge operators, and railroad crews in those countries. Although he was headquartered in Washington, his tour of duty took him behind enemy lines on several major underground assaults, and at one point he infiltrated enemy positions within Germany itself. Goldberg was a civilian when he began his O.S.S. assignment, but became a captain in the United States Army and was a major when he left the service in 1945. He then returned to Chicago and private practice as a labor lawyer. He was also named professor of law at John Marshall Law School and lecturer at the University of Chicago School of Industrial Relations.

In 1948 Philip Murray, president of the C.I.O. and the United Steelworkers, called Goldberg to Washington as general counsel of both labor organizations. Murray was embroiled in a struggle with communist infiltrators in the union. When Murray's general counsel, Lee Pressman, resigned to join Henry Wallace's Progres-

sive party, Goldberg was summoned to fill the post. A former
C.I.O. official describes the feeling at the time: "It was an interesting thing. I remember many of us had watched Goldberg in the
early days of the C.I.O. For all their policy differences Phil Murray
and Lee Pressman had quite a close rapport. Lee had a position
of influence and power and the question in a lot of people's minds
was whether any successor to Lee could ever attain the same role.
And lo and behold, Arthur not only filled the role but they gave
him more policy responsibility, too."

In taking this dual job Goldberg accepted two different assignments. For the C.I.O. he was to be legislative expert and lobbyist.
The Taft-Hartley Act had just been passed and the C.I.O. was
waging an intensive campaign in Congress to overthrow the new
law. For the Steelworkers he was to be chief negotiator, which involved as much legal courtroom work as it did collective bargaining. Goldberg scored his first major victory in the latter job when
he led the fight for steelworker pensions at the bargaining table
and eventually through the courts. Not before the union had struck
for forty-nine days did it win, however. While Goldberg was chief
strategist and negotiator, the Steelworkers were involved in three
major strikes: fifty-nine days in 1952, thirty-six days in 1956, and
one hundred and sixteen days in 1959.

Out of this profusion of strife Goldberg had gained a reputation
not only as a tough bargainer (he has been described as "the steel
in the steel union") but also as a mediator who could reconcile
opposite points of view. To Goldberg this involves no conflict.
"A good labor lawyer," he says, "if he's any good at all, is a good
mediator."

An associate, in describing Goldberg's tougher side, says, "Arthur is a very partisan advocate for what he is persuaded the
union is entitled to win. You can't budge him when he thinks he's
right." In 1952, despite their close friendship, Goldberg fiercely
fought Steelworkers' President Murray, who was willing to give
up premium pay for Sunday work. Goldberg felt strongly that
extra pay for Sunday labor was something to which the Steelworkers were entitled. Again, in 1959, Goldberg was adamant, through-

out the Steel Union's one-hundred-and-sixteen-day strike, against an industry demand to change work rules.

Goldberg also has a talent for seeing the *other* side. A former law partner says, "He's always had an understanding and sympathy for the employers' problems when they are really important to the employer in terms of proper production. And he has not only had that, but he has communicated it. And for that reason people on the other side, who are reasonable people, are very glad to work with him."

In 1959, during negotiations at the height of another Steelworkers strike at the Kennecott Copper Corporation, Charles Cox, Kennecott president, asked for a no-strike contract clause. Goldberg agreed it was a reasonable request although union members were strongly opposed. "We knew it was going to create a terrific reaction back at the local level," says a labor lawyer who was involved. "Frankly, it took us a week to sell it to our local people, but this is the sort of thing Arthur will take a stand on. If he thinks our people are going overboard on something and the management makes a telling point, he will turn to our negotiators right at the table and say, 'I think the fellows are right on the other side of the table. We've got to deal with facts and reason here, we can't just be emotional.' " Kennecott's Cox recalls that the no-strike clause was approved by all but three A.F.L. unions and "we could not get them to take it. I went to see Arthur and told him I might open the plant but that this could bring a lot of bloodshed. Then he started to work on these other unions. If it hadn't been for Arthur we might have been out another six months."

Collective bargaining is not only a test of will power or fairness. To the negotiators it is also a game of bluff, and Goldberg is rated a master at knowing just what the other side has to give. He is credited with having a sixth sense about what is obtainable. In the 1955 steel negotiations with United States Steel Goldberg met with industry representatives in his Pittsburgh hotel room. Deadline was a few hours away. "Arthur thought the industry had another penny in the kitty," a union man at the scene remembers. "So he suddenly claimed he had a headache and ushered everybody out of the room. The strike started on schedule but it lasted only a few hours when the industry came in and upped the ante." In the last hours of the 1959 steel strike, while negotiating in a downtown Washington office building, Goldberg kept a plane warmed up at National Airport. It was to fly to Pittsburgh at a signal from him for a court order that could have meant an automatic four cents cost-of-living raise for the union under the old contract. Goldberg had held off this legal step, pending settlement of a new contract. Throughout the session industry negotiators nervously kept asking whether the plane had taken off. The settlement was made at 4 A.M.

Goldberg has a knack for clarifying issues when they become too involved and for getting at the heart of a matter. In recent steel talks both sides were fighting over an incentive plan that attempted to define a theoretical normal work load as the amount of energy expended by a man walking three miles an hour over level ground empty-handed. When Goldberg heard the argument, he interrupted. "Forget it," he said; "you can't measure sweat."

From the beginning of his own career in Washington Goldberg's tasks went beyond those of the usual labor lawyer. C.I.O. President Murray fell ill soon after Goldberg's arrival in 1948 and Goldberg assumed the responsibility for the C.I.O.'s relations with Congress, often testifying in joint appearances with President William Green of the A.F.L. He became the C.I.O.'s chief of staff and the organization under Goldberg "just rolled along as though it was on tremendous ball bearings," an associate recalls.

Perhaps Goldberg's most notable accomplishment was his role in the A.F.L.-C.I.O. merger. He first felt the tremors of the warring factions within the labor movement as a young student in the 1930's. At that time attempts were being made to form new unions in the mass-production industries, such as steel and automobiles. Old-line A. F. of L. craft unions were generating almost as much resistance to the newcomers as industry was. They fought efforts at organizing along factory-wide or industry-wide lines. Then John L. Lewis led his United Mine Workers Union into the fray, supporting the efforts to create industrial unions, and the foundation for a new labor federation, the C.I.O., began to be laid.

Philip Murray and William Green, head of the A.F.L., had put out feelers in 1946 concerning a possible alliance between the A.F.L. and C.I.O. Neither, however, really had his heart set on merger. The A.F.L. was an amalgamation of nearly one hundred unions and Green felt the C.I.O. should "come back to the house of labor." The thirty-seven-union C.I.O., on the other hand, was a lively organization which, Murray believed, would only be inhibited by unifying. It wasn't until after both leaders had died in 1952 and George Meany and Walter Reuther succeeded them that merger began to be taken seriously. Even then the impetus for merger came not from positive convictions but because feuding leaders threatened to tear the C.I.O. apart. At this point, eighteen months before the alliance actually took place, Goldberg saved the project.

Goldberg worked for President David McDonald as general counsel of the Steelworkers. In the same post for the C.I.O., he represented Walter Reuther. These two union leaders shared a mutual disaffection and it became a "remarkable acrobatic feat" for Goldberg to hold down both jobs. Together, McDonald's Steelworkers and the United Auto Workers, which Reuther headed along with the C.I.O., formed the hard core of the C.I.O. But McDonald rankled under Reuther's leadership, and early in 1954 made overt signs that he might pull his union out of the C.I.O. A war of nerves developed between the two leaders which McDonald capped by meeting on May 2, 1954, amid much fanfare, with John L. Lewis of the United Mine Workers and Dave Beck of the Teamsters Union. The trio met the press after their conference and refused to deny they were thinking of a third labor federation. The *Wall Street Journal*'s accurate comment on the meeting was "they have a common enemy rather than a common purpose." If they had joined together, the C.I.O. almost certainly would have fallen apart, or at the least its bargaining position with the A.F.L. on merging would have been all but destroyed.

Goldberg wanted the merger to succeed and he talked to Mc-

Donald. A union associate describes the events this way: "During a steel executive board meeting about that time Arthur had breakfast with McDonald, and I gather this must have been a crucial turning point in the whole history of the labor movement. He somehow convinced McDonald that he was moving up a blind alley by dealing with Lewis and Beck. Goldberg said it was all very fine if it was what McDonald wanted to do, but it wasn't going to get him anywhere, because Lewis was old and isolated and Beck was a curious character, and that if McDonald really wanted to be effective he shouldn't be playing around with these fellows. Instead, he should be in the C.I.O. yelling for merger, because this represented a realistic road toward some progress in which Dave could play a part. Dave bought this, and at the next Steelworkers' convention not long afterward he laid down a sharp challenge to Reuther to get on with the job for merger."

The merger plans began to gain momentum, but in the negotiations both sides indicated they still had serious reservations. The highest hurdle they faced was a proposed pact that would prevent rival A.F.L. and C.I.O. unions from raiding each other for members. In his talks with Meany, Reuther insisted that a firm ban be placed on union raiding before the merger took place. Meany was just as insistent that the A.F.L. unions could not agree to be bound by such an agreement. Goldberg became the mediator, meeting Meany as an emissary of Reuther's but at the same time as an individual intent upon patching up the differences between the two.

While he represented Reuther "Arthur had a very good relationship with Meany," says a union attorney. "Meany recognized that Arthur was genuinely interested in trying to work toward unity. And Arthur was the guy who could talk to both sides and who could understand their problems." The no-raiding issue was explosive enough to hold up the merger and was even threatening to kill it altogether when Goldberg found a solution. Goldberg's plan took care of both points of view. Instead of a firm ban on raids, he proposed that the principle of no raiding be included in the constitution of the new federation. This was the substance of

Reuther's position and one that Meany could sell to the A.F.L. unions. In 1958, some three years later, the A.F.L.-C.I.O. Executive Council took the final step and ordered the affiliated unions to obey the no-raiding clause in the constitution.

One problem remained, and it, too, required the Goldberg touch; this time his talent for bridging gaps with language. The new organization needed a name. The old, proud A.F.L. wanted its name perpetuated. The C.I.O. was also determined to be recognized, if necessary by a subordinate body of industrial unions within the federation that would bear the initials C.I.O. for Council of Industrial Organizations. Leaders on both sides were wary, however, that a C.I.O. division could become a separate power bloc and the merger would be in name only. One morning at breakfast Goldberg was reading a recently merged morning newspaper. He picked up the telephone and called a friend. "Well, if it can be the *Washington Post and Times Herald,* what's wrong with the A.F.L. and C.I.O.?" An associate adds this postscript: "After it was announced that the name would be A.F.L.-C.I.O., someone from the Washington paper said to Arthur, 'Isn't that an awful unwieldy name?' Arthur replied, 'And is this coming from an editor of the *Washington Post and Times Herald?'* Guess it sort of set the editor back."

Labor racketeering was one of the hottest subjects in the merger negotiations. The union leaders knew it existed but it wasn't until several years later, through the work of the Senate's McClellan Investigating Committee, that they discovered just how deeply corruption had penetrated the labor movement. In 1953 A.F.L. President George Meany had forced the expulsion of the International Longshoremen's Association at the A.F.L.'s convention in St. Louis. Reuther insisted that the newly-merged organization continue the attack. Goldberg later wrote in his book, *AFL-CIO Labor United,* "A few locals affiliated with the C.I.O. had at times fallen under the control of racketeering elements. . . . In contrast the A. F. of L. not only had a more serious problem with respect to racket-controlled locals . . . but at various times other internationals were faced with the threat of serious racketeering influences."

The unity committees agreed to make the fight against corruption a major plank in the constitution of the new federation. Goldberg took on the job of defining the criteria by which corruption could be judged. In a series of documents, since proclaimed for their legal excellence, the labor attorney wrote the ban on racketeering and a code of ethical practices for union leaders. The codes, which spelled out the proper behavior rules for union leaders, became the foundation of the A.F.L.-C.I.O.'s own internal campaign against corruption.

The International Brotherhood of Teamsters, headed by Dave Beck and later by James R. Hoffa, was the A.F.L.-C.I.O.'s main target, although corruption had also been uncovered in the Bakery Workers, United Textile Workers, the Jewelry Workers, and other small unions. Once the anticorruption program got under way, however, it aroused strong opposition among some A.F.L.-C.I.O. officials who objected to public exposure of members of labor's own family. Some officials favored outright forgiveness, others preferred that the matter be handled within the privacy of A.F.L.-C.I.O. headquarters. But for a majority the time had come for a clean break with corruption. Goldberg was among this majority.

Even this group hoped to avoid the painful process of expulsion of individual unions from the A.F.L.-C.I.O. When the offenders were brought to trial before the federation's five-man ethical practices committee, prosecutor Goldberg presented the evidence. A union attorney describes the general attitude: "This was not a lot of prosecution for the sake of prosecution. Really, in presenting the material against the unions, the objective was not to convict the unions as such, but to put the material on the record. This wasn't an adversary proceeding of the court in which the idea is to get a judgment against the other party to win a case." It was hoped that with the evidence presented, the offenders would voluntarily depart. When they refused, however, the charges were laid out, this time before a jam-packed A.F.L.-C.I.O. convention in Atlantic City in 1957. The accused went to the rostrum, one by one, to make their unsuccessful pleas against expulsion. This scene, publicly exposing the soul of the labor movement, today remains vivid in the minds of many of the participants.

The Teamsters Union was expelled first. Before any others were tossed out, however, differences erupted between Meany and Goldberg as to how to handle the Bakery Workers Union and its president, James Cross. Cross had been involved in questionable moral and financial practices in running the union. Meany and Goldberg agreed on the action against the Teamsters, but Goldberg felt that in the case of Cross the punishment of expulsion would be unnecessarily severe on his members. "Arthur gets away from the black-and-white aspect that so many of us have, particularly in the labor movement," a friend comments. Goldberg suggested that Cross be demoted to a local office in the Bakery Workers where he could be controlled. To Meany there were no shades of corruption, and Cross and his union were ousted. This was one of the few defeats for Goldberg's measured approach.

Goldberg worked closely with the McClellan Committee and particularly with the Kennedy brothers during the A.F.L.-C.I.O.'s own efforts to clean house. He used the evidence uncovered in the committee's hearings for his work with the A.F.L.-C.I.O.'s ethical practices committee and, in turn, helped in the McClellan investigation on Capitol Hill. Robert Kennedy, in his book *The Enemy Within,* describes a meeting that took place soon after the McClellan Committee went to work: "George Meany and his associates in the A.F.L.-C.I.O. were sicker about the corruption our Committee revealed than anyone else in the country. Shortly after our work started I sat down to lunch one day in the noisy bustle of the dining room of the Senate Office Building with Mr. Meany and Arthur Goldberg. . . . The luncheon had been arranged so we could explain to Mr. Meany the tremendous tasks we faced and so we could try to understand the problems that our work would create for him.

"All he asked from us at that meeting or any time was that we be fair," Kennedy continues. "Several times afterward he disagreed with what the Committee was doing and said so. There is no question that we made mistakes but his criticism was not always justified or based on fact in my judgment." Many times during the three-year investigation the blunt-spoken Meany became openly resentful of what he felt was unnecessary extension of the committee's work, and at one point he snapped, "God save us from our friends." Goldberg, acting as mediator, prevented on more than one occasion an open break between Meany and John Kennedy by persuading the union leader that the Massachusetts Senator was being fair to labor. In Kennedy's subsequent campaign for the Presidency Goldberg played a major role in lining up union support. Bob Kennedy described Goldberg in his book as a "wise and skillful" lawyer and when Kennedy was sued by Hoffa for remarks he made on a national television show he hired Goldberg as his lawyer. The suit was dismissed.

Arthur Goldberg shares his professional life, when he can, with his family. Mrs. Goldberg has often watched from a spectators' seat his frequent appearances as labor counsel before the Supreme Court, government boards, and congressional committees. When the Senate Labor Committee convened to considered Goldberg's nomination for Secretary of Labor, Goldberg introduced his wife to the legislators before the hearing started. Their children, Barbara, twenty-four, a graduate student at the University of Chicago, and Robert, twenty, a sophomore at Amherst College, were often present at public events until their college careers took them away from home.

Home for the Goldbergs is a comfortable nine-room, three-story brick house overlooking Washington's Rock Creek Park. Because their life has always been fairly public, Mrs. Goldberg has kept it a flexible household. Quiet evenings may find Goldberg reading a book (his taste ranges from Nero Wolfe mysteries to politics and archaeology), taking in a movie, or swinging a cane as he walks with Mrs. Goldberg along the Chesapeake & Ohio canal in nearby Georgetown. But quiet evenings alone, or with a small group of intimate friends, are a rarity now, and the Goldbergs more often entertain large numbers of people from a wide variety of professions.

Mornings on the way to work, his frequent companion is a little girl, a next-door neighbor, who shares the back seat of the cabinet officer's chauffeur-driven black Cadillac. Goldberg drops her off at Alice Deal Junior High School on his way downtown and sees to it that her playmates are properly impressed as the chauffeur makes a special ceremony of opening the limousine door to help his young passenger alight in front of the school playground.

One of the highlights of the year at the Goldberg house is the Seder ceremony, a religious occasion commemorating the deliverance of the Jews from Egypt in ancient times. Goldberg, one of the two Jewish members of the Cabinet, has evolved over the years a special version of this ceremony for his guests, many of whom are not Jewish. A friend who has attended the service many times describes it this way: "The Goldbergs over the last few years have run quite a big Seder. A Seder is nothing more than a dinner celebration with a traditional form and readings. Part of the tradition is that the youngest child present reads four questions and then there is a long answer in Hebrew by the elders. What Arthur did was work out something with a Rabbi Weinstein of Chicago in which the emphasis was put almost entirely on matters of ethical evaluation. The whole thing was shortened and simplified so the kids could understand it as well as the adults. It is a very moving thing." Goldberg breaks with tradition, too, in serving sparkling burgundy along with the ceremonial heavy sweet wine. The number of guests invited has increased recently (there were forty-four seated guests last year) to the point where Mrs. Goldberg has had to hire extra help for what is traditionally an intimate family gathering.

Goldberg does not smoke, will occasionally nurse a scotch and soda, and prefers Sanka to coffee, even at breakfast. He frets at clutter and is as meticulous and organized at home as he is at the office. He picks up after himself and, even when in a hurry, his sense of order forces him to pull things from his drawer one by one. The Goldbergs have sentimentally, without fail, exchanged Valentine's Day cards for thirty-one years, usually the humorous variety. (Despite the pace of her husband's life this past February Mrs. Goldberg received a valentine on time.)

The Goldbergs have traveled a great deal for pleasure, and

their children have usually accompanied them. The children, however, remember that the only "real" vacations were the times the family went to the small summer place on Lake Michigan that Goldberg gave his wife as a tenth anniversary present ("a shack with a kerosene stove and a W.P.A. outhouse, but with no running water, lights, or refrigerator").

Mrs. Goldberg shares her husband's interest in the labor movement. In the days when they lived in Chicago she studied labor problems at the University of Chicago and attended summer sessions of the Wisconsin Summer School for Workers. She became an active member of the Women's Trade Union League of Chicago and, a friend recalls, "with her artistic skill, she relieved the drabness of the League's announcements and pamphlets with her lively drawings."

Goldberg derives a tremendous satisfaction from his wife's established talent in painting. Her work has received prominent critical recognition in gallery showings in New York and Washington and she has had five one-man shows. A great deal of her time is spent at the art gallery she runs with three other women in Washington. An abstractionist, Mrs. Goldberg describes her technique as "poem paintings, an attempt to fuse paintings and words." Many of her paintings are of labor subjects, some with a personal meaning for her husband and herself.

Goldberg has special favorites which hang in his Labor Department office. One of these is a convention scene. "This long predates the merger," Goldberg explains. "It is a modern abstract that was done after the 1949 settlement of the great pension strike. Actually Mrs. Goldberg painted it when she was sitting there at the C.I.O. convention in Cleveland when Mr. Murray announced that I was to report on the steel settlement. I think it is a fine painting. It had been hung at the Corcoran in a show there and in several other shows. But for me it has great sentimental attachment."

Another is a picture called "The Wall." "It looks like a picture from antiquity," to Goldberg. "If you stand back you see faces emerging, oriental faces and faces from the past. I have always liked archaeology. I have always said if I were to be reincarnated

I would like to be an archaeologist, which I think is a great job in life. It has all the elements of a detective story and the search. Lawyers do that, too, when they search for evidence. You dig into the past, so this has always appealed to me, and this painting is really a little bit of archaeology."

Despite his twenty-three years' experience with the labor movement, Arthur Goldberg is on the spot in the Kennedy Cabinet. He brought as much expertness to an assignment as any official in the Administration. But he faces conflicts as Secretary of Labor that are inherent not only in the Labor post itself, but in the broader role he has carved for himself in the Kennedy administration. Goldberg has actively sought the challenge.

As long as he is in the cabinet, Goldberg cannot hope to shake completely the critics who cite his labor background as the basis for their suspicions that he will favor labor over management when the chips are down. During the Senate Labor Committee hearings on his confirmation Goldberg told Senator Barry Goldwater, "I cannot in all candor say that the views I held as a private citizen disappeared when I was given this high honor." But he said then and has repeated many times, "The Labor Department is a department of our government. It is not the private domain of any special interest group . . . it is intended to represent fairly and vigorously the interest of all the groups who have important concern with the work of the Department."

Goldberg's disclaimer, to most businessmen, does not erase the memory of his effective union career. Indeed his success as counsel to labor has brought charges that he helped build a powerful labor monopoly while emphasizing moderation from both labor and management, "sort of talking out of both sides of his mouth." It is Goldberg's very success and effectiveness as a labor spokesman that bring many businessmen to doubt, at heart, that he can switch his role so smoothly to that of a business-labor statesman. "I have a historic distrust of union leaders," complains one critic, "especially the smart ones like Goldberg and Reuther."

Yet a substantial portion of the business community, including those members who look skeptically upon him, oddly enough

prefer a Goldberg to a James Mitchell, a businessman who es-
poused many of labor's causes as Eisenhower's Labor Secretary.
"Mitchell was a wolf in sheep's clothing," the reasoning goes, "but
Goldberg, at least, is a wolf in wolf's clothing."

Not all businessmen take a dim view of Goldberg. A hard core
of prominent industrialists, including General Lucius Clay of Continental Can Corporation, Charles Cox of Kennecott, and Edgar
J. Kaiser of Kaiser Steel Corporation, are outspoken in their praise
of Goldberg's fair-mindedness. Kaiser, who has frequently faced
Goldberg across the bargaining table, says "he bends over back-
ward to appear not to favor labor." Goldberg's problem is to
convince management in general that he shares its interests as well
as those of labor—a problem he has been working on from the
moment he entered the Cabinet.

For several years, even as union negotiator, he warned that
labor and management were drawing farther apart, and increasing
bitterness was making communication between them more difficult.
President Kennedy established, at Goldberg's suggestion, the President's Labor-Management Advisory Council. This gave Goldberg
the chance to demonstrate that through the council he can reconcile differences between employers and union leaders so they can
make a common approach to such critical matters as automation,
foreign competition, and ever-rising levels of wages and prices.
Goldberg views this as his most important assignment in the Cabinet job. It is an unenviable task which could further tilt the prejudice of either labor or management. But it is one which, if
successful, would be the final capstone to a philosophy he has
followed all his adult life.

George Meany says Goldberg "can't do a Jekyll and Hyde, he
can't change his thinking." But union leaders who still think of
Goldberg as one of them may find themselves in disagreement
with him on labor and other issues in the new administration.
Goldberg pledges a vigorous enforcement of the Landrum-Griffin
Reform Law which makes labor officials accountable to the Labor
Department for the way they run their unions. This conceivably
could find Goldberg pitted in legal contests against some of his
former associates. As enforcement officer for the Administration's

anti-discrimination program Goldberg may be required to move against unions which discriminate against Negroes and other minorities in their membership policies.

While Goldberg has been a prominent public figure in his role as counsel to organized labor he has been fairly free of public criticism; the barbs have been fired mostly at the union leaders, who are the symbols of a particular point of view. In a sense, Goldberg served no master as a private attorney. But neither was he the general on the firing line. He noted his extraordinarily favorable reception in the press at the time of his appointment, remarking, "There is only one regret I have, and that is that I am not leaving on this note, but entering on it. This presents obvious difficulties."

Indeed, Goldberg's intimates say he is thin-skinned. He follows his exploits closely in the public press and is sensitive to personal criticism or comments about him that don't conform to the image he has of himself. Goldberg sees himself as a serious man acting in a serious manner. Once he complained privately to his wife when a news magazine used the word "grandly" in describing an action he took. Another time he called in for a personal interview a British journalist who described a tie Goldberg wore as "gay." The tie was not gay, claimed Goldberg, but "sincere." Although the confrontation was good-humored, friends say it illustrated how Goldberg will react to comments about himself that wouldn't faze other people in the slightest.

But his critics haven't slowed Goldberg down. Uncomfortable unless he is on the move, Goldberg is cutting a wide swath through the Administration. He is interpreting in the broadest way possible the mandate for the Labor Department, which achieved Cabinet rank in 1913, "to foster, promote, and develop the welfare of the wage earners of the United States, to improve their working conditions, and to advance their opportunities for profitable employment."

In past years the Labor Department has been something of a stepchild in the federal family, its stature ranking below most other government agencies. But Goldberg may change all that. "I'm no

jurisdictionalist," he says, as he moves outside the specific responsibilities of his department into the broad regions of economic
policy, civil rights, legislative goals, and other issues vital to the
Kennedy administration. Thus far, at least, he has been a welcome
member of the innermost councils of government strategy.

12.

PROTECTORS OF THE
NATURAL RESOURCES

Orville Freeman
Stewart Udall

By CARROLL KILPATRICK

ON NOVEMBER 7, 1943, A VOLUNTEER PATROL OF SIXTY MARINES cut its way through the dense, malaria-ridden Bougainville jungle in the Solomon Islands. It was trying to find the Numa Numa trail used by the Japanese as an overland supply route for an air base. After two days of tortuous but unsuccessful search the patrol turned back toward its base at the west end of Empress Augusta Bay. Lieutenant Orville L. Freeman was in command at the head of the column.

Suddenly, only fifteen feet ahead of him, Freeman saw a group of Japanese soldiers. They were as surprised as he but quickly opened fire. Freeman dived behind a log and began shooting. As he drew a bead on a crouching Japanese, an enemy bullet crashed through his left jaw joint, passed through his neck, and lodged under the skin of his right shoulder blade.

With his right hand he gingerly felt the hot, open wound and began vomiting freely. A few moments later, the Japanese having been dispersed, a corpsman reached his side and gave him a shot of morphine. It was the worst thing that could be done for a man with a wound near the brain. But somehow Freeman survived. His men carried him forward through the dense jungle, dropping him once when they came upon another small Japanese patrol.

291

That night Freeman suffered acutely. Once he ordered his men to leave him behind. "Skipper," replied one of his charges, "we aren't about to leave you. You're going out with us." It was sunset the next day when the Marines reached camp.

For two days Freeman was treated in the primitive Bougainville beach hospital, then taken by ship to the field hospital on Guadalcanal. There a surgeon extracted the bullet by squeezing the skin between his thumb and forefinger. Then followed a month in the hospital in New Caledonia, where Freeman's jaw was wired shut, and six months in a hospital in Oakland, California, where he painfully and slowly regained the use of his jaw and learned to speak again.

The Japanese bullet which put the twenty-five-year-old Freeman out of the war was fired just three months and seven days after a Japanese destroyer, not many miles distant in the Blackett Strait in the Solomons, knifed through PT 109, commanded by Lieutenant (j.g.) John F. Kennedy, U.S.N.R., then twenty-six, and ended his naval career.

Eight months later, on the other side of the world, Technical Sergeant Stewart L. Udall, twenty-four, waist gunner on a B-24 bomber named *Flyin' Home,* began a flight from Foggia, Italy, to bomb the Goering tank works at Linz, Austria. On that particular day the nose gunner was ill, and waist gunner Udall was ordered to take his place. A youngster from upstate New York took Udall's customary place at the waist gun.

As the *Flyin' Home* neared its target there was a furious battle. The flak attack was bad enough, but even worse were machine-gun and 20-mm. cannon fire from a flight of German ME-109's. The *Flyin' Home* was riddled with bullet holes. One cannon shot found its mark, tearing through the waist of the ship and instantly killing the waist gunner substituting for Udall. But the B-24 made it to target, dropped its bombs, and headed home. The badly damaged ship was leaking so much gasoline that the men were in constant fear of an explosion. The captain ordered all matches, lighters, and cigarettes thrown overboard to make certain that no one would thoughtlessly light up. When, at last, the crippled plane reached its base, the brakes failed to function. The *Flyin' Home* careened wildly across the field, narrowly missed several other planes and a hangar, and came to rest at the end of the field. It did not explode.

A short time later, having completed fifty missions, Technical Sergeant Udall was sent home. His war experiences left as deep an impression on him as the even more intimate brushes with death left on Kennedy and Freeman. At the end of the war Udall tried to record his feelings and convictions on paper. He wrote a personal credo, pledging his future "efforts to secure the climate of peace." At the end of the paper he listed these as his "compass points":

"When my loyalties require that I offend persons for whom I feel affection and respect I shall offend them;

"When an idea I champion is at stake I shall not retract my hand, though good manners would dictate its withdrawal;

"When people of minority groups are unjustly accused in my presence I shall take their part, as I would expect them to defend me if my own minority were attacked;

"When my convictions invite steps which will be regarded as 'radical' I shall take such steps;

"And when to speak out will involve loss of prestige or material gain I shall not hold my peace.

"I shall do this quietly, with humility, but with the vigor of dedicated purpose, realizing always that in a day of atomic destructiveness 'men must learn to love one another or die'—must see clearer than ever before the great lessons of a Jewish Galilean that men have never quite learned and never quite forgotten."

The war is by no means the only common ground of President Kennedy and the two men responsible for the nation's natural resources. Secretary of Agriculture Freeman and Secretary of the Interior Udall, like the President, were tested under fire of many kinds—in sports, where they all excelled, in intellectual competition, where they won top honors, and in politics, where they learned the habit of success and the meaning of power.

More important, their mental processes are akin. They are pragmatists rather than dogmatists. They are suspicious of doctrinaires and men with easy answers. They are accomplished political organizers who know that detailed planning and long hours of dreary, meticulous work are the first requirements of victory.

In ideology they are moderates but activists; they believe that problems must be sought out and solved, that they seldom just go away. Each has learned the importance of compromise, though at heart each is a tough fighter. They are more interested in gaining an objective than in dreaming about it. And they belong to the same generation (Freeman is forty-three, Udall forty-one, and Kennedy forty-four).

In family background and religion the three men are as different as the states from which they come. A Catholic, the President was born to wealth on the eastern seaboard. Freeman, now a deacon in the Lutheran Church, knew poverty. Even when working his way through the University of Minnesota he had to help support his family. Udall's Mormon family, although prominent in Arizona, was not wealthy. His strict parents frowned on smoking, drinking, and dancing. Unlike the outgoing Kennedys and the hard-driving Freeman, Udall led a sheltered and even lonely existence as a youngster.

In 1960 Kennedy's Catholicism was a problem not only for him but for Freeman the Lutheran and Udall the Mormon. In Arizona Udall's critics whispered that he was a "Jack Mormon," one who does not fully abide by the teachings of the church and devote as much time to its good works as the faithful deem necessary. Even worse, the critics said, he was in the forefront of the fight to elect a Catholic to the Presidency. Udall was re-elected to Congress over a Mormon Republican challenger, but it was by the narrowest margin he had ever had, and Arizona voted for Richard M. Nixon for President.

In Minnesota, where Freeman had been governor since 1954, the religious issue contributed to his defeat in his bid for a fourth term. Four days before the end of the campaign Freeman delivered a major speech in an attempt to stem the anti-Catholic tide sweeping not only Minnesota but all of the Midwest. "I was not prepared for the kind of opposition that says I must be 'punished' for having nominated, and for supporting, a Catholic for President of the United States," Freeman said. Referring to the great volume of anti-Catholic letters and literature he had received, the Lutheran deacon said: "They lead me to conclude that there has been more consideration given to the religious issue, in the minds and hearts of the voters, than to any other issue in this campaign. It has been discussed from the pulpit more than it has been mentioned on the political platform."

When the votes were counted, Kennedy narrowly won in Minnesota, but Freeman, the dynamic, intense governor, lost by a narrow margin. The defeat hurt Freeman deeply. It was not his first defeat at the polls, and he had known adversity many times. But he was proud of his record as governor. He believed that he, more than anyone else, was responsible for building a strong Democratic party in the state. He had been on the scene, on the firing line every day. Yet his old friend and colleague, Hubert H. Humphrey, who had worked at a safer distance, easily won his bid for a third term in the United States Senate. It was not easy for Freeman to reconcile himself to the fact that the election simply was further proof that tenure is easier to establish and maintain in Congress than in a governor's office. As governor, Freeman had gotten into "too many fights," said one Minnesotan. "He had worn out his welcome."

The year had seen a series of frustrations for Freeman. He had worked hard as co-chairman of the Humphrey-for-President organization, only to see Humphrey lose to Kennedy in the Wisconsin and West Virginia primaries. When Humphrey withdrew from the presidential race after the West Virginia primary debacle, Freeman, who had been a strong Stevenson supporter in 1952 and 1956, turned to Kennedy—against the wishes of many in the Minnesota Democratic-Farmer-Labor party. After all, Kennedy had wrecked the chances of the party's hero, Humphrey; the New Englander was too conservative for many Minnesota labor officials, and he had a bad farm record in the view of many of the state's farm leaders.

When the Minnesota delegation assembled in Los Angeles it was badly split. The Governor, who should have been able to control it, was buffeted from every side. Humphrey at first refused to say whom he wanted for President. Minnesota's other Democratic senator, Eugene J. McCarthy, a Catholic, was for almost anyone but Kennedy. The division in the delegation, as everyone knew, was a handicap to Freeman's ambitions to win the vice-presidential nomination.

On the day the convention opened Freeman spent an hour with Kennedy discussing strategy. "Freeman was surprised when Kennedy accompanied him to the door of the Biltmore Hotel's ninth-floor suite to meet reporters," the *Minneapolis Star* reported. "To the newsmen's questions Kennedy called Freeman 'one of the foremost vice-presidential candidates.' "

There followed interminable conferences in an attempt to swing the Minnesota delegation to Kennedy. On Wednesday midnight the delegation began a lengthy caucus that almost ended the friendships of everyone present. Freeman knew that he faced an uphill fight for re-election as governor; he much preferred to run for the Vice-Presidency with Kennedy. Over the years friction had been developing between Freeman and Humphrey, but that night it erupted into sharp rejoinders. When the Senator emerged he said that he was for Freeman for Vice-President, but he would not say then whom he supported for President.

A few hours later Humphrey said he was for Stevenson, whom McCarthy was to put in nomination. None of this helped Freeman, who, at the last moment, was picked to put Kennedy in nomination. When that happened, political tradition told Freeman he would not get the vice presidential nod. To cap it all, when Freeman began his nominating speech the teleprompter in convention hall failed to work properly. He waved to an assistant to bring him a copy of his speech, but the assistant did not understand. Freeman delivered his fiery speech without benefit of text.

When the roll was called, Minnesota's divided delegation threw its votes away on Humphrey, despite the fact that one of its members had nominated Stevenson and another had nominated Kennedy. Minnesota Republicans read the headlines and knew that

Freeman had been wounded by his fellow Democrats. The Republicans were sure they could finish him off at last.

Like many Minnesotans, Orville Freeman is of Scandinavian descent. His grandfather came to this country from Sweden and was a homesteader on a farm near Zumbrota, Minnesota. Freeman's father ran a small men's clothing store in Minneapolis. Born May 9, 1918, Orville attended Minneapolis public schools and the University of Minnesota. It was at the university that the pattern of his life was set. "Even then," according to Humphrey, "Orville was a demon for work. He always had about four jobs." According to Evron M. Kirkpatrick, their political-science professor, Humphrey "just soaked up knowledge" while Freeman had to work for what he got. "Freeman had the most dogged determination I ever saw," Kirkpatrick said. "He's a thoroughly disciplined individual, not flashy like Humphrey. Freeman has a Rock-of-Gibraltar quality about him. He's hard to move once he has made up his mind."

Despite his many jobs Freeman found time to play quarterback on the football team and to make Phi Beta Kappa. In 1940 he was graduated *magna cum laude*. After the war he returned to the university to get his law degree. It was while an undergraduate in the depression days, under Kirkpatrick's influence, that Freeman left the G.O.P., to which his family was devoted, and became a Democrat.

The year after graduation Freeman volunteered in the Marine Corps and was sent to officers' training school at Quantico, Virginia. Before he was sent overseas he married Jane Shields of Winston-Salem, North Carolina, a political-science student two years behind him at the university. Also a Phi Beta Kappa, she has been a stabilizing influence in the family and one with whom Freeman talks out his problems. After his defeat in 1960 she was invaluable in bringing him back to an even keel.

Both the depression and the Marine Corps left their marks on Freeman and on his style as a public official. "The depression showed me the need for action programs," he says. The Marine Corps drummed into him the lesson that "when you're halfway up a hill on a frontal charge you don't decide you should have used a flank attack." He recognizes that the problems of peace are different and that there must be adjustment and compromise of views. "But when you're in a fight," he insists, "you don't back out." His enemies have come to know the strength of that determination. The first who found out about it after the war were the communists in Minnesota.

The fight to force the communists out of the Democratic-Farmer-Labor party "was the toughest, most disturbing, most disillusioning struggle I've ever been in," Freeman has said. "Many fine people were misled, but by the time we started the fight it was black and white as far as I was concerned. We knew what we were up against."

In 1946 Freeman, then an assistant to Humphrey who was mayor of Minneapolis, was elected state secretary of the D.F.L. Humphrey had his eye on the Senate race in 1948, and he knew that to win it his party must undergo a housecleaning. The Humphrey-Freeman campaign to capture control of the D.F.L. was organized down to the last vote. Nothing was left to chance. As one method of arousing members to the communist danger they joined Americans for Democratic Action (A.D.A.) and organized chapters in various parts of the state. They went to one political meeting after another to rally support. By early 1948, shortly after Henry A. Wallace had announced his presidential plans as the Progressive party candidate, Humphrey and Freeman were ready to move.

The 35-member state executive committee under control of former Governor Elmer Benson was pro-Wallace. So a meeting of the 217-member state central committee was convened. In this group the anticommunists held a majority, thanks to the preliminary efforts of Humphrey and Freeman. During the session one of the left-wing leaders falsely accused Freeman of failing to notify the full membership in advance when the meeting was to be held. Freeman, furious, started toward his accuser. "I'll never forget that scene," recalls one of those present. "Before Freeman could reach that fellow he had fled the hall."

The Freeman-Humphrey group had the votes. Freeman was elected state chairman and a slate of electors was chosen pledged to the re-election of President Truman. The Benson group bolted and named a slate for Wallace, which the Republican secretary duly certified. Freeman and Humphrey took their case to the state Supreme Court, which reversed the Secretary of State and ordered him to certify the Truman electors. With the communists expelled, Humphrey, with Freeman as his campaign manager, ran for the Senate and was elected.

Two years later Freeman was a candidate for attorney general, and lost. In 1952 he made his first race for governor, and lost again. In 1954 Freeman, then thirty-six, won the governorship. He was Minnesota's first Democratic governor in sixteen years.

Freeman's inaugural address on January 5, 1955, sounded somewhat like Kennedy's call to arms in 1961. "Our state stands at a point of intense crisis," the new Governor said. "The present challenge we face in Minnesota is, in a real sense, more complex and difficult than our previous periods of crisis." He said the state faced crises in education, in finance, in farm prices, and in the organization of the state government. He promised action.

A strong organizer, Freeman put through a revamping of the government structure that stepped on many bureaucratic toes. He instituted a continuing self-survey project in each department and agency to improve procedures and keep officials alert. The *Minneapolis Star* wrote that Freeman "soon became the best-grounded governor on operations of the administration since the one man elected to the office at a younger age, Harold E. Stassen." Freeman developed a wide program of state-welfare aid, extended social security for state and local employees, and made himself unpopular by raising taxes to pay for his reforms. He ended every year in office with a treasury surplus.

Republicans charged that Freeman was too stern, too dictatorial, too unyielding and inflexible in his relations with the legislature. A major weakness, according to one competent observer, was his "hard-nosed stubbornness, his inability to find the line between leadership and dictatorship. He was still the Marine lieutenant."

His friends concede that Freeman is not quite an effervescent personality and may lack wit and gregariousness. But they think he makes up for any such shortcomings in effectiveness. He dislikes frills and small talk. He pushes and drives hard when he has an objective in mind. After he became Secretary of Agriculture, he discovered that a civil servant, whom he regarded as incompetent, occupied a key post. "Humphrey would have used every roundabout method in the books to transfer that man," an associate said. "But Freeman said: 'I'm just going to call him in and tell him I don't want him.' " The man was in another department within less than a month after Freeman took the oath as Secretary.

In his 1960 campaign against Freeman Republican Elmer Anderson successfully used the slogan: "Minnesota needs friendly, not angry, government." Anderson knew that the slogan would impress many Minnesota voters, not only because of their recollection of the many fights Freeman had had with the legislature but also because of a labor-management row which developed around Freeman's head in late 1959. Some one thousand United Packinghouse Workers struck the Wilson & Company plant in Albert Lea on November 3. A short time later the company began hiring farmers and other nonunion members to operate the plant. Strikers hurled stones, and overturned cars of the workers attempting to enter the plant.

Freeman sent his chief labor conciliator and the state highway director to the scene for an investigation. They sensed more serious trouble. On the night of December 11 Freeman was speaking at the dedication of a new elementary school at Kandiyohi, west of Minneapolis. His secretary reached him just as he was leaving the building to report that his agents at Albert Lea were trying desperately to get in touch with him. After conferring by telephone from the school for almost two hours, Freeman ordered the National Guard to Albert Lea, with instructions to maintain the peace and close the plant. Freeman's advisers had told him that there would be bloodshed if he failed to call the Guard and the plant remained open.

James D. Cooney, president of Wilson & Company, denounced the Governor at once and called his action "completely arbitrary and capricious." Freeman acted, Cooney said, not to maintain law and order but to "close down the plant." The *Minneapolis Star* disagreed. "The violence that flared at Albert Lea was deplorable," it said, "but calling out the National Guard troops was necessary when the local law-enforcement officers asked for assistance to prevent the spread of trouble."

As a result of Freeman's action there was no bloodshed. But the company successfully maintained in court that its rights had been violated. It sought and obtained a restraining order to compel the removal of troops from the plant and the reopening of the packing house. The federal court said that there was no need for military rule in Albert Lea. Moreover, the court criticized Freeman for "surrendering to mob rule." Freeman complied with the court order, and a settlement finally was reached six weeks later.

In angry reply to the court, however, Freeman said that if the same situation arose again "I would act just as I did at Albert Lea." That comment, which sounded to some voters as though he were saying he would act in defiance of the law, was used against him. Critics charged that he had dictatorial ambitions. It was another of the factors in his 1960 defeat.

The experience as governor tempered Freeman's theories and taught him there are always at least two sides to a question. He has promised as Secretary of Agriculture, for example, to remember the consumer's interests and to take a practical rather than a theoretical approach to the farmer's problems.

When Freeman appeared before the Senate Agriculture Committee for confirmation, he said: "I do not present myself to this committee as an expert. I do not think that I have the answer to all the problems of agriculture." But his own farm record is clear, and it is about as firm on one side as Ezra Taft Benson's was on the other. He is firmly in favor of high price supports and production limitations. As Minnesota's governor he testified frequently before the House and Senate Agriculture Committees in sharp criticism of the Benson philosophy.

"Millions of individual farmers acting individually cannot make adjustments necessary to meet changing demands," the Governor told the Senate Committee in 1956. One of the fallacies of the Benson program, he said, is the assumption that if surpluses could be eliminated the law of supply and demand would function and resolve the problems of agriculture. "This is not the case," Freeman

said. "Lower prices do not cut down production but rather increase it."

What farmers need, he testified later, is a program based primarily on the adjustment of supplies to demand so that the market
price will bring the farmer a fair return. Instead of using acreage
limitations, which he called ineffective because farmers can boost
the yield on each acre, he proposed national sales quotas on each
commodity. Each farmer would be assigned his share of the total
and prohibited from selling more. "Growers of a particular commodity should be able to draft a program of their own in cooperation with the Secretary of Agriculture," Freeman feels.

"Government should provide a structure under which farmers
can, like business and labor, control the amount of their production at a level of supply that would bring to them a fair price," he
has said. "Such a price would amount to parity in income, and
would insure them a return on their labor, management, and invested capital that is comparable to the return received by those
engaged in nonfarm occupations."

Specifically, the Kennedy-Freeman plan, which already has run
into major congressional opposition, would permit each farm group
to write its own program subject to veto by Congress. Marketing
quotas and orders, commodity loans and purchases, direct payments, payments in kind, export subsidies, and other means would
be employed if the farmers wished to develop commodity programs
designed to assure parity income. Farmer-selected committees
working under the broad direction of the Secretary of Agriculture
would write the commodity programs for submission to Congress.

Despite his intimate knowledge of Minnesota farm problems,
Freeman told three or four of his close associates after his defeat
on November 8, 1960, that he wanted to be "spared" the ordeal
of being secretary of agriculture. Humphrey took him at his word,
and some of Freeman's supporters thought Humphrey was indeed
overzealous in pushing Freeman for a lesser, non-Cabinet post. On
November 11 Kennedy telephoned Freeman to express regret over
his defeat and to ask him to delay making any plans until there was
another opportunity for a talk. No job offer was made, and Freeman
left with his wife for a Latin-American tour in company with sev-

eral other governors and their wives. On the trip he saw many things which interested him. He saw the need for surplus food shipments and the agricultural experiments being carried forward in many countries. The realization that he might really be able to accomplish something important in the Agriculture Department began to dawn on him. His wife urged him to consider the Cabinet post if it were offered. As he came out of the depression that followed his defeat as governor, the thought of a challenging post once more not only intrigued him but excited him.

"I had been on the firing line for fifteen years," Freeman said later, "and I was exhausted from the campaign. I thought I wanted something less demanding than the Agriculture Department. But when I reflected on it I could not say no. I realized that it represented one of the great challenges of our times. If we are to survive as a free people we must meet this challenge of abundance in agriculture."

There were strong congressional pressures on the President-elect to name someone other than Freeman. But from the beginning Kennedy leaned toward the Minnesotan. He wanted someone from the Midwest. He liked Freeman because of his toughness, his drive, his ability as an organizer. Kennedy was reluctant, however, to put a lame duck in the Cabinet. He looked over other candidates. But one by one he found them lacking. The more he reflected, the surer he became that he wanted Freeman.

On December 15 the President-elect telephoned the Minnesota governor and asked him to be Secretary of Agriculture. "He didn't have to persuade me," Freeman said later. "I was ready." Late that same day, from the snow-covered steps of his Georgetown home, Kennedy announced his selection of Freeman. "He brings to this job energy, executive ability, and dedication to the interest of our country, and I believe that he is the best man that we could get to take on the job of Secretary of Agriculture," Kennedy told the freezing reporters in front of his house on N Street.

Humphrey has kidded Freeman, "and he doesn't go for this," by telling him it was a good thing the Minnesota voters kicked him out of the governor's office. "I said it was good for him because it gave him a new challenge. He was a little tired of the old ones, and now he's pitched into his new problems like a man possessed."

Like many men possessed, Freeman has developed a gnawing ulcer which he must feed with buttermilk and crackers several times a day between meals. "I tell him there is nothing wrong with his ulcer that a good fight or a good victory won't cure," Humphrey said. "He's a far cry from the Prophet Ezra who preceded him as Secretary of Agriculture. Orville is earthy. He speaks like a Marine lieutenant, but he's a good churchman, too."

One day after Freeman took office a group of farm lobbyists (he thinks there are too many lobbyists, too many farm pressure groups, too many commodity spokesmen splitting farmers into competing organizations) called on him to urge a special course of action. He listened attentively to their arguments, then replied bluntly: "My statistics don't show that." That was that.

Can this hard-driving, sometimes inflexible, and dedicated man succeed in an inordinately difficult and complicated assignment where diplomacy and flexibility are also required? Can anyone, for that matter, even begin to resolve the farm dilemma which has eluded solution for decades? "Orville will do an awfully good job," said one of his oldest friends after his appointment, "or he'll be a real disaster."

No one would expect Stewart Udall to be a disaster at Interior. He is probably the most logical of the Cabinet appointments. By all objective tests he should be the one most likely to succeed. His problems are less perplexing than Freeman's, and Udall has spent all his life with his problems. Although he is a fighter with a strong will to win, Udall has something of the poet and scholar in him. That, combined with his love of the outdoors and his experience of six years in Congress, has made him a bit more even tempered, somewhat less disposed than Freeman to think that the shortest distance between two points is necessarily the best route.

One day in 1959 Congressman Udall heard that Robert Frost, poetry consultant at the Library of Congress, had complained that no one in Congress ever bothered to consult him. Long an admirer of Frost's work, Udall and his wife invited the poet to their home for dinner with a group of congressmen. That was the beginning of the Udall-Frost mutual-admiration society. Each is fascinated by the other. The picture of the slightly stooped white-haired New Englander attending the inaugural ceremonies on the arm of the strongly built black-haired young man from Arizona is one that Washington will not soon forget.

The relationship with Frost has been "one of the really big things in my life," Udall says. "He has a great deal to teach about life. We throw the term 'great' around loosely. But Frost has inner greatness. Yet he is a very simple man. He tells us that life is revealed in the simple things, the little things."

Years ago Frost wrote that a poem should "begin in delight and end in wisdom," a haunting thought which Udall cannot forget. "Frost still personifies this combination of wit and good sense," he says. When Frost visited the Udalls in Arizona in 1960, the Congressman took a snapshot of the poet with Denis, aged four, the next to youngest of the six Udall children. The picture now has the place of honor on the desk of the Secretary of the Interior.

At about the time that Udall was discovering Frost's "inner greatness" he was learning something about the steel in another New Englander half Frost's age. Udall learned that this relationship, too, could "begin in delight and end in wisdom." Despite Senator Kennedy's personal charm, Udall had some doubts about him as a candidate for President. "But as we got into the thick of the fight over the labor reform bill I saw more and more the qualities that everyone is seeing in him as president—quick insight, firmness, and toughness," Udall recalls. "The writing of any labor bill obviously brings management and labor into collision and generates the most terrific pressures. Kennedy stood up to these superbly. In fact, he thrived under pressure. This is a quality a President must have, to be able to work well under pressure."

The other thing that impressed the Arizona Congressman about the Massachusetts Senator was that he "surrounded himself with able people." Arthur J. Goldberg, now Secretary of Labor; Archibald Cox, the Solicitor General; Ralph A. Dungan, Special Assistant to the President, and Udall worked side by side in the long struggle over the labor bill.

Udall made up his mind about Kennedy only after the fight was ended. "On the night Congress quit I went over to Kennedy's office about 3 A.M. and told him I was going to work for him," Udall says. He returned to Arizona and went into every part of the state quietly plugging for Kennedy. Most of the Democratic leaders in Arizona were for Lyndon B. Johnson, and it was generally taken for granted that the state would support its Texas neighbor. But Udall took nothing for granted, and he ignored such chieftains in the party as Senator Carl Hayden and Ernest W. McFarland, a former senator and governor. When the state Democratic convention met in Phoenix in April 1960 Kennedy captured 25 of the 34 delegate votes. And at Los Angeles Arizona voted solidly for him.

"I saw the 1960 election as a real watershed affair, the most important election of my generation," Udall says. "You had to decide whom you were for and go down the line for him win or lose."

Just as Kennedy sold himself to Udall during the two-year labor bill struggle so Udall sold himself to Kennedy. Both became involved in bitter fights with the Teamsters; both fought for what they considered a "moderate" bill against extremists on either side of them. In the course of long wrangling in a House Committee in 1959 Udall was bitterly assailed by the Teamsters. Sidney Zagri, a Teamsters attorney, "came to my office and bragged about calling Teamsters and A.F.L.-C.I.O. leaders back in Arizona and telling them about my votes in the Committee," Udall said. Zagri warned him that labor would get him in line.

"That really got me angry," Udall said. "I asked what right he had setting himself up as the great judge of what was right and wrong. Before I finished he backed down and said I might be right regarding what was right for the labor movement. I made it plain I wouldn't be a rubber stamp for him or anyone else."

On another occasion, less than a month after he became Secretary of the Interior, Udall demonstrated his political bluntness with equal and unusual frankness by saying publicly that he knew how to play the great game of politics. "My objective is not to do a good job in this department but to get the President's program passed in all fields," Udall said. "All strong Presidents of the past have used all proper means to generate support. And I want my President to be a strong President."

The fight was over the Administration's attempt to increase the size of the House Rules Committee so that Administration bills could get by this traditional roadblock and onto the House floor for a vote. Udall pitched in and began urging certain congressmen with particular interests in Interior Department decisions to vote for the Rules reform. When House Republican Leader Charles A. Halleck of Indiana heard about Udall's activity he complained that the Secretary was bringing undue pressure on Congress. Questioned at a press conference about his activities, Udall said he had done nothing new or improper.

"Charlie Halleck . . . styles himself as a 'gut fighter' and a guy who plays the game to the hilt," Udall said. "I am afraid he does not like it when other people play the game to the hilt, too."

An astonished reporter asked: "Did the people you talked to vote right?"

"I got a result or two," the Secretary replied with a grin.

Udall was born in St. Johns, Arizona, on January 31, 1920. His forebears were among the earliest Mormon settlers of the area. His great-grandfather, Jacob Hamblin, was one of the early explorers and Indian peacemakers, known in western history as the "Mormon Leatherstocking." Stewart's father, the late Levi S. Udall, was for many years Chief Justice of the Arizona Supreme Court.

"He chose a public career as a way of life," Stewart once said of his father. "He didn't leave much in the way of material things, but he left the best in the way of an example. He left us all with the feeling that the finest thing a person could do was to render a public service."

Five years ago, when about one hundred and fifty members of the Udall clan gathered in Phoenix for a family reunion, the Arizona *Republic* said that "if Arizona has a 'royal family' it is undoubtedly this remarkable group of Udalls. They have supplied members of Congress, the Arizona Supreme Court, the superior courts, the state legislature, and more county and city offices than anyone has bothered to record. . . . They have a Democratic branch and a Republican branch. Like their fellow Mormons, they have worked industriously, lived frugally, and helped build Arizona from a desolate territory to a flourishing state."

After attending public schools in St. Johns, Stewart went to Eastern Arizona College for a year and then transferred to the University of Arizona. He interrupted his studies for two years as a Mormon missionary in Pennsylvania and New York. When the war started Udall sought an Air Force commission but was washed out of a bombardiers' training school and became a noncommissioned officer. His accuracy as a bomber was not satisfactory. He was sorely disappointed. "I threw myself into reading and study," he recalled recently. "I read through every post library I was in. This was one of the really fruitful things in my life."

After the war Stewart returned to the university and received his law degree in 1948. In 1946, when he was an all-conference guard on the university's basketball team, he played in the Invitational Tournament in Madison Square Garden. But Arizona lost to the University of Kentucky 77 to 54. That same year Stewart married Ermalee Webb of Mesa, Arizona, whom he had met at the university while he was studying law and she was an undergraduate. An attractive blonde, with as much energy as her husband and as many interests, Mrs. Udall has been a big help to him politically and socially. "I like Stewart, but Lee is wonderful," is a common remark of their friends. She is warm and effervescent, while her husband, although friendly and generous, is somewhat austere, his mind ever on the job at hand. Stewart would be called, critically by some, "bookish," and despite his many human qualities he is not gregarious. There is little that is light and gay about this nondrinker, nonsmoker except when he is engaged in sports or is out hiking with his family. He has a great love of the outdoors, but cannot bring himself to hunt or fish. Despite their busy life, the Udalls and their six children are a closely-knit family with an abiding interest in camping, hiking, and mountain climbing. They would like to explore together all the public parks under the Interior Department's jurisdiction.

When Udall began practicing law in Tucson with his younger brother, Morris, time then was as elusive as it is for today's busy

Cabinet officer. His friends recall that, partly for exercise, partly to avoid waiting on a slow elevator, he often ran up many flights of stairs to his office in the Valley National Bank Building. He took an intense interest in local civic and Democratic political affairs and served on two different school boards in the area. (Years later, after Udall was in Congress, a Tucson high-school principal said that the most "logical step" in getting federal aid for education was for other congressional districts "to elect more congressmen like Stewart Udall.")

In 1954 Udall won the Democratic nomination for the second congressional seat, from which Democrat Harold A. Patten was retiring. Henry G. Zipf, formerly administrative assistant to Senator Goldwater, won the Republican nomination. Zipf tried to pin the label "left-winger" on his Democratic opponent. According to Zipf, Udall was associated with the ultraliberal American Veterans Committee set up in opposition to the American Legion, was opposed to right-to-work laws, championed the United World Federalists, supported formation of the Progressive party, and accepted support from the left-wing International Union of Mine, Mill, and Smelter Workers.

Udall replied that he did oppose right-to-work laws. But he denied that he had accepted Mine, Mill, and Smelter Workers' support. He declared that Zipf's statement "that I supported the Progressive party in 1948 is a bald-faced lie." What he did was to sign a petition to permit the Progressive party to be placed on the ballot in Arizona. "That was not an act of endorsement of the party in any way," Udall told the voters in 1952, "but rather an act indicating my faith in our democratic processes."

His record supports his claim that he was never enamored of the Wallaceites. In 1948, the year that Henry Wallace was the Progressive party candidate for President, Udall vigorously supported Democrats in the primary and in the general election. In the primary he was Tucson campaign manager for Congressman Richard Harless, a candidate for governor. In the election campaign Udall was vice-chairman of the Pima County Democratic Central Committee. "I worked strenuously for the election of President

Truman and the entire Democratic ticket," Udall asserted. "I did not support nor assist the Progressive party in any way."

Udall told the voters it was true that he was a "left-winger," pointing out that the term was derived when the nobles and aristocrats sat on the king's right while spokesmen for the people sat on the left. "In that sense, I plead guilty to being a left-winger," he said. "Now let's have no more nonsense about it." Udall thinks he is still a left-winger in that sense, and those who oppose his policies may find that he can be as stubborn as an earlier Interior Secretary, Harold Ickes, was in protecting what he believed to be the public interest against those who speak for special interests.

But even in his first campaign Udall showed that he knew the importance of bipartisan support and action. Like many other Democrats that year, he recognized President Eisenhower's great popularity. If his attempt to ride the President's coattails seemed to be purely tactical it also was a forerunner of things to come. He would never be narrowly partisan. He told the voters in 1954 that he would back the President more often than Zipf, and he cited the record of "Zipf's quarterback, Senator Barry Goldwater," who, he said, opposed Ike "on more than one-third of the key votes during the session of the 83rd Congress." Udall won the election with 62.1 per cent of the vote.

Udall's congressional district embraced all of Arizona except Phoenix. He had more Indians, more Indian reservations, and more national-park areas in his district than any other member of the House. Reclamation and power development projects were a basic concern for him then as now. His district was, in fact, a microcosm of the Interior Department. When he reached Congress, it was natural that he should seek and be assigned to the House Interior and Insular Affairs Committee. His other committee was the House Education and Labor Committee, embracing his other chief interests.

More than most congressmen, Udall quickly showed a wide-ranging concern for nearly all the problems before the House. He read widely and was far from parochial in his viewpoint. He readily took stands on issues in an independent manner. He criticized President Eisenhower on occasion and supported him other times. When the Republican President refused to affirm his support of the 1954 Supreme Court decision barring school segregation, Udall was critical. "I think the . . . decision was necessary and wise," Udall said. But he fought the Powell amendment to the federal aid-to-education bill, which would have denied funds to nonintegrated schools. Udall took a constructive position. He offered an amendment to provide additional aid to those school districts which complied with the Court's order but found integration especially costly.

In 1958, when Paul Butler, Democratic national chairman, attempted to read Southern Democrats out of the party, Udall sprang to their defense. "The big majority of Southern Democrats are moderates on civil-rights issues," the Congressman said. "They are people who will work toward a solution of the problem and are a credit to the party. We need them to work our way out of the civil-rights problem. . . . Butler is way off base if he wants to read out the moderates. If he wants to read out the extremists only, I second the motion."

That same year Udall read a lecture to powerful Democratic senators who, in his view, were hurting the party by talking constantly of spending more for defense. "The great advocates of the arms race," he said, "are presenting a face of the Democratic party, which, if regarded as *the* face of the party, could be very harmful to it." He said that he was for a strong defense, "but it is equally important to work to an end to the senseless arms race." The development of each new nuclear device, he said, instead of giving the country greater security, actually gives "further emphasis to the dangers of a nuclear Armageddon."

In 1956 Udall asked permission to testify before the House Foreign Affairs Committee against a measure that was of little concern to his district but which he felt strongly about. The committee was considering a resolution calling for revision of treaties that deny foreign countries criminal jurisdiction over American servicemen stationed within their boundaries.

Udall testified that the resolution was an "attempt to bully President Eisenhower." He said he was impelled to appear because not a single member of the House had come forward to oppose it. "Why, you ask, should a member of the Democratic party take the part of the Administration in this quarrel? The answer is quite simple. The treaty is a prime example of the bipartisan approach in foreign affairs." The resolution was eventually killed.

In a House speech the year before Udall noted that a *Congressional Quarterly* computation listed him as a 100 per cent supporter of the Eisenhower administration on foreign policy. "As a Democrat this does not embarrass me in the least," he said. "In fact, I take pride in it." He told his colleagues that if the President and Secretary of State, as a result of the Geneva summit conference, found it necessary to do some things that might be unpopular he hoped the House would be slow to criticize. "We should be ready to be persuaded and to support them if they are right," he said.

On the subject of agriculture, Udall's independence, or parochialism, as some might call it, may cause friction with his colleague, Orville Freeman. Udall opposed high-price supports and acreage controls while a member of the House. On several occasions he supported Ezra Taft Benson's recommendations. He explained that he did not believe that acreage controls would be "advantageous to Arizona's efficient cotton producers." Udall charged that the farm bloc, made up of Midwest Republicans and Southern Democrats, had "fixed and controlled farm policies" long enough. "The time has come to bury once and for all the myth that our present farm programs protect the family farmer." It was time, he added, for Congress to write "a sensible farm program that will look to the future, and not to the preservation of a stagnant *status quo*."

As a result of Udall's early experience on the conservative-dominated Education and Labor Committee, he quickly became interested in efforts to strengthen the organization and the effectiveness of the House. Chairman Graham A. Barden, a North Carolina Democrat, ran the committee with an iron hand and opposed minimum-wage, labor-reform, and education bills which Udall and liberal Democratic colleagues favored. In 1957 they attempted to take away some of Barden's power over staff appointments and the organization of subcommittees. The attempt failed, but Barden saw the handwriting on the wall. The next year he surprised them by proposing a new set of rules embracing most of what they had sought.

Among the other reforms Udall campaigned for were four-year terms for members of the House, limitations on the power of committee chairmen, and increased and improved use of the congressional power of investigation. To encourage small campaign contributions he offered a bill to make political contributions of up to $100 tax exempt. He campaigned at length in favor of repeal of the Twenty-second Amendment limiting a President to two terms.

A Udall proposal that won much sympathy in Washington, and which as Secretary of the Interior he is in a position to help put into effect, was to prevent the erection of a statue in Washington to any person until at least a half century after his death. "A man's contemporaries are notoriously bad judges of his place in history," Udall told the House. "It is an act of foolish presumption for any generation to pass judgment on its leaders." He noted that the Lincoln Memorial was dedicated sixty years after the death of the Great Emancipator and that the Jefferson Memorial was dedicated more than a century after Jefferson's death. "Those memorials which have the most meaning and artistic integrity were conceived and carried out by posterity and not by personal friends," Udall said.

The memorial Udall wishes to leave behind him is the record of a great conservationist. He wants President Kennedy to be ranked with Theodore Roosevelt as one who took giant steps to protect the nation's resources. "I have some big ideas for the sixties," Udall said after he was chosen to be Secretary of the Interior. One example of what he has in mind is to find a cheap way to convert saline water. "If we could beat the Russians to finding a low-cost, efficient way of making saline water usable, this could be far more important in some areas of the world than competition on the fringes of peace."

When Republican Senator Gordon Allott of Colorado asked Udall's views on public versus private power development, the Arizonan said he believed in a mixed system and that he held no doctrinaire views. "I might say, however," he added with emphasis, "it does seem to me, with the great river systems we have, that many of these resources are public resources and we need to develop them for the good of the whole nation . . . but I do not have a fixed view that you follow one plan and follow it rigidly under all circumstances."

He has made it clear many times that he favors "full and comprehensive developments in all the river basins of this country." In a 1955 speech Udall expressed his philosophy for basin developments and power projects as well as all the other intricate problems facing him as Secretary of the Interior. His experience in Congress had taught him the need, he said, to "place the national purposes first." It was essential to build, he said, "a broader sense of responsibility and put competing local prejudices into a proper perspective."

Udall is committed to a pragmatic course, with the public interest foremost in mind, in protecting the public lands, the oil and forest resources, in pressing for water- and air-pollution control, in the development of what he calls "an all-embracing national water program," and in the management of the Indian tribes. Each tribe is different, this man who had 100,000 Indians in his congressional district believes, and each needs to be approached differently.

Those who think Udall's moderate words are a sign of weakness may be in for a surprise. Udall is somewhat less openly aggressive than, say, Freeman. But he has the same impatience to get things done and the same quick eye for irrelevancies. The New Frontier to frontiersman Udall is more than a phrase. He sees the nation in a race against time. For example, because so much of the open land is being rapidly developed, he believes that Kennedy "has the last real opportunity to make a record as a conservationist which will compare favorably with that of Theodore Roosevelt." Udall is pledged to carry out "a very aggressive" national program for improvement of the public parks. "Our population is outrunning our recreational resources," he believes. "I think we need to make a new breakthrough, a great new effort."

Both the President and the Secretary of the Interior would like to develop more playgrounds, especially in the East, and buy more land on the seashore for public recreational areas. They have their eyes on lovely Cape Cod, where Kennedy has spent many summers, which is rapidly seeing its beaches fall into private hands.

Udall may not be committed to a rigid formula. But in all the fields in which Interior has an interest he is committed to action. This man with an inner compulsion to foster and protect the great outdoors can detect an "obstructionist" at first glance. Where Interior is concerned there are many obstructionists, men who think the Government should play a passive role. Udall wants results that can be measured, and where individuals cannot protect the national welfare he thinks that the Government can and must do so. "I would like to think of myself," Udall says, "as being constructive, to bring new ideas and imagination to the job. That is the main task."